(Continued from front of jacket)

drawn irresistibly to follow the country's fading frontiers.

There was Papa Bosworth, who was a mystery never wholly explained. In a Studebaker wagon which served as home and transportation for a good quarter of a century, he went up and down and across Texas and into New Mexico Territory looking for something he never found: a new country scantily peopled and without fences, where a man could be himself. Out of time and wind and flash floods and desert dust, stories were born—of Papa and the Panic of 1893, of Papa and the Texas Skinning War, of Papa championing quail and cutting barbed wire and roping a house out of the river—until Papa grew to be ten feet tall in the imagination of his youngest son, Allie. Papa lived and died a legend.

There was Mama, proud that she came of fine-haired people, who was looking for a home and an education for her children. The only mystery about Mama was her strength, which enabled her to hold her head high in hovels, to cling to her aristocratic vanities in public wagon yards and in solitary camps that were always either dusty or muddy, hot or cold. Mama married Papa for true love, bore him ten

(Continued on back flap)

BOOKS BY ALLAN R. BOSWORTH

NEW COUNTRY

THE CROWS OF EDWINA HILL (FICTION)

THE LOVELY WORLD OF RICHI-SAN

ALLAN R. BOSWORTH

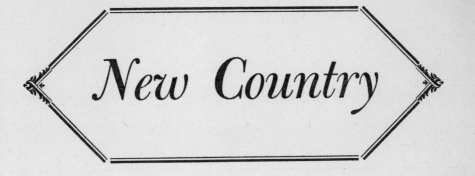

New Country

HARPER & BROTHERS · PUBLISHERS · NEW YORK

NEW COUNTRY

A PORTION OF THIS BOOK

ORIGINALLY APPEARED IN

"THE NEW YORKER."

LIBRARY OF CONGRESS CATALOG CARD NUMBER: *62-9885*

To Bettie Ivanhoe Rucker Bosworth

1864—1949

Happy he
With such a mother! faith in womankind
Beats with his blood, and trust in all things high
Comes easy to him; and tho' he trip and fall,
He shall not blind his soul with clay.
                    —ALFRED TENNYSON

List of Illustrations

[vii]

8. *Papa liked San Angelo. Ranch wagons outnumbered the buggies, some of the freight outfits had twelve-horse teams, and cowboys rode festively down Chadbourne Street.*

9. *Dee was to grow up the tallest of all my brothers, and the most valiant.*

10. *People said the name of Claudia Ivanhoe Bosworth sounded as if it came out of a novel. She married Willie Jones.*

11. *When Dee was twenty-three, he became the real head of the family, and Mama drove the wagon nearly a thousand miles to be with him again.*

12. *Illness, worry and emotional strain showed on Mama's face in her mid-forties. She looked older then than she did in her fifties.*

13. *"Old Lady," Jay teased Mama when he was twenty-one, "why should I work for thirty dollars a month when I can make a quick clean-up? I'm going to hold up the Angelo stage."*

14. *Floyd went to John Tarleton College for a while when he was sixteen. He had almost worn himself out, the past several years, trying to make a man of me.*

15. *Papa found the Stradivarius in Mexico in 1909. "I will give it to you," he said, "on one condition."*

16. *At thirteen, Floyd talked and acted like a man. Mama said he was "just born grown-up."*

17. *Bert was known as "Speck" when he was eleven, because of his freckles.*

18. *When I was six, it was handy to have brothers of all ages who could lick any old brother anybody else had.*

19. *Floyd and Bert were both good shots, and they taught me to use a gun. Floyd teased Mama, too—he was going to rob the Southern Pacific.*

20. *After his return from Mexico, Papa helped Uncle Nick build a house. He never built a house of his own.*

21. *In 1917, Mama's children had all grown tall.*

22 and 23. *Mama's first house, unsoftened by shade or shrubbery, had a chapped and blistered look. It wasn't as big as the house Papa roped, that time.*

24. *The first schoolhouse in Ozona had been the courthouse when Crockett County was first organized.*

25. *The new stone schoolhouse was one of the finest in Texas.*

26. *Fifth and sixth grades at Ozona's new school building, in 1911.*
Front row, left to right, *Mason Joslin, Peery Holmsley, Jeff Owens, Allie Bosworth, Massie West, Ben Gilbert, Walter Augustine, Claude Russell, Welton Bunger.*
Second row: *Willie Baker (mouth open), John Patrick, Robin Adair, Joe Patrick.*
Third row: *Tip Smith (on banister), Jesse Angermiller, Wesley Berry, Armond ("Hop") Hoover, Joe Chapman, Wilma West, Ora Mae Cox, Miss Glee Stafford (teacher), Maggie Davidson (peeping over teacher's shoulder), Alice Friend, Maude Burchett, Alpha Westfall, Lela Johnigan.*
Fourth row: *Daphne Meinecke, Frances Barker, Daisy Robertson, Annie Wigzell, Alma Chapman, Irene Kincaid, Cora Burchett, Marian Marlin, Willie Kirby.*
Back row: *Warren Clayton, Charlie Perner, Joe McMahan.*

27. *The Crockett County courthouse overlooked the town square and a little park of mulberry trees. Just behind it and to the left was the jail;*

behind and to the right were the windmills on Waterworks Hill. Mama could sit on her gallery and hear guitar and fiddle music drifting from the courthouse during the Saturday-night dances.

28. Ozona was already becoming a "millionaire's town." The bank was small, but wealthy, and friendly. "Mammy" Kirkpatrick's hotel stood nearby.

29 and 30. West from the water tower, or north along the main street past the Baptist church and the old high-school building, the town was rubbing the rough edges off the thorny and rocky frontier.

31, 32 and 33. Many an old Studebaker wagon, with high, hooped hickory bows, and with a water barrel and a slope-fronted chuck box in the endgate, served as chuck wagon on the cattle and sheep ranches. They were handsome when catalogue-new, and they provided reliable transportation. But the first automobiles were chugging along the ranch roads—huge, high-wheeled, right-hand-drive Buicks and carbide gas headlamps. Some of them cranked from the side.

Some Acknowledgments

Some of the material used in this book was stored away in my own earliest rememberings, without awareness of purpose, when we rode in the Studebaker wagon and camped beside it. I added bits and fragments a half-century ago, sitting with Mama and my brothers on the gallery of the house on the rocks, watching the twilight shadows deepen and talking about Papa and the old times, and the places we had been. By the time I knew that ours was a story which might be written, I had to make a living, and then two wars intervened. Finally, in 1960, just after I had been retired from the Navy, I went back to Texas to round up the rest of the material.

I carried a tape recorder, and spent delightful hours capturing the remarkably clear and vivid recollections of my oldest brother, Dee, and my oldest sister, Norah. I drove several thousand miles up and down and across Texas, retracing routes traveled by the Studebaker wagon, checking the records in county courthouses, talking to people who were unfailingly kind and helpful. I returned to Virginia and began to write, remembering a Saturday night on Friday Mountain, which is a beautiful piece of Texas owned by Dr. Walter Prescott Webb, reliving my Texas boyhood days through Norah's gentle voice and Dee's soft drawl, and recalling the courtesies extended to me in Hallettsville by Judge Paul C. Boethel.

It would be an impossible task to name all who have helped me. I should like to thank Dr. Webb for his interest and his inspiration, and his insistence that the book be attempted. Miss Llerena Friend, of the University of Texas Library, furnished invaluable source material. Charles J. Strauss, Clerk of Lavaca County, welcomed me to his files. Judge Houston S. Smith of Ozona, Crockett County folklorist and historian, deserves much more credit than he knows. He refreshed my memories of my old home town, but, more than that, it was he who gave me a feeling for history many years ago, as my high-school teacher. Miss Anne Dobie Peebles, past president of the Virginia Federation of Women's Clubs, educator and civic leader, researched the records of the Confederacy and lost a gallant fight in attempting to run down my mysterious grandfather, Thomas Rucker, but uncovered Bosworths, Mauldings and Hannas along the way.

I am indebted to Mrs. Jack V. Silva, of Anahuac, Texas; to my cousin, Mrs. J. C. Cook, Pettus, Texas; to Maude Van Fossen, Historian of East Carroll Parish, Louisiana; to Mr. Leon Wheeler, Geneva, Ill.; to Mr. Monroe F. Cockrell, Evanston, Ill.; to S. G. Tarkington, Jr., Postmaster of Cuero, Texas; to C. L. Sonnichsen, Dean of the Graduate Division of Texas Western College, and man of letters.

I owe many thanks to Miss Miriam Dozier of Austin; to Mr. Val D. Huvar, Clerk of Victoria County; to Mr. Earl Hanna, Baton Rouge, La.; to Mr. J. W. Hanna, St. Amand, La., and his daughters. I was assisted by Mrs. Richard D. Owen, of Jackson, Miss.; by Mr. J. R. Bradshaw, Clerk of Rankin County, Miss.; and by Miss Mercedes Duecy, of Dallas, whose family had traversed much the same route as mine.

I am deeply grateful to Miss Rachel MacKenzie, of *The New Yorker* magazine; to Elizabeth Lawrence and others at Harper & Brothers; and to my agent and counselor, Marie F. Rodell.

In addition, my sincere appreciation goes to the anonymous but courteous staff members in the University of Texas Library, the Archives of North Carolina at Raleigh, the National Archives at Washington, D.C., and the Virginia State Library and the Headquarters of the United Daughters of the Confederacy, both at Richmond. Mrs. Robert P. Kline, of the Roanoke Public Library, and

Mrs. Mary Linda M. Smiley, also of Roanoke, have my special thanks.

Two chapters of this book, written as fiction, were printed some years ago in *Farm Journal,* under the titles "A Cowboy For to Be," and "The Time I Robbed the Santa Fe." A longer, factual article appeared in *The New Yorker* in February, 1960. The publishers of both magazines have graciously consented to use of the material here.

Author's Preface

For more than twenty years before I was born, and for a considerable time within my own memory, the Bosworth family followed the fading frontier of Texas in an old Studebaker wagon. Up and down and across and back again, we followed it for thousands of miles.

PAPA was looking for something he never found. His search became more compulsive with the years, and Papa grew more difficult to understand, or to explain. Nothing in this book is likely to clear up his private mysteries.

MAMA was looking for a home, and an education for her children. The only mystery about Mama was her strength. This enabled her to hold her head high in hovels, to cling to her aristocratic vanities in public wagon yards and in solitary camps that were always either dusty or muddy, hot or cold. It enabled her to keep her brood washed clean, and to live out eighty-five years—not all of them unhappy. Neither time nor Texas succeeded in wearing Mama down.

THE CHILDREN—I was the tenth born—went along, there being nothing else we could do. We knew the pains and pleasures of a way of life that is now long gone, and perhaps we found things for ourselves on the far sides of the hills where Papa searched in vain.

ALLAN R. BOSWORTH

Roanoke, Va.
September, 1961

New Country

One

*T*here was a time in Texas when the rimrocked hills were higher, and the mornings always came younger, with a sparkling dew-washed look and a fresh, exciting smell. There was a time when a mile was a respected distance, not yet sullied by gasoline fumes nor devoured with a steel-throated roar. The sounds of passage were softer. They were the low basso rumble of steel wagon tires, the fiddle squeak of harness and oboe squeal of brake shoe, a banjo jingle from the trace chains, and always the dull, patient tympany of horseshoes on a sunbaked dun-colored dirt road. These sounds conspired to make a slow and lazy music, a melody akin to earth and wind and sun, and the rain that hummed on the wagon tarp.

The road reached westward, longer than the day, and just as unhurried. Those days had more hours in them, before sundown and after; dusk was a time to alight and stretch growing limbs with the lengthening shadows, and to make a fire that had all manner of dreams in it. The wind came up to breathe on the fire and spray bright showers of sparks from it, and to throw a magic-lantern show of shimmering shine and shadow on the faded wagon tarp. The horses stamped, and blew muffled notes of contentment into their *morrals*—

a day's honest labor and ten to twenty miles behind them. And the old Studebaker wagon made mysterious settling noises long after the wheels had stopped rolling and the tongue had been propped up with the singletree. . . .

The day and its travel belonged to Papa, but the camp at night was Mama's domain, and for months at a time she had only the wagon and a circle of flickering firelight on some lonely stretch of prairie for her home. There had been ten children, down the gypsying years, eight of them hardy enough to survive. The children and Papa had to be fed.

Mama greased the skillet lid with a bacon rind and leaned it carefully toward the outer coals of the mesquite fire, so that when she covered her biscuits they would brown evenly, top and bottom. The smoke got in her eyes. There was an old saying that campfire smoke always blew toward the prettiest member of the company, and even after bearing ten children Mama was an uncommonly pretty woman.

Papa sat impassively on a box by the fire after the horses had been unharnessed and watered and fed. The children foraged in the mesquites for dry wood or sunbaked cowchips while there was still light enough to see.

"You children!" Mama called into the prairie wind. "Look out for rattlesnakes, now—you hear me?"

The firelight showed Papa's face under his wide-brimmed hat, but neither firelight nor any other illumination ever disclosed the things that made up his nature and drove him on. The firelight only added mystery to the dark, brooding restlessness in his eyes; it softened the angles of his high cheekbones and the set of his lean jaw, and showed the quickness with which he reacted to any sound in the gathering darkness. He was resting peacefully by his fire, but let a horse's hoofbeats come drumming down the wind, and Papa was what the Mexicans called *muy alerto*—all at once high-strung and hair-trigger. Nobody ever knew why.

Papa was not a communicative man. Sitting tonight in his camp near a ranch windmill, he disclosed no plans for tomorrow. The camp might be only for the night. It might turn out to be for three days, three weeks, or six months—and in Papa's case the latter period passed for permanent tenancy. His plans depended upon many things. He had left some places hurriedly, and later said only, "My horses wouldn't drink the water there."

It might be that he would want to scout the surrounding country, if it had impressed him at all favorably. In cotton country, and in the cotton-picking season, Papa could offer the services of a considerable crew. Sometimes he looked for temporary work as a ranch hand, or for labor as a carpenter—Papa had some skill with hammer and saw, and built many houses in Texas, but never one of his own. On needful occasion, he did whatever job came to hand; he was interested in none of them on a long-term basis. Nobody would ever have thought of Papa as a career man.

Upon arrival at any new place, Papa needed to look around and see how badly the country had been fenced up, and whether or not all the cattle had been branded. Even when he had money, which was not often, he was averse to buying his fresh meat from butcher shops.

There was another very considerable factor to be weighed, and one Papa regarded as beyond his control. If Mama, stooping over the skillet and the stewpans at the campfire, happened to be far along in pregnancy, it might be advisable to pitch the tent.

After breakfast in the morning, Papa very probably would saddle the extra horse he always had along, and ride off for a couple of hours. When he came back, the family would learn whether he had decided to stay or move on. Tomorrow, Papa would have the reins again.

At the moment, Mama was indisputably in charge. She was chief cook and bottle washer, major-domo and wagon boss. Unless they could help her, even the children stayed out of her way.

II

The chuckbox was in the endgate of the wagon, with a lid that could be let down to table level and propped with a hinged wooden stake to serve as pantry shelf and kitchen sink. Mama mixed biscuit dough

[5]

by lantern light, kneaded it with vigorous slappings and poundings, flattened it with a quart whiskey bottle used as a one-handled rolling pin, and cut the biscuits with the greased rim of a tin can. Coffee was already boiling in a blackened pot at the edge of the campfire. It would not be *good* coffee, because even when ten-pound bags of Arbuckle's Four X coffee beans sold for a dollar, Mama never threw out this morning's, or even last night's, grounds—not until the pot was half-filled with them. She simply freshened the pot by adding a few more spoonfuls of coffee ground in the hand mill that was secured to the chuckbox. To have used fresh coffee for each brewing would have been to go against the frugalities she had learned during the lean years of the Reconstruction.

Now she heated yesterday's red beans—Mexican *frijoles* liberally seasoned with fiery Mexican chili peppers—and put more beans to soak so they could be cooked in the ashes overnight. She fried thick slices of sowbelly bacon until the rinds curled and turned white and were as crisp as popcorn, and made thickening gravy by stirring flour into the smoking hot bacon grease and adding water. For sweetening she had stewed dried peaches or apricots. The children had learned not to eat much of the stewed fruit, but saved it, instead. There was no refrigeration, and in a few days it would begin to bubble and foam. Then Mama would add more sugar—an expensive item—and boil it again until the syrup was thick. This was not merely stewed fruit, but "preserves," and much more palatable.

There was always a jug of strong blackstrap molasses. All the children had heard about occasional unwanted or untended pickaninnies found sorghum-sodden at the bottom of vats in molasses-making time. The stories may or may not have been purely apocryphal; at any rate, sorghum molasses was tasty when poured over hot biscuits, with melted beef tallow used for butter.

Other children called thickening gravy "heifer dust." Mexican beans were known as "Texas strawberries," and molasses was "lick." Mama would not allow any of us to use these terms.

When she announced that supper was ready, one of the older boys was sure to shout: "Come and get it, before I throw it out!" This was a borrowing from the *cocineros* (cooks) of the cow camps, and Mama did not like it either. She would frown, and sniff disapprovingly, and declare that she just didn't know, bless Patty, what our "raising" was coming to. A family meal, to Mama, was still somehow a dinner by candlelight, with gracious silver and snowy linen. And still it pleased her to cater to young appetites, and she secretly liked to be teased.

We sat on bedding rolls, on the propped-up wagon tongue, or on the ground when it was dry, and ate from tin plates. The campfire was our family hearth, and around it was the only family unity we had ever known, but it was hardly a place to gather on winter evenings for reading or the singing of hymns.

The wind changed again, and somebody was sure to laugh and say that the smoke was blowing Mama's way because she was so pretty. Mama always had stock answers for this compliment. She said, "Pshaw!" or "Fiddlesticks!" or "Pretty, my foot!" But she smiled, and the color came warm and high in her cheeks to show that she was pleased. Mama was a very vain woman, proud of what she called her "blue blood." She reminded all of us, quite often, that we were "fine-haired people."

"You children! I won't have you playing with those young'uns over at that other wagon—you hear me? They're nothing but poor white trash. I declare, I just don't see how anybody could let their children get so dirty!"

After supper was finished and the dishes had been washed, Mama made beds in the wagon for the younger children and herself. Papa and the older boys unrolled their tarps on the grass if the stars were shining, or spread them foot-to-foot under the wagon box if it looked like rain. Mama did much of her darning and mending by lantern light, and her day was long.

Tomorrow, if Papa came back from scouting the country and said he had decided to stay awhile, whole new vistas opened for her. Papa would get the old tent out of the rawhide cooney—it was a cowhide slung under the wagon like a hammock, and it served as a carry-all—and would set it up, cutting and driving pegs for the tent

[7]

stays. He would unload the cast-iron cookstove with its joints of rusty pipe, and get down Mama's old tin trunk.

While this was being done, Papa might talk—even with an initial enthusiasm—about settling here permanently. He would take up a "squat" of land. A man, he said recklessly, could build himself a little frame house over yonder on that high ground, with that liveoak tree for shade in the front yard. Maybe drill a well, he went on, and put up a windmill, and start running a few head of cattle. . . .

Papa never mentioned building a fence as one of the improvements necessary to prove up a piece of Texas land. He was a staunch advocate of free grass, or the open range system. He hated fences with a passion.

But Mama's eyes would be shining by now. She would have the boys take her old pedal-operated Singer sewing machine out of the wagon and put it in the tent, along with a couple of cowhide-bottomed chairs and her rocker. Then she would climb into the wagon bed herself, to get her large gilt-framed looking glass out of its protective wrapping of homemade quilts. This had belonged to her mother, and was her most cherished possession. Not many women, roaming Texas in a wagon, owned a full-length mirror.

She propped the looking glass on a box draped with dimity, or leaned it against a tent pole. After things had been straightened up, she spent hours before it, brushing her hair very carefully—Mama's auburn hair was so long she could sit on it—and powdering her nose with prepared chalk.

When the children saw her doing this, when we saw her spreading the featherbeds on the grass to sun, or boiling clothes and bed linen in a five-gallon can of soapsuds, when we saw her emptying the chuckbox so she could scrub and scald it from top to bottom, and polishing the monogrammed family silver with wood ashes, when we heard her singing softly to herself as she did all these things, we knew that camp was permanent.

That is, for a little while. . . .

The wagon was already old by the time I was born, but age in a wagon was never really important. It had been built to last, and in those days the makers of vehicles neither designed their body styles to appeal to women, nor changed them every year—or every ten years. Wagons were designed for men. The Studebaker may not have been beautiful to anyone but Papa, who loved all wagons, but over the years since the ungainly looking Conestogas first lumbered across the Plains, Studebaker and Bain and a few lesser manufacturers had evolved a utilitarian product that came near to perfection in performance and durable service. Ours was a ranch or farm wagon, smaller and lighter than those used for freight hauling; two horses could pull it, with a load, whenever the road was reasonable. It had tall rear wheels with moderately broad tires, sturdy hubs, and strong wooden spokes. The wagon box and the spring-mounted seat and dashboard had originally been painted forest green, with tasteful yellow trim and graceful scrollwork, and it bore a modestly small Studebaker mark. The colors had been faded by sun and rain and abrasive blowing sand; the once bright red of the running gear was weathered to a brownish teat pink. The tarpaulin cover had to be replaced every several years, being given to mildewing in damp weather and fraying out over the hickory wagon bows and around the edges in the nearly incessant Texas winds. At both ends were reinforced hems threaded by small Manila ropes. By tightening these to draw the canvas into puckered circles, the wagon could be almost completely closed.

Under the wagon sheet when the wheels were rolling was everything the family owned—the stove, the sewing machine, a trunk or two, the nested chairs, the featherbeds and gay patterned homemade quilts, Mama's quilting frames, some precious china she seldom used, and a few equally precious books. The featherbeds and quilts were on top, so that the children rode in cushioned comfort, sitting almost as high as the sideboards.

We carried water in a six-gallon keg which was racked outside on the left of the wagon box and had to be kept covered with a piece of tarpaulin to keep out the dust of travel and the suicidally thirsty yellow jackets and wasps. On rough roads, the water keg made great bowel-rumbling sounds and sloshed some of its precious contents against the cover and over the sides; on extended dry drives across some parched stretch of prairie where the windmills had not yet come, the staves shrank and began to collapse inward from the top.

The slope-fronted chuckbox held all our perishable food, and such indispensable medicines as Mama had read about. She believed all printed words and had great faith in patent remedies; she never traveled without Castoria, Sloan's Horse Liniment, paregoric, Cloverine Salve, Black Draught and Cardui, and—if she could afford it—a bottle of Dr. Pierce's Golden Medical Discovery, or his Favorite Prescription. Papa admired Dr. Pierce, too: he kept a book this eminent medical man had written on home remedies, and felt qualified to treat all manner of ailments by consulting it. A member of the family had to be desperately ill indeed, before Papa thought it necessary to summon a doctor. . . .

Mama carried asafetida, mercifully sealed in a tight can, to hang in little bags from the necks of the children in winter. It fended off colds and fevers, as well as people.

When the chuckbox was opened, the smells of freshly ground Green Stamp Arbuckle Four X coffee beans, dried apples, sorghum molasses, vinegar, salt pork, onions and spicy dried Mexican chili peppers mingled and blended with all the other odors, rich and strong under the hot Southwestern sun, that went to make up the aura of the wagon. For there were smells about the wagon itself: the sharpness of linseed oil coming from a pair of old Fish Brand slickers, the turpentine odor of axle grease applied thick and yellow to the wheel hubs, only to ooze thin and black after the friction of a few miles, neat's-foot oil rubbed into harness that already smelled pungently of horse sweat, and kerosene spilled from the dust-coated bullseye lantern and from the gallon can we always carried in reserve, a shriveled Irish potato impaled on its spout.

The wagon had its signature sounds, too, and they were sometimes melodic. It was always filled with mysterious creaks and rattles, like an old ship in heavy weather. The wind that billowed through the front and rear openings of the tarp produced a soft and rhythmic drumming of canvas on the hickory bows. When the team was in a trot on some downhill grade, the steel trace chains acclaimed our lively progress, and in bursts of affluency Papa even had bells on the hamestraps of new harness. When we rolled across the smooth limestone ledges of the hill country, we carried a personal thunder, and I was always certain that the earth beneath us was honeycombed by caves, some of them undoubtedly filled with long-buried Spanish treasure.

For some reason, Papa had never been a sixshooter man. He had a .30-.30 Winchester behind the wagon seat, after that gun appeared on the market, and he also carried it in his saddle scabbard. The saddle was in the wagon for the extra horse that was led behind except for times when he allowed one of the older boys to ride ahead, scouting for wood, water, and camping sites. Mainly, the saddle horse was for Papa's personal use. He rode well, and it was very apparent that he felt more of a man when he was mounted.

Whoever first called the Plains wagons "prairie schooners" was perhaps more apt in his choice of description than he knew. There was considerable similarity. Many a stretch of Texas prairie looked like the sea, with cloud shadows chasing one another across waves of wind-rippled grass, and perhaps another wagon hull down on the far horizon. The wagon was a complete entity, as was a sailing ship in its day. It carried its own crew, and was provisioned for a long voyage; it had a spread of wind-filled canvas, and even the spare horse was towed astern like a small boat and served the same purposes. The horse was used as a whaleboat in the pursuit and slaughter of maverick beef, a dinghy or gig for short errands, a lifeboat in times of emergency or disaster.

Papa probably never knew how eminently fitting this was. Some of his forebears—he cared nothing for ancestry, and had lost track of them—had settled, much earlier, in New England. A number of them followed the sea. Papa would have snorted scornfully at any suggestion concerning hereditary instincts; he would have insisted that he did things out of custom and training, or in the practice of common sense. But his wanderings were akin to voyages on the sea, and sometimes, when there were no roads on the prairies, he made camps with his wagon tongue pointed toward the North Star, Polaris, ever the guiding light of mariners.

Nothing ever went seriously wrong with a wagon, and if a man took care of his team he could keep it rolling. But we carried simple tools: an axe, a clawhammer and nails and a saw, a single combination wrench that fitted wheel hubs, body bolts and wagon rods, and an awl that was needed for mending harness. There was also a pair of wire cutters.

The latter had to be kept hidden at times. In 1883 and 1884 the mere possession of such a tool might have landed a man in jail. The family was in Brown and Lampasas and Coleman counties in those years, and Papa became somewhat involved in the beginnings of the notorious Fence Cutter's War, just as he always managed to get embroiled in quarrelsome enterprises. But there was one thing in Papa's favor. He had wheels. He was extremely mobile, and usually he could pull out ahead of the sheriff.

On downgrades, when the wagon threatened to override the rumps of the horses, Papa could throw and notch a brake handle at the right of the seat, just as we set parking brakes today. This applied friction to the steel tires of the rear wheels, and set up an unearthly screeching if the pressure had to be maintained. The friction blocks were easily relined by nailing entire old shoes or scraps of discarded harness to their working surfaces, and in hill country these were sometimes doused with water to increase their gripping power and reduce the noise they made. In dry weather wheels shrank, spokes began rattling emptily in their sockets, and steel tires wobbled and threatened to leave their rims. Papa knew the remedy for this. He let the wagon stand long in any creek that had to be forded; he removed wheels and soaked them overnight in waterholes or stockmen's tanks. If no water was handy, the tire and rim could be wrapped with a wide thong of green rawhide, or with dried rawhide moistened from the water keg. The family might go thirsty for a little while if the last available water were needed for this use.

Thongs of wet rawhide exert incredible force when they begin to dry and shrink and pull: they have been known to cut fence posts or small trees in two. I heard stories about rawhide when I was much too young to understand them, but I enjoyed the delicious chills of horror their telling produced. They were mostly Mexican legends, about wayward wives and luckless lovers being bound together with green rawhide in an embrace much closer than they had ever enjoyed, and left to a pitiful, squeezing death under the desert sun. . . .

The history of Texas might well be burned into rawhide. Rawhide held Texas together until barbed wire came. Clothing was made from it in the earliest days, and it was used to fashion the *riatas* by which some men made a living and others their fortunes. It belonged in a raw frontier land; it expressed and symbolized the supple strength and toughness of the pioneer. It yielded and stretched and pulled, but it never wore out.

Mama had known about the properties of rawhide since she was a baby. A Negro servant—freed as a slave only the year before—made a hide-bottomed chair for her when she was only two years old. All of Mama's children sat in this chair. It is still strong and steady, with the original bottom, after a hundred years.

But in the beginning, Mama really knew very little about wagons, and certainly she had never thought about a wagon as a home. Her interest in them had been that of an observer who watches travelers go by; she had seen many a wagon outfit roll along the liveoak-shaded roads of Sweet Home, in Lavaca County, where she was born. The freight outfits came that way from Brownsville and Matamoros. The trail herds were gathered there to be driven to faraway rail points in Kansas.

The very word "romantic" comes from the name of a people who traveled in wagons, with their alluring campfires and their compelling gypsy music. As a young girl, Mama may well have been attracted to those campfires on the holding grounds at Sweet Home, and to the idea of travel. But she did not know how far things might go when the wagon wheels started rolling down the years.

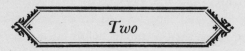

Two

*P*apa left skillet prints in the ashes of dead campfires all the way from the Gulf Coast to the New Mexican Territory, and from the Red River to the Rio Grande. These showed where his caravan had rested; they were his marks upon the land. And when he had hitched his horses and gone, the wind came up and blew them away. . . .

Since I am the youngest and last of his children, it was not given to me either to enjoy or endure Papa's company for very long, and I never felt that I knew him. Growing up, and defensively inclined to picture Papa as a legendary figure, ten feet all, I consulted Mama and my older brothers and sisters. All confessed to the same feeling. Nobody ever really *knew* Papa.

"Well, I kind of hate to say it," my oldest brother, Dee, told me not long ago. "But it was kind of like Papa was running from the law, because he was always going over the hill. I don't know how many squats of land he took up, but he would just file on them and then go off and leave them."

After he told me that, I tried earnestly to arrive at a better understanding of the things that moved and drove Papa by tracing his origins, only to find that the records were almost as evanescent as the ashes of his campfires. His family, and his forebears, were not given to writing journals or putting their names on documents. This, of course, was characteristic of the early-day Texans: a man had all he could do merely to survive the Comanches and the Mexicans and the floods and the fevers, and to make some sort of crop. There was a notable lack of communications. For example, Texans fought the last land battle of the Civil War at Palmito Ranch, near Brownsville, on May 13, 1865, and did right well—they captured eight hundred Union troops, and then learned from their prisoners that the war had ended more than a month before at a place called Appomattox.

It was that difficult to get important word to a place so far away, and so wide and wild; it was easy to lose track of origins in Texas, or to misplace an occasional relative. When records existed at all, they were likely to be so informal as to be misleading. It is remembered that the bill of sale on a certain horse was "all right if you ride him west, but back east of here, where he come from, it ain't so good."

And there was a reluctance, born of something more than courtesy, about asking a stranger's name in those days. The impolite and curious few who broke this unwritten rule of etiquette had to be prepared to punctuate the question with gunshot. A portion of the population—surely exaggerated, but still considerable—had scrawled "G.T.T." on doors or barn walls or gateposts all through the troubled South, or neighbors had chalked it for them after finding the house deserted and the horse stalls empty. It stood for "Gone to Texas." The people who wrote it for themselves did so with a special kind of desperate, high-hearted and exuberant finality: they wanted the dead past to bury its dead without historical epitaph, and never mind the reasons.

My grandfathers, on both sides of the family, left that kind of mark—one in Mississippi, the other God knows where, but most likely either in Virginia or Tennessee. Having written it, they were gone to Texas in a hurry.

By dint of long and arduous research, I have been able to track down the Mississippian—after a fashion. The other grandparent rests somewhere in Texas, secure in the anonymity he desired.

II

Both Papa and Mama were born in Lavaca County, Texas. Papa is listed in the 1860 Federal Census as Woodson Bosworth, three years old, then the youngest son of Grandpa Henry C. Bosworth. Mama, Bettie Ivanhoe Rucker, first appears in the 1870 Census, when she was six.

Thomas Rucker, the tall and courtly and deliberately mysterious Southerner who was Grandma Hester Ann's second husband, the love of her life, and my grandfather, had died just before the 1870 Census was taken. Nobody knows anything about him. Nobody knows how old he was, or where he came from, or when, or why he was in Texas. Mama remembered him out of her early childhood:

"Your Grandpa Rucker was a polite, soft-speaking man, and very tall—six feet four. And proud—I declare! You never saw a man so proud! He carried himself at his full height, and kind of looked down his nose at folks, but he was well-liked and respected. He could read and write several languages and was a Greek and Latin scholar, and I remember that he told me he was a professor of astronomy and botany, but I don't know where. We had some of his books till that time when your Uncle Bob's ferry dropped the wagon in the Pecos—that was when we were coming back from New Mexico, and you were just a baby. He was a mysterious kind of man, and sort of hinted that he was a disinherited younger son. He said that someday he would tell us all about himself. But he was riding out around the plantation when a cold rain came up and he got soaking wet and took a chill. It turned into pneumonia, and he died without ever telling us a word. . . ."

Whatever the reasons for his cloak of mystery, Thomas Rucker wore it with all the romantic dash of an Inverness cape. Surely he had a middle name. He never used it. There have been many Thomas Ruckers since John and Thomas (sons of Peter Rucker) came to America in 1699. A genealogy and a family history—both excellent

[16]

—tell about the Ruckers who settled in Virginia, founded Ruckersville in Madison County, and later went on to lend the name to towns both in Georgia and Tennessee. Several Ruckers fought in the Revolutionary War; scores of them fought for the Confederacy.

But there seems to be no record of the Thomas Rucker who wrote "G.T.T." on his gatepost.

That "disinherited younger son" hint intrigued and even haunted Mama all her long life, and she was ever hopeful that one day a much forwarded letter would arrive saying that she had heired an estate. She imagined the property would be in England or Ireland; she was certain that the letter would end all hard times for us, and I think she really believed it was coming. Someone actually did write her to solicit funds needed to press the legal fight for a vast fortune, rightfully due the heirs of a "T. Rucker," held in chancery in Ireland. I suspect this was a genteel and lucrative racket, not much different from the notorious "Spanish Prisoner" swindle that parted a great many Americans from their hard-earned dollars over a long period of time.

Mama had no money to send, but the letter rekindled her dreams. These were actual nocturnal dreams, not mere daytime fancies.

"Last night," she said once, her eyes shining, "I dreamed I met a mysterious stranger. He told me that if I would go to a place called Richland Springs I would learn something of great advantage. Those were just the words he used—I could see him, just as plain! I wonder if there is a place named Richland Springs?"

(There is. I was about twelve at the time, big enough to catch the fever, and I looked it up on the Texas map at school. Richland Springs was in San Saba County, not much more than a hundred miles from where we lived. I urged Mama to go there at once. But she never did.)

Her dreams were highly contagious, and I vowed that one day I would trace the lineage of Thomas Rucker and see that Mama came into her own. But I neither had the money to begin the search nor would I have known where to start. With the years, the dream faded

[17]

and grew brittle, and skepticism came. Why had Mama been named Bettie Ivanhoe? (She pronounced the middle name "Ivanna" and passed it along to my second-oldest sister.) Why did Grandpa Thomas use the term "disinherited"? He used it, and added it to Mama's vocabulary when she was no more than six. What had happened, back in Virginia or Tennessee, to send him to Texas? He was sadly out of place, down on the frontier, with his Greek and Latin; he could find little use for his astronomy and botany.

The dream died entirely. I came to the sad conclusion that not much had happened, anywhere, except that Grandpa Thomas Rucker had been caught up in the novels of Sir Walter Scott, which were popular in his day. He must have been especially enamored of Ivanhoe. And, if you remember, Ivanhoe's shield bore the legend "Disinherited."

In short, I fear that the tall ancestor I have vainly tried to track down, splendidly educated for his time and gone to Texas for reasons unknown, was simply an incurable romanticist. Grandma Hester Ann loved him a great deal more than she had loved her first husband, DeWitt C. Maulding; she loved him much more than she did her third husband—for there *was* a third. Thomas Rucker was tall and handsome. He had manners and charm. And if he had no money at the moment—I suspect he was dead broke—there was always the chance that the Old Earl would relent, at death's door, and would draw up a new will. Old Earls did this, quite often, in novels. Mama always loved the books in which it happened. She was an ardent fan of Mrs. E. D. E. N. Southworth. . . .

It was, after all, the Age of the Mysterious Stranger. Samuel Clemens caught its spirit with brilliant satire when he related the doings of the king and the duke in *Huckleberry Finn*. Grandpa Rucker's "someday I will tell you all about myself" went well with the time and the place.

It went well in Texas, where tall tales were always popular, and the distances were so great that nobody could readily check on the tales that were told. In the middle nineteenth century, Boston was a cultural center, and traditions were already old and honored in

Philadelphia, in Williamsburg and Charleston. But Texas was a hundred years behind.

The Texans were building a new empire and establishing a culture of their own, based on values and circumstances far different from any existing in the East. They were still fighting the Indians and the Mexicans, and exploring their new and vast land. Their log cabins, with "dog runs" and stick-and-mud chimneys were only expediences. They were beginning to fashion a new world—one based on symbols burned with red-hot branding irons into the hides of cattle.

Grandpa Thomas Rucker was utterly devoted to his little daughter. He had high and loving plans for her: she would go to Virginia for her schooling, she would become a lady of refinement and culture, at ease in the drawing rooms he remembered, and among the people who had been his own. He could not foresee that she would grow up to marry a man almost exactly his opposite, except for being even farther gone in his own individual brand of romanticism.

Grandpa Rucker died inarticulate, out of time and out of season.

III

As I was out walking one morning for pleasure,
I saw a young cowboy a-riding along,
His hat was throwed back and his spurs were a-jingling ...

Papa was heir to the coonskin cap, but had been born a little too late to wear it. As a very young man he was bold and dashing in the frontier concept of manhood, although he had avoided shooting scrapes. He sported a black mustache (for some strange reason, the males of the time were able to grow mustaches in their teens) and he went booted and spurred. His hat brim was turned up in front, as if he had been riding hard against the wind, and he walked awkwardly in high-heeled boots that were not meant for walking. But his spurs made music.

Papa had been working as a cowboy since his early teens. He rode a lot and knew horses intimately; he spent a great deal of time in the

[19]

cow camps and thought nothing of loneliness. He would have been very ill at ease in Grandpa Rucker's remembered drawing rooms because he was essentially antisocial. Being antisocial in those Texas years was not only a natural thing, but also an aid to longevity: most of the men who were killed died in saloons or gambling halls. Papa felt most secure beside a campfire, and even then he knew enough to keep in the shadows and listen for hoofbeats on the wind or the stealthy sound of a squeaking saddle nearer at hand. He was branding no cattle for himself, but the ranch outfits he worked for were always at war with some bigger, more powerful outfit.

It could hardly have been expected that Papa would have any understanding of women when he led Mama to the altar. He had an older and a younger sister, but his upbringing had been purely masculine. As soon as he could toddle he was off to the corrals to watch the work going on there; when he was six he admired Grandpa Henry's freight wagons, leaving for Matamoros and Veracruz with contraband cotton, and sometimes Grandpa let him ride a little way. He worshiped his older half-brother, Gus, who was big enough to rope and ride. He learned about horses, and how to spit like a man who chewed tobacco, and he early walked like a man.

It was the era in which Texas was all right for men and dogs, but hell on women and horses.

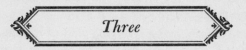

Three

*C*arried back far enough, genealogical research can become a fascinating adventure, a demanding hobby, and—in terms of time and expense—an incurable and wasting disease. Mama and Papa certainly were not ordinary people. Now—in an attempt to show what Mama was, and why—I write a love letter to a gallant lady who died too many years before I was born. It is an expression of my affection, and my respect, for Grandma Hester Ann.

In the search for origins, she stands out vividly, with none of the vague and romantic shadows that still conceal Grandpa Thomas Rucker. Hester Ann can be documented more than once; she comes alive, full-bodied, proud and tempestuous, from the yellowed pages. All of her descendants owe her much more than the mere accident of birth, since birth is an accident that would have happened at some other intersection of life anyway. One thing should be remembered: those who had known both said that Mama was the spit and image —I prefer *spirit* and image—of her mother, Hester Ann.

This explains a great deal. Grandpa Thomas Rucker lived only long enough to give Mama a memory of his mysteries, real or fanciful, and perhaps to add to the aristocratic pride that would be her shield and buckler in the prairie camps and wagon yards and transitory tents; she did not really grow up with him, or enjoy his tutelage long enough to absorb much of his culture and education. Her formative years were lived with Hester Ann. And from this pretty auburn-haired woman, utterly feminine and deceptively soft, Mama inherited more pride, all her outrageous vanity, and all the courage and spirit and rawhide pioneer stamina that would see her through the gypsying years with Papa. Grandma Hester Ann had lived out the rockiest of rocky times in Texas. . . .

She was pure female, and a marrying kind of woman. She divorced her first husband on proven charges of bigamy, but delicately refrained from citing the fact that for three years he had been under indictment for murder. She survived the untimely death of her second husband, my grandfather. I do not find evidence that she ever bothered to divorce her third husband, but in getting rid of him she committed the only unladylike act of her entire life: she literally rode him out of the house and across the gallery and halfway to the yard gate, sitting astride the small of his back, boxing his ears vigorously and yanking out strands of his thinning hair.

It was the era of the sidesaddle. Ladies *never* rode astride. Not even in an emergency.

To my older brothers and sisters, who can remember her living, she was always, affectionately, "Little Grandma." Grandma Martha Bounds Bosworth, on my father's side, was inclined to weight in her middle years and was known as "Big Grandma."

The two were acquainted in Lavaca, back in the 1860's. Their houses were not too far apart, and they were curiously related to each other by marriage ties too complex to figure out.

A Texas newspaper, the Columbus *Old Capitol* (which waited until after Little Grandma's death to publish "a bit of Lavaca County history"), described her as "a beautiful and accomplished lady." The more I learn about Hester Ann, the more I find myself comparing her with a famous and exceptionally well-drawn fictional contemporary. She and Scarlett O'Hara had much in common. They were of an approximate age; their upbringing and environment and heritage were largely similar. Each had heired the Old South at a fateful time, when all they had known was doomed. Both owned slaves and considered such ownership a desirable and natural thing, and a responsibility to be discharged with kindness. Both met wreck and ruin in the Reconstruction.

But there the similarity and resemblance end. Hester Ann, purely female but not entirely feline, had no claws. She could not be hard or shrewd. She had no head for business.

The slaves she had owned were as bewildered by their emancipated status as was Hester Ann, herself. She summoned all of them to tell them that they were free.

They stood respectfully, hats in hand, and the more comprehending wept.

"But whah we go, Miss Hetty?" they implored piteously. *"Whah we go?"*

"I don't know!" Hester Ann answered. She began weeping, too. "I don't know. But go—please go! Because it's your right to go— you're free. Don't you understand? You're all free!"

They did not really understand. In the end, most of them stayed, having no money and finding it difficult to get jobs. Their lot was hard; one of their more substantial privileges was to be buried in the newly-established Freedmen's Cemetery, and that proved a fleeting reward. In 1891, the town of Hallettsville dug into the east bank of the Lavaca River to get earth for a street building program. They found skeletons there, and assumed they were the remains of some ancient Indian tribe—until somebody remembered where the Freedmen's graveyard had been established.

They stayed, the tragic black people, and Hester Ann fed and clothed them as best she could, and cared for the new children who were born free. This was during the worst of the rocky times. There was barely enough to eat. Corn, if the crop was good, and sweet potatoes. They used molasses for sweetening, and parched the corn to brew for coffee; they dyed clothing a tiresome brown color with an extract made by boiling pecan shells. No boy under twelve ever owned any clothing except a long shirt that was more like a nightgown than an article worthy of masculine apparel, and all clothes were handed down.

Hester Ann sold her land in driblets so that she could take care of her kin and her "people." She insisted upon payment in gold, or at least in "coin dollars."

"And then she got married for the third time," Mama used to say, with her nose wrinkling in a faint memory of distaste. "Oh, I know—she needed a man around the place at Sweet Home, after your Grandpa Rucker died. But she married a Yankee—a carpetbagger! He was nearly thirty years older than your grandma. That was when I was maybe eight years old—around 1872."

It was May 24, 1872, to be exact. And in telling about it, Mama committed a libel which I have laid to her love for Hester Ann and her deep Texas resentment of the Reconstruction. Because Little Grandma married Thomas Carpenter. The records show that he had been around Texas longer than Hester Ann herself, and that he wasn't a Yankee carpetbagger at all. The hated word "North" had been connected with his name—but that was because he hailed from *North* Carolina!

"No, it wasn't Thomas Carpenter who beat Little Grandma out of all she owned," my oldest brother, Dee, told me. "It wasn't him at all. Mama had some cousins named Chapman—let me see, Till Chapman, he was one of them. There was another Chapman who had one leg that just ended at the knee, with a perfectly shaped little foot on it—he rode a special saddle, I remember, with one stirrup shorter than the other. Well, the Chapmans had mighty long fingers. They were always selling cows. And they butchered beef and sold it, and they never owned a single steer. A lot of other people were doing that. No . . . it was the times and the customs that made Little Grandma go broke . . ."

The War had been over a quarter of a century when Hester Ann died of a heart attack in her garden at Sweet Home. She was only in her middle fifties, and she came of long-lived people. But, in a way, death was kind. She had outlived the time she knew and loved, and had entered an era that she could never understand. She never got over the Reconstruction.

Papa and Mama were in Karnes County, less than a hundred miles away, at the time of her death. But there were no telephones, and not even telegraph facilities in the vicinity. The news had to come by mail.

The morning after Little Grandma died, Mama awoke deeply disturbed. At breakfast, she related her dream. Her mother had appeared—"Just as plain as I can see you, right now! And she said, "Bettie Ivanhoe, I have come to tell you good-bye . . ."

Two days later, a letter arrived from one of Mama's half-brothers. Grandma Hester Ann had already been buried at Sweet Home.

II

The Hannas ran to red hair and independent, explosive natures. They had come from the Middle Border country, where the Highlanders used to steal the Lowlanders' cattle and women, and vice versa; they settled early in the Carolinas and married their own kind, and moved on into Georgia, and, eventually, into Louisiana. They moved when their cotton land wore out, which was often in the days before chemical fertilizers were known; besides, they were a restless and tempestuous breed, and very property-hungry. They traded in land and slaves and livestock, and had recourse rather frequently to the courts of law. If it had not been for this latter tendency, I might not have been able to trace them at all.

Little Grandma was born Hester Ann Hanna, in the lush, green, bearded-oak and cypress country near Clinton, Louisiana—in East Feliciana Parish—in the year 1834. Judging from her mother's age, she must have been the eldest of several children born to Robert O. Hanna and his wife, Elizabeth.

This Elizabeth Hanna, my great grandmother, set off the Texas migration for numerous other members of the family when she went there in January, 1844. For reasons which will never be known, she had just obtained a divorce from Robert O. Hanna.

Elizabeth took her three children and eleven slaves along with her. She went to Lavaca County, and by 1846 she had remarried. Her second husband was Walter Hinckley, who had a plantation six miles northwest of Hallettsville, the county seat. Hinckley became the legal guardian of Elizabeth's children, and had the use of her slaves and owned twenty-three of his own.

The tax rolls for that year listed him as the second-largest slave owner in Lavaca County—only old Greenwood Foley owned more blacks—and he was assessed for having a carriage. He paid taxes on 83 head of horses, 200 head of cattle, twelve yokes of oxen, and 40 head of sheep.

This, in 1846, was wealth.

In 1846, Hester Ann Hanna was twelve. She was swiftly developing into womanhood at that age, as her mother had done before her, and as her daughter (Mama) would do.

Was this a blood heritage, the early ripening? Was it because of the warm sun of the South? Or did Nature, in some mysterious and prescient way, produce women earlier to meet the needs of the frontier?

The girls of Louisiana and Texas still marry at the ages of fifteen and sixteen—but not as often as they used to do. More of them go on through high school and college, now. The same sun is shining; the same biological demands assert themselves. But the need of the frontier is not there any more, because the frontier has gone. And who is to say what really brought about those early marriages, and whether or not they were wise? The age had no Dr. Kinsey to probe its sex mores. It was quite Victorian, and would have been thoroughly shocked if anyone had tried such a survey.

Great Grandma Elizabeth was extremely well-to-do around the year 1850—a circumstance that has no part in this narrative beyond the fact that my mother was born wealthy and died poor, and the recurring wonder on my part: *what happened to our money?* The only thing of actual importance here is to show that Mama had to leave a lot of things behind when she went adventuring in a Studebaker wagon.

In 1846, slave ownership in Lavaca County was something like a rating in Dun & Bradstreet. There were only thirty-eight people who owned slaves. In 1850, there were 1,571 people in the County—the slaves were not counted that year. As a ten-year-old child in Louisiana, Little Grandma Hester Ann already had three Negroes in her own name, and they came to Texas with her.

Then the Hannas met the marrying Mauldings. In the long run, the results were rather confusing, and a little tragic.

Little Grandma Hester Ann Hanna, not yet fifteen, became the bride of DeWitt C. Maulding on the 27th day of July, 1848. She was a grown-up young lady of property. DeWitt C. Maulding was eighteen, and a man, big and handsome, the son of old Major John W. Maulding.

Little Grandma Hester Ann moved just over the line into Victoria County, probably on land she already owned, with her new husband. The 1850 Census finds them there: DeWitt C. is listed as a herdsman, and they have a year-old son named John W., who did not survive.

Walter Hinckley, second husband of Great Grandma Elizabeth Hanna, had opened a hardware store in Hallettsville, and continued to prosper. In June of 1854 he died, and before a year had passed Great Grandma remarried.

A Lavaca County planter, writing to his daughter in an Alabama school, on February 22, 1855, said, "I do not know that I have one word of news that will interest you. Mrs. Hinckley was married to old Major Maulding, the other day. One of his sons, you know, had married one of her daughters long since . . ."

The wedding took place on February 13, 1855. According to Federal census records, which did not always get ages right, the bride was the grandmother of a five-year-old boy when she was only thirty-five. But, then, let us remember that this was in Texas.

Great Grandma sued for divorce three years later. But in her suit she charged that Major Maulding had left her bed and board on the third day of August, after their February marriage. During those three years she had been in court rather frequently, attempting to hold together an estate which Major Maulding seemed bent upon liquidating.

On the 12th of August, 1855, he sold to J. O. Wheeler of Victoria a whole family of slaves: "Harry, a yellow man, 35; Martha, his wife, (yellow) 25; Frank, 9, Ann, 5, Maria, 3, and Alice, 1—children of Harry and Martha, all yellow." Added was, "Tom, black boy, aged 14, together with a sorrel horse and buggy."

I consider it very white of Major Maulding to have put the black boy, Tom, before the horse. This was protocol in a day when nobody knew what the word meant.

The transaction netted thirteen hundred dollars. It is interesting because of things Major Maulding could not have known at the time. J. O. Wheeler was a former ship captain and a pioneer railroad builder. He went to France two years later—in 1857—and died there. His body was put aboard ship for return to Texas, and superstitious members of the crew refused to sail. Finally, the casket containing J. O. Wheeler was sent home under a cargo manifest listing it as a piece of granite. . . .

But, back in 1855, Major John W. Maulding was selling off my great grandmother's estate in an alarming fashion. Six hundred and seventeen acres, for $600 cash in hand, to Z. N. Hanna. Other smaller deals. Great Grandma Elizabeth went to court and deeded 446 acres to her daughter Louisa, who by this time was married. She went to court again in October and had her husband put under bond of ten thousand dollars, and got an order taking the property completely out of his hands.

She waited three years before suing for divorce, but, meanwhile, she was rid of the Major, who seems to have been a liability. Besides, it was very confusing to be married to the father of your daughter's husband, which made you your own daughter's mother-in-law.

III

The marriage of Little Grandma Hester Ann to DeWitt C. Maulding lasted fifteen years, if one counts the three years he was not in residence because of the murder indictment and the war. They lived in

Victoria County for a while, probably on land owned by Great Grandma, and then they came back to Lavaca County. The first baby had died. They had two other sons, Ed Maulding, born in 1856, and Lee Maulding, who arrived two years later.

"I can remember Uncle Lee Maulding very well," my brother Dee told me. "He was Mama's half-brother, you know. I remember when he was running a little country store down at Runge, in Karnes County. It was the first time I ever saw a music box. Uncle Lee had a music box in his store—you put in a paper roll and turned a crank and it played a tune. . . ."

Hester Ann and her husband were not keeping a store in the early days of their marriage, but like the other Hannas and Mauldings they bought and sold human chattels. The price varied. The market fluctuated, and what a slave was worth depended upon current values, sex and fertility, age, and the condition of the teeth.

On the 17th of October, 1849, "for and in consideration of the sum of 176 Dollars, paid by Collatinus Ballard of Lavaca County," Little Grandma and her husband and his father, Major Maulding, sold "a certain Negro child, named Elizabeth, of yellow complexion, about four years old, and a slave for life." (The title was guaranteed.)

On the 27th of April, 1855, Grandma Hester Ann paid John W. Maulding "900 Dollars for a Negro boy, Jim, of yellow complexion, and two Negro girls—Mima, dark, about 21, and a slave for life—and Tizza, of yellow complexion, about 10."

This was the year that Major John W. Maulding had to be stopped, by court order, from selling off the whole damned plantation. It is nice to find that some of the transactions were within the family . . .

This transaction also shows that seven years after her marriage, Little Grandma Hester Ann was plainly the manager of her property, and DeWitt C. Maulding was head of the family in name only. Occasionally he affixed his signature to a deed or a bill of sale, but it was always after that of Hester Ann.

But then, in 1860, when they were living in a gray house on the west bank of Little Brushy Creek, not far from where it empties into the Chicolette, DeWitt C. Maulding came quite suddenly into the limelight of notoriety.

The fires were already smoldering, that year, and needed only a wind to fan them into open flame. The national issue had been pretty clearly defined; the few Abolitionists in Lavaca County were well, but not favorably, known. The population had grown to nearly 6,000, and slaves (who were not counted in the census) numbered 1,882 on the tax rolls. The history of Lavaca County written by Judge Paul C. Boethel, of Hallettsville, says these slaves represented an assessed valuation of $1,143,730.

"National developments were closely followed in the county," Judge Boethel wrote. "The large planters were kept informed on the issues by the State press. The people as a whole, however, were dependent on the local press, the Hallettsville *Lone Star,* and their leaders, the majority of whom were violent secessionists. As a result, the sentiment for secession developed early, and assumed such proportions by the fall of 1860 as to include practically everyone in the county."

(On the day after Sumter had been fired upon, James Gordon Bennett's New York *Herald* had a total circulation of 287,750. California was receiving a comparatively imposing number of these papers, with a circulation in that state of 5,525. But Mr. Bennett's voice was hardly even a whisper in Texas. He had 35 subscribers in the Lone Star State.)

The Comanches had moved westward, but the other public enemies—the cattle and horse thieves, highwaymen, crooked gamblers, common murderers, and now the Abolitionists—were still around. On November 12, 1860, the *Lone Star* printed a full-column front-page advertisement that revealed something of the temper of the times. It extolled the merits of Colt's Revolving Breech firearms—pistols, rifles, carbines and shotguns.

"Simple Reason for preferring Colt's Arms to all others" listed such things as:

They do not endanger your eyesight and brain, as do the arms with patent primes, which fly like shells into many pieces.

They do not stick fast, refusing either to open or shut without the aid of an axe when heated, as do the guns which open like molasses gates or nutcrackers.

Treat them well, and they will treat your enemies badly.

They are always worth what they cost—in the Far West much more— almost a legal tender! If you buy anything cheaper, your life, or that of your companion, may balance the difference in cost.

If you buy a Colt's Rifle or Pistol, you feel certain that you have one true friend, with six hearts in his body, and who can always be relied on.

(Prices ranged from nine dollars for a five-shot, .31 caliber pistol, to twenty dollars for a six-shot .44, with a 7½-inch barrel, and $32.50 for a six-shot, .44 caliber carbine. The .44 holster pistol with the long barrel weighed four pounds and two ounces; it could do much to establish peace and quiet when brought down upon a rowdy's skull.)

IV

When the census enumerator came around in 1860, he listed the dwellings by number in the order of his calling upon them. The result shows a sprawling but closely-knit rural community of people who were either then, or later, largely related by marriage. John Hanna was in House 284, Hester Ann and her husband DeWitt C. Maulding were in House 285. William Maulding was not far away. In House 346 was the family of Thomas Carpenter, who would one day be Grandma Hester Ann's third husband, and his daughter Josephine, then ten, who would marry Papa's half-brother Gus. Farther on, in House 478, was the family of young William Bounds, and in House 480 lived Grandpa Henry Bosworth and his wife, who had been Martha Bounds.

In House 410 was Joseph Ammanecker. He had been making himself exceedingly unpopular in Lavaca, and around the town square at Hallettsville, and at the crossroads village of Sweet Home. He owned no slaves himself, and was given to cracker-barrel oratory denouncing those who did. He was remembered as always making trouble of some sort: there had been the time, in 1852, when he voted illegally in an election concerning the location of the county seat. His ballot was thrown out on grounds that he was an alien—he had been born in France, but spoke with a thick German accent.

They called him "the Old Dutchman." He was only forty-nine, but he wore a long gray beard. Now he was championing Abolition, and making much of a title he may or may not have owned. It was "Freiherr von Ammanecker," and he boasted that "Freiherr" meant he was a free man, and that the "von" showed he was of the nobility.

The Texans—if they had liked him—would have greeted the title with loud guffaws and pants slappings, and let it go at that. Instead, they told it around that the Old Dutchman was in league with the Devil. They said he had owed one Sandy McGuire the sum of $14.45 and, instead of paying, had induced Sandy to swallow some pills of his own manufacture. These "exploded in the stomach," and Sandy McGuire was no more. They said he had a grudge against a Dr. Beach, and took revenge by pouring quicksilver into the ears of the doctor's faithful horse, which also shortly was no more.

The Old Dutchman rode a big sorrel stallion with arrogant Prussian pride, and for this his neighbors liked him even less. Then, on March 7, 1860, he committed an overt act.

On the farm adjoining his, in House 411, lived a sixty-one-year-old farmer named Major Smith, who had come from North Carolina more than twenty years before, and had a wife and five children. He and Ammanecker had an argument, and the Old Dutchman cut him with a knife.

This assault, unlike the mercurial mischief done to the doctor's horse, or the time bombs he allegedly fed Sandy McGuire, is of record. He was convicted of assault with intent to murder, and fined $100 and costs. (State of Texas *vs.* Joseph Emmenecker, No. 411, District Court of Lavaca County. The Old Dutchman's name was spelled variously.)

The 1860 Census enumerator came and went, the knife attack rankled, and Major Smith was still limping on the evening of October 12, when a meeting of sorts was held at Little Grandma Hester Ann's house on the Little Brushy. She owned the hall, but the meeting was men's business, with a jug of the circulating kind. Grandma Hester Ann stayed off the front gallery, and saw to it that the slaves cleaned her kitchen and washed the supper dishes. She put her sons Ed and Lee Maulding to bed early.

Six men were on the gallery, chewing tobacco, spitting into the yard, and passing the jug. DeWitt C. Maulding was the acknowledged leader. Major Smith was there, and James Coleman, John Goss, and a circuit rider named John Morris. Another Maulding was there, too, which is not surprising—the woods were full of Mauldings and Hannas. The only thing strange about this one is that he was listed, later, as Ed Maulding, and somehow he became confused with the child Ed Maulding who was asleep in the house.

The jug went around again. Circuit Rider Morris was moved to lead his comrades in a rousing rendition of a song meant to be mournful called "We are Passing Away, Away." The group had not yet gotten around to discussing the object of the meeting, the Old Dutchman.

Then the singing ended abruptly in mid-chorus. There was the Old Dutchman swinging down from his big red stallion at the front gate.

Ammanecker had heard about the meeting. Some notion of strategy was in his mind: he could best frighten his enemies by putting on a bold front. So, in his thick accent, and in a tone both jovial and challenging, he demanded, "Vell, boys—vhen you hangs Old Ammanecker, hey?"

Subsequent proceedings must have surprised him considerably. There was a shocked interval; the six men looked at each other in the twilight. DeWitt C. Maulding had the jug. He tilted it with grave deliberation while Ammanecker waited for an answer. The jug gurgled musically. Maulding wiped his mouth on the back of his hand.

"By God, boys!" he said. "What's wrong with right now?"

They fell upon the Old Dutchman as one man, and after a rather violent struggle helped him back on his horse, which they led to a convenient liveoak tree, and there the horse went away without a rider after being smartly quirted on the rump. Old Ammanecker's long gray beard, they say, waved well in the wind.

The old newspaper accounts of this lynching tell that Freiherr von Ammanecker pronounced a lurid curse before the rawhide *riata* shut off his wind. It was meant for all present, but it was directed with particular feeling against DeWitt C. Maulding, then a large and handsome man of thirty, owning a beautiful and well-to-do wife and a number of slaves. According to the Columbus *Old Capitol,* years later, the curse was quite effective.

Meanwhile, somebody found the Old Dutchman in the next day or two, and cut him down. His long beard was tucked into the coffin. The grand jury met and dutifully voted murder indictments against DeWitt C. Maulding John Morris, Major Smith, John Goss, James Coleman, and Ed Maulding.

The handwritten true bills are now yellowed with age and breaking at the folds, so that a few words are illegible. They allege that the defendants "did beat, bruise and illtreat and inflict two wounds" upon the person of Ammanecker, and that they "feloniously, wilfully, and of their malice aforethought did make an assault with a certain rope which they [illegible] around the neck of him. . . ."

That grand jury was told that each of the six defendants was "not found."

V

To use an expression of the time, all six of the indicted men had joined the birds, which is to say they migrated, and yet perhaps few of them were ever far away. Hiding out in the brush would have been pretty hard on Major Smith, turning sixty-two; I wonder how far he went and how long he stayed? There is no record to show whether the six fled immediately after the lynching, or whether they stayed until the grand jury was called, next year.

During that interim, the Civil War broke over the land with its larger violence. Every year, the process servers went through the motions, and made new "not found" notations on the warrants. Who wanted to prosecute anyway? Had anybody liked the Old Dutchman, in the first place? He was an Abolitionist, wasn't he?

None of the six was ever prosecuted. When DeWitt C. Maulding finally came in and surrendered to the law in Hallettsville, in 1871 —eleven years after the lynching of the Old Dutchman—his attorneys promptly obtained his release on a writ of habeas corpus. The case was never called to trial, and DeWitt C. Maulding was not seen again in those parts.

But the curse that had been pronounced by the Old Dutchman remained. It was a thing to gossip about when the ladies of the community gathered to rock and dip snuff on some shaded front gallery; its telling made Little Grandma a legend in her own lifetime. The Columbus *Old Capitol* more than did justice to the legend in a three-column story published shortly after her death, and this was reprinted in the Hallettsville *Herald & Texas Farm and Ranch* as "a bit of Lavaca county history," on April 4, 1889. It formed the basis, in 1959, for a chapter in a second book written by the scholarly Judge Paul C. Boethel, of Hallettsville. He called the chapter "When the Dutchman Cursed the Vigilantes" and through research was able to correct the names that had been thinly disguised by the *Old Capitol*—probably because Texas libel laws in 1889 were rather drastic.

I have a photostat of the story as it appeared in the *Herald,* describing Hester Ann as "a beautiful and accomplished lady," and giving her husband, "a gentleman of wealth," the courtesy title of "Major." It relates the events that led up to the lynching bee, and then goes on to tell about a horseback ride to Port Lavaca which DeWitt C. made a few days later, in the company of one of the Hanna boys—whose name was changed to "Hare." The two men encountered a rain and lightning storm after dark, and suddenly discovered the presence of a third horseman riding between them. There was a flash of lightning. . . .

"My God!" exclaimed Mr. Hare. "It is Old Ammanecker on his big sorrel stallion!"

"Nonsense," replied the Major. "Let us gallop on and outstrip the storm."

They put spurs to their horses. But the ghost of the Old Dutchman (and the imagination of the reporter) also went into full gallop. The specter rode stirrup-to-stirrup with Maulding, and began to chant:

> *A buzzard shall feast on her bosom so fair,*
> *As you fly, as you fly, as you fly for your life;*
> *You may seek her at home, but she'll never be there,*
> *Yet, you'll meet her again as another man's wife!*

With a wild, devilish laugh, Old Ammanecker's ghost veered away when Maulding grabbed for the red stallion's bridle rein. Then it came back, and the Major shook his fist into the face of the grinning specter, and shouted:

"Cease thy insults, sirrah! I would to God thou wert flesh and blood, that I could wreak my vengeance upon thee, thou accursed spawn of hell!"

(It seems rather remarkable that DeWitt C. Maulding, a herdsman certainly accustomed to the language of cow camps and cattle hunts, should suddenly talk like that.)

The ghost would not be silenced. It waxed even more prophetic:

> *There is yet a scene I gloat o'er, a grave*
> *Where the hangman his work has performed but too well;*
> *You may call on the powers of Heaven to save,*
> *But together we'll sup in the nethermost hell!*

The newspaper account goes on to tell of Hester Ann's second marriage, and how, years later, she is summoned to the grave of her son, Ed Maulding. In this story, Ed has become involved in the

Sutton-Taylor feud. He is pulled out of jail in Clinton (then the county seat of DeWitt County) and hanged by a lynch mob.

At the graveside, Little Grandma meets her former husband, the "Major," now fragile and bent. I quote:

"Hester!" he said in a voice hoarse and unnatural.

"Mr. Maulding," she replied; then, overcome by the intensity of her emotions, she found relief in tears.

"Hester," he continued, "we laid him to his final rest the other day, the body of our loved, wayward boy, the last severed bond of even a remote communality between us. Henceforth, I ask no favors of life, and I trust it will soon relinquish all claims upon me. But *you*, Hester, you have ties that yet bind you to earth, to life, to society; return to your home, resume your duties; and around this hallowed spot, this altar, upon which we have laid the sacrifice of our hopes, our love, and our sorrows, I trust that our souls will hold communion forever, Hester, goodbye, and may God bless you, my . . ." his voice sinking, refused expression to the sentiment, and scalding tears shut in his vision.

It is a shame to spoil what was a rousing good newspaper story when it was reprinted in Hallettsville, at a time when Grandma Hester Ann was well and favorably remembered. A great number of readers must have accepted it as the truth. It called for rocking chairs and snuff bottles and wagging tongues again. But it was one of those newspaper stories that remains forever exclusive, being fashioned of half-truths and whole cloth.

Hester Ann's son, Ed Maulding, was not the Ed Maulding indicted at the time of the Old Dutchman's hanging—he was no more than five years old when the true bills were voted. He was never a "wayward boy"—Mama remembered both her half-brothers, Ed and Lee, as well-behaved young men. And Ed Maulding was still around and counted in the Census of 1880, when he was twenty-four and the father of three children.

There were many of the marrying Mauldings at the time. The Ed Maulding named in the indictment could have been a brother or a cousin of DeWitt C.; the sentimental graveside reunion of Little

[37]

Grandma with her former husband must have been dreamed up by a correspondent who was getting space rates.

I know what happened to DeWitt C. Maulding. Microfilm records of the Confederacy in the National Archives show that he enlisted as a private in Company E, 19th Louisiana Infantry, when the war broke out. (He had gone to Louisana, apparently, to wait for the hanging case to blow over.) He served principally at Corpus Christi, and found relief from the monotony of military life by making frequent trips to Goliad. There was a twenty-one-year-old widow, or divorcée, in Goliad, named Virginia Harmond. She had a two-year-old son and had come from Mississippi, like the Mauldings. It is possible that DeWitt had known her or her family before.

He married her on February 19, 1863, without having done anything toward dissolving his matrimonial ties with Hester Ann. It was a few months before Little Grandma learned about this. When the fall term of the Tenth Judicial District Court convened, she was there with her attorneys, McLean and Tate, and a certified copy of DeWitt C.'s bigamous marriage license.

Her divorce petition brought out her personal ownership of the woman June (now forty-two), and the boy Bob (now twelve), and the boy William, whose years are still blank. It discussed parcels of land purchased with her own money, and the gray house on the Little Brushy, which she also had bought, and it prayed for the custody of the two children Ed and Lee.

The court granted her pleas in their entirety. It decreed, also, that Hester Ann resume her maiden name, but that portion of the judgment was stricken out. It may well have been that Little Grandma informed the court that she was about to change her name again anyway.

Once free, she lost no time. On September 20, 1863, she married the tall and mysterious Thomas Rucker.

County Judge B. F. Wrote performed the ceremony. Grandpa Rucker looked down at his pretty bride, who was then only twenty-nine, and squeezed her hand affectionately. Someday, he promised, he would tell her all about himself.

[38]

Mama was born on the fifth of the following August. She never used to say that she was born in 1864. It was always "the year the War broke up."

As everyone knows, the war didn't end until 1865. But it "broke up," in the sense of shattered Confederate dreams, during the year previous.

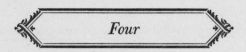

Four

No place ever had a lovelier name than Sweet Home, where Mama was born; and in those days, before too much of the timber had been cut and too much of the land fenced and broken by the plough, few places could have owned a more serene and pastoral beauty. You can still find Sweet Home on the map, down on the rolling Texas coastal plain: it is in a green and gentle land watered by two rivers—the Lavaca and the Navidad —and by many a winding little creek, leaf-shaded and lazy, and intriguingly named. Across the pastures in springtime the tall grass runs in the wind like a flowing green sea, and turns tawny and golden with the early summer ripening; anyone with half a cattleman's eye can see that this was meant forever to be cow country, and the river's old Spanish name, and that of the county—Lavaca—meant "the cow." Spanish moss drapes the shoulders of the spreading live-oaks like gray lace *mantillas,* lending them even greater dignity and age, and recalling the land's heritage. The moss sways in the wind of moonlight nights, when ghosts of the past walk again along the banks of Mustang and Chicolete creeks and the Little Brushy; the moon lays its silver on the glossy liveoak leaves, and the wind sets them whispering.

The land that looks so peaceful has a remarkable history of violence. Here stood the tree—it was pointed out for many years—where they found old Ammanecker hanging that morning, his gray beard bending like a strand of moss in the wind, his stiffening body turning from side to side like an indecisive weather vane. Here on Ponton Creek, not far away, was where William Ponton's horse did not quite clear a gully, and the Comanches caught him. They cut the skin from the soles of his feet and made him walk quite a way before they scalped and killed him. This and many another Indian horror were still fresh in the memory of older settlers when Mama was a little girl.

The Indians had gone a little west of the Lavaca when Grandma Hester Ann came, and quite a bit farther before the Bosworths got to that country. But the violence went on. Somebody murdered old Frank Vanlitzen because he wouldn't reveal the source of the lead he had been molding into bullets—a vital commodity of the time. Along in 1870, there was another memorable hanging bee. A mob lynched three Negroes who had killed a German settler named Newman, together with his wife and baby and a Negro servant. The story goes that the bodies of the three were never cut down—at least not for a very long time. Eventually a music lover living on Honey Creek retrieved a portion of one of the skeletons, and whittled keys and a tailboard for his fiddle from the sun-bleached bones.

There were scores of such stories for Mama to hear when she was a child. And Grandma Hester Ann was fond of telling her the legend of Pirate Jean Lafitte and the million dollars' worth of treasure he had buried near Maulding's Motte the time a prowling revenue cutter bottled up his ship in Matagorda Bay and drove it up the Lavaca River. Little Grandma believed the treasure was still there—maybe on land that had belonged to her first husband's family. So, for a long time, did a lot of other people.

The causes of violence were simply changing with the changing economy. The Indians killed because they were losing their land and their way of life, old Ammanecker was lynched because he attacked an economic system at a time when feelings about it ran high, and somebody wanted the other old Dutchman's lead mine badly enough to commit murder. And the economy changed suddenly and drastically just after the Civil War, when the cattle that had been running wild in the brush became all at once worth more than cotton. Men died in Texas because railroads building deeper into Kansas made it possible for New York to eat Texas beef. The longhorn herds began bellowing past Sweet Home on their long and dusty way north; there were people with too many branding irons in the fire, and some of them got shot.

Then came the Sutton-Taylor feud. It was reported to have "started back in the Carolinas, flourished in Georgia in the '40's, and was brought to Texas with the household goods of the Taylors and Suttons, who, oddly enough, elected to settle in DeWitt." DeWitt County was at first its principal shooting preserve, but the dispute and its tributary quarrels spilled over the boundaries into Victoria and Lavaca counties, and the twentieth century had dawned before the peaceful-looking country really knew peace. . . .

Sweet Home has been moved a little way from its original location near Mustang Creek, nine miles west of Hallettsville. Today it has two stores, two churches and a modern school, the usual filling stations, and a scattering of neat farmhouses with fat shorthorn cattle grazing behind the fences. There are two cemeteries, and the older one is sad to see—a net wire enclosure of rank, waist-high grass that mercifully conceals memorial stones leaning awry or fallen into the pitifully sunken spaces that once were mounds. Even the returning dust that lies here in the inexorable collapse of pine box and bone rib cage is not the older dust of the first settlers. The stones mostly bear Germanic names. The roster of early-day taxpayers was almost entirely Anglo-Saxon; it might have been a list of the people who settled at Jamestown. Arnolds, Ballards, Bests, Billingses, and Boatwrights; Browns, Butlers, Clarks, Dodds, and Dowlings; Foleys, Fosters, Greenwoods, Heaths, and Hinckleys; Kellys, Kents, Laughlins, and McDonalds; Millers, Murphys, Ryans, Shaws, Tates and Tollivers and Watts—these were only a representative few, and the names of

Hanna, Maulding, Rucker, Bounds, and Bosworth blended well with them.

In the seventies and later, successive waves of immigration came to Lavaca County from western Europe. Germanic tongues were heard around the Hallettsville town square, several newspapers were being printed under names like *Obzor, Nachrichten, Der Anzeiger* and *Treue Zeuge,* and one could no longer single out any man by referring to him as "the Dutchman."

The newcomers were fine people, fair-haired and neat and thrifty. They had come to Texas because they needed room, but they did not need as much room as the Tennessee mountaineers or the people from the pines and bayous of the Deep South. Furthermore, having liked what they found, they stayed there.

II

Old Sweet Home was never more than a crossroads village. But when Grandma Hester Ann married Thomas Rucker and moved there, it shared a common importance with some other strategically situated villages around the world, such as those along the ancient Silk Road of Cathay or, contemporarily, with stations on the recently constructed Panama Railroad, which was hauling California gold across the Isthmus. Sweet Home was becoming the rendezvous and tallying point for Texas herds being thrown on the Long Trail, and for two decades, beginning in 1866, the riches flowing through Sweet Home rivaled the wealth of the Indies.

The little town experienced a mild sort of boom. Several of the earlier-day cattle kings lived there, among them Willis McCutcheon, and George West, who married one of Mama's cousins. In 1866, the first year of record, 260,000 cattle went north. Then cotton staged a temporary comeback and the drives dwindled for two years, but in 1869 the volume was 350,000 head, and the year of 1871 would be the biggest of all. Texas' famed J. Frank Dobie, who knows more about long-horned cattle than any other living man, says the total for that year was 700,000.

This made a number of Texans rich, and a few of them richer. Sweet Home had more than its share of wealth at that time. To be sure, herds were gathered and started for Kansas at other points, but in the beginning most of them came up from southwest Texas along the old road from Matamoros to Alleyton. Contraband cotton had been hauled in the opposite direction during the Civil War blockades, and Grandpa Henry Bosworth had freighted a great deal of it.

Old Sweet Home became a cowboy capital, perhaps as much as Dodge City ever was, except that by the time the trail drivers reached Dodge City they had a larger thirst. The spurs jingled by; the campfires blazed on the prairie. There was usually a dance somewhere, and now some of the violence would start out to be only good-natured fun, it being somebody's night to howl.

Grandpa Thomas Rucker died circa 1871, the year of the record drives. Little Grandma Hester Ann married Thomas Carpenter on May 29, 1872, but now her whole life was devoted to her little daughter, Bettie Ivanhoe. She very carefully sheltered Mama from everything harsh and unseemly. Mama remembered nothing but happiness in her childhood, except that during Reconstruction there were pinches of poverty, and Little Grandma Hester Ann was not accustomed to poverty. She dipped snuff, like all other Texas women of the day; she had started a border of brown snuff bottles along the walk to the front gate, and could not finish it when snuff prices went out of sight.

The boy Bob remained to work for "Miss Hetty," along with her other personally-owned slaves, even after they were freedmen. He was still assigned to look after little Miss Bettie, who romped and played over the place, swung on grapevine swings along the creek, and ate wild mustang grapes. These were sweet enough, inside, but "if you ate the skin it would just take the hide off the inside of your mouth." Mama had only one real, store-bought doll; the boy Bob, clever at working with tools, made her some wooden dolls. She was still very young when she learned needlework from her mother, and she fashioned doll dresses from scraps of calico and gingham and other materials, increasingly scarce, that came out of a large old leather-bound trunk Grandma Hester Ann kept under her high four-poster bed.

The trunk fascinated Mama. It was a treasure chest of things Grandma Hester Ann probably never could have worn on the Texas frontier—even if they had still been in fashion—without having been accused of putting on airs. It contained hoop skirts of crinoline, lacy pantalettes, saucy bonnets decked with ribbons and lace, a pair of dainty ballroom slippers (Little Grandma and Mama were both extremely vain about their small, high-arched feet), and an ivory-handled folding fan. In Texas, ladies fanned mostly with palmetto leaves or with turkey wings; if there were no turkeys around, somebody was sure to have shot a hawk that was swooping over the chicken yard. . . .

The boy Bob went into the kitchen and made Mama a "sugar-tit" by tying a lump of brown sugar in a piece of clean bleached domestic. Mama was admiring a silk dress when he came back.

"That Miss Hetty's dancin' gown," he said. "My Mammy told me—my Mammy belong to Miss Hetty's folks back in Louisiana. She daid, now."

Mama tried to fold the ballroom gown and put it back in the odor of camphor, but her arms were too short and her hands too small. The boy Bob shook his head as he helped her.

"Sho' is a pity, Miss Bettie!" he lamented. "Miss Hetty, she done lost all her money, and Ah reckon you cain't never wear them kind of clo'es. But you remember one thing: you come from quality! Don't you ever 'sociate with no po' white trash!"

One day Grandma Hester Ann came into the room to find that Mama had most of the contents of the trunk draped on the bed or strewn about her where she sat on the floor going through the scraps for new doll dress material.

"Sakes alive!" Little Grandma exclaimed. "Bettie Ivanhoe, don't you ever do this again! If you want something out of my trunk, you ask me to find it for you—hear?" And she made a hasty inspection of the trunk bottom before she began repacking it.

[45]

Mama always remembered that incident. "I think," she used to say, "that your Grandma Rucker kept money hidden in that trunk—that is, what little money she had left." Even though Hester Ann married Thomas Carpenter, Mama always referred to her as "your Grandma Rucker."

But she remembered the scene for more than the thought of money in the trunk. Hester Ann was kneeling on the floor as she repacked the fading souvenirs of another era, the trappings of a life more gracious and more gay. The late afternoon sunlight came through the window to catch her auburn hair and strike glints of gold and burnished bronze from it, and Mama watched with love and envy, wondering if she could ever be that pretty. She was about eight at the time, but she had been born vain, and her vanity sustained and nourished her all her life.

Human memory is marvelously kind, but a poor keeper of the books. The veterans of the past three wars, now grown pot-bellied and bald and even palsied, gather in conventions and weep (by the generations) into their beer as they recall what wonderful times they had in the forests of the Argonne, or in the steamy jungles of Guadalcanal, or on the tomb-pocked ridges of Korea. The facts are that nobody ever had a good time in any of those places. We remember the good things and conveniently forget the bad; to uncover a traumatic experience suffered at the age of six, we have to resort to a psychiatrist's couch.

Mama remembered the good things. I regret being the last of her children. By the time I realized that she had lived a most unusual life, and began to feel a reporter's curiosity about it, she had forgotten much. She did not remember the exact date of Grandpa Thomas Rucker's death, that having been a bad thing; it was, she thought, "when I was six or seven." But she could recall sitting on her father's lap while he read to her from good books; she could describe the color and pattern of a new dress she got as a child, or tell fondly about an occasion when one of the rich cattle drovers was kind to her. She liked going to school near Sweet Home, where she learned to write on a slate and study aloud from McGuffey's *Readers,* Webster's *Blueback Speller,* and Davie's *Arithmetic.*

It seemed to her that the summers of her childhood saw "just one camp meeting after another." Some of these lasted for two weeks, and folks came for miles around to camp beside their buggies and wagons under the liveoak trees, to fan themselves in the shade of the brush-covered arbors when the hellfire and damnation preaching made them break out in a sinful sweat, to enjoy the singing, and the shouting of those unmistakably moved by the Spirit. And the baptisms in the cool waters of the creek—Mama loved them. She was early immersed as a Baptist, but that did not stop her from going to the Mossy Grove Methodist Church when it had revivals—although she never held with "sprinkling" as a means of salvation, because certainly it did not wash the sins away. Nor did she pass up the Negro camp meetings, where the shouting was something to hear, and the Spirit moved penitent sinners to fall and grovel, to claw at the grass roots and talk in the tongues. And the singing!

> *Wade in de water,*
> *Wade in de water, chillun,*
> *Wade in de water—*
> *God gwine to trouble de water!*

Or, again and again, and never growing old:

> *One o' dese mawnin's, bright and fair,*
> *Gwine to hitch mah wings, and try de air. . . .*

Reconstruction times were still rocky. During the short period of her widowhood, and after she married Thomas Carpenter, Grandma Hester Ann was forced to sell parcels of her land to feed the family and the former slaves. July 6, 1871, to Leonidas Hudspeth, 7½ acres of land northeast of Hallettsville, for $300 in gold. (This deed was signed by Hester Ann alone, indicating that Thomas Rucker had already died.) December 8, 1871, a hundred acres twelve miles south of Hallettsville sold for "four hundred coin dollars." On August 6, 1872, less than three months after her marriage to Thomas Carpenter, she sold a hundred acres on Lost Creek to C. C. Haynes, for $348. Haynes was probably a neighbor; a Henry Haynes was one of the witnesses who had been called in the lynching of the Old Dutchman.

Rocky times, indeed. Still, Grandma Hester Ann managed to live graciously. At least once during each summer she took Mama and her Maulding stepbrothers to Port Lavaca, where the boys swam and the womenfolk bathed in the waters of the Gulf. No young lady of the time was athletic; Mama never learned to swim. The bathing was done wearing cotton dresses and stockings, and even then not in mixed company, because wet clothes clung too intimately.

Mama came to the season of her lovely blossoming without ever having been told anything. Perhaps it was better so, since the alleged facts of life are not nearly so beautiful as a young girl's dreams. She had been thoroughly protected: all the lusty violence of the cattle trail had passed her by, and all its spur-jingling bravado did not impress her much. Hester Ann, pressed for money, had opened her house in Sweet Home to a select clientele, and ran something of an inn. Only the owners and the trail bosses stayed there; the cowhands bedded down with the dry cattle, out on the prairie, where campfires lay scattered like fallen stars. Men got drunk, and rode through old Sweet Home with their sixshooters blazing in the air; if they had time, they went to Hallettsville and scorned the hitching posts and rails around the square. They delighted in riding directly into the stores and transacting their business from the saddle—until the year 1888. That was the year a railroad came to town, and the city fathers enacted an ordinance making it a misdemeanor to ride a horse indoors.

There must have been fancy women about; the law of supply and demand would have taken care of that. But if there were, Mama never knew about them. She had been exposed to cattle business— a rough enterprise, at best—since her birth, and fifty years later she would suffer a violent Victorian blush if anybody used the word "bull" in her hearing. To Mama, a bull was always a "gentleman

[48]

cow," or a *"toro."* I don't think she ever learned that the only gentlemen among cows are steers, or that *toro,* after all, is "bull" in Spanish.

III

Not long before he died, Thomas Rucker had talked about sending his daughter to Virginia to school, when she was old enough. Cousin George West, who had the money, talked about the same thing now, as Mama grew into her teens. But Grandma Hester Ann dreaded the idea of being separated from Bettie Ivanhoe, and they kept putting it off.

Besides, Mama didn't want to go anywhere. She had grown up kitten soft and pretty, and now she was having a wonderful time— first at the play parties, and later at dances.

The Texas play party and a dance were two different things entirely. One could attend play parties and not be thrown out of the Baptist Church, which did not countenance dancing. There were times, of course, when a play party descended (or ascended) to the status of a dance—times, say, when a fiddler chanced to drop in— but this never occurred at the Baptist parsonage or the home of a Baptist deacon. Play parties were social gatherings, such as candy pullings, where the young people played Forfeits and Charades, and sometimes—with great giggling and blushing—Post Office. They played lively games like Drop the Handkerchief and Spin the Plate, and there was Skip to My Lou, coming dangerously near to being a dance with its circle and its merry tune:

> *Flies in the buttermilk,*
> *Skip to my Lou!*
> *Flies in the buttermilk,*
> *Skip to my Lou!*
> *Flies in the buttermilk,*
> *Skip to my Lou!*
> *Skip to my Lou, my darling!*
>
> *If you can't catch a redbird,*
> *A bluebird will do;*

[49]

> *If you can't catch a redbird,*
> *A bluebird will do;*
> *If you can't catch a redbird,*
> *A bluebird will do;*
> *Skip to my Lou, my darling!*

These were fun at twelve and perhaps thirteen, and then they suddenly seemed childish. By all present-day standards Mama *was* still a child; by the standards of the Texas frontier in the 1870's, she was a young lady. Everything conspired, in that time and place, to shrink the tender and beautiful span between the child and the woman to nothing at all. The warmth of the sun and the length of the growing seasons had their way with the child's body; the marriage mores were such that census takers listed unmarried girls of twenty as "spinsters," which even then was a synonym for "old maid," and the hot-eyed young men who were drifting into Texas from all over the South greatly outnumbered eligible women. Mama was quite an old woman before she ever heard the term "teen-ager," and it puzzled her. She could understand its application to boys: when she was young, the Lavaca boys in their teens were painfully shy and awkward children, stumbling over their own immaturity. They were antisocial, to begin with, and no young lady of thirteen or fourteen gave them a second look. Girls, on the other hand, were never really teen-agers, but became grown-up, coquettish, and highly desired from the age of thirteen on to their marriages.

The frontier was short of women. Nature moved swiftly to fill the demand.

Mama had grown up in the same community with young Woodson Bosworth. He was eight years older, which made things about right: it gave him a chance to outgrow his gawkiness before Mama reached the mature year of fifteen. Woodie was past twenty-one before Mama ever gave him a second glance; he looked at her one day when she was fourteen, and things were never the same for him thereafter. They began going to dances.

Nobody ever taught Mama how to dance—she already knew. She loved the gay and lively ones; the schottische and the polka were her favorites, and they brought out her high, glowing color, and made her eyes shine. She could do the Virginia Reel and the quadrille, and of course the square dance.

"Sometimes we rode ten or fifteen miles, on horseback, to go to a dance," Mama recalled, her eyes shining again at the memory. "They had the big Saturday night dances in the courthouse at Hallettsville—had them upstairs. There would be a lot of buggies around the square, and of course the boys had jugs in some of them, and sometimes there were fights and shooting scrapes. But mostly they behaved themselves. And there wasn't any of this hugging out on the floor the way young folks do today—I declare, I don't blame the church for throwing them out!"

"But you belonged to the Baptist Church, Mama. And you danced."

She smiled a mischievous smile. "I danced out of the church, one night in Hallettsville—somebody turned in my name. But it was like your Papa said—you're only young once. And after we were married and I had quit dancing, I was baptized again."

The smaller dances were held in homes, or in country schoolhouses, in the summertime. There were still puncheon floors in Lavaca. The sparse pieces of furniture were moved into another room, or put outside in the breezeway that was called a "dog run." There was seldom a rug to be rolled up. They sprinkled corn meal on the floor, and the fiddlers tuned up, and the excitement mounted; there might be a guitar or banjo, or someone who could play the French harp—the harmonica. "Money Musk," "Sally Goodin," "Turkey in the Straw," "Old Dan Tucker," and "Pop Goes the Weasel" were the favorites, although Mama always liked the more sentimental tunes such as "Nellie Gray," "Gentle Annie," and "The Little Old Log Cabin in the Lane."

"We used to dance the moon under and the sun up, and just never thought of getting tired! We didn't pay any attention to what time it was—we just danced!"

✿

There was a square dance, one night, near old Sweet Home, with the fiddles squealing and the prompter calling the numbers, and the dust coming down from the shaken rafters:

> *Toes to the center! Backs to the wall!*
> *Take a chaw of tobacco, and promenade all!*

This was Tuesday evening, October 7, 1879, and Mama was two months past her fifteenth birthday. She had a stock of cream-colored lace at her throat, and wore a dove-gray princess-style dress fitted closely at her whalebone-corseted waist, and the skirt swirling wide to her slender ankles. It was a special occasion, and she had borrowed Grandma Hester Ann's ballroom slippers. . . .

> *Chicken in the bread tray, kickin' up dough;*
> *Granny, will your dog bite? No, by Joe!*

Grandma Hester Ann had gone to the front windows that afternoon, to see who was raising such a commotion. It was that young Woodie Elliott Bosworth, riding up and down the road at a full gallop. He yelled and yipped and slapped his leather *chaparejos* with a plaited Mexican quirt; he showed off his cutting horse, and did everything but lean out of the saddle to pick a handkerchief off the ground with his teeth. He was being *muy caballero*.

"I declare to goodness!" Little Grandma said. "What on earth has got into that young Bosworth boy? Riding by here like the prairie was on fire!"

Mama smiled, and said she guessed it was just because Woodie was taking her to the dance that evening. But her heart began beating fast. Woodie's wild riding was a prearranged signal. It meant that he had obtained the marriage license. . . .

> *Ducks in the river, going to ford;*
> *Coffee in a little rag, sugar in the gourd!*

This was the night they did not dance the moon and stars out

of the sky. Sometime after twelve o'clock, there was a pause. The
two fiddlers and the banjo player took out bandanna handkerchiefs
and wiped their heated brows. Somebody thoughtfully passed them a
brown jug with a corncob stopper. They had recourse to this and
thanked their benefactor right kindly; then the fiddlers resined their
bows and the banjo player tightened his keys. The prompter stamped
his boot on the puncheon floor, and bawled:

> Now, how'll you swap, and how'll you trade
> That purty little gal for this old maid?

And young Woodson Elliott Bosworth and Bettie Ivanhoe Rucker
danced right out the open door.

Mama waited at the gallery while Papa went to untie and saddle
the horses. A mockingbird was singing in the moonlight, and the
world was a lovely place. Her heart beat faster again.

Papa came back riding his own horse and leading the mare with
the sidesaddle he had rented from the livery stable and wagon yard
in Hallettsville. He helped Mama to the sidesaddle with a kiss, and
they rode away from the music. It was ten miles to town, and it
was well past three in the morning when they aroused a sleepy justice
of the peace and showed him the marriage license.

The Judge called for his wife to come down and serve as witness.
Then, growing more awake, he looked at Mama over his steel-
rimmed spectacles. In the soft light of the coal-oil lamp, she was
beautiful. And she was very, very young.

"And how old are you, young lady?" the Judge inquired.

"I'm just over eighteen," Mama answered.

In all her long life, Mama never told a downright lie. She had
written the figure 18 on two slips of paper, and these were tucked
carefully into the bottoms of Little Grandma's dancing slippers.

The Judge pushed his spectacles back up his nose, cleared his
throat, and opened his Bible. Mama began to weep softly, happily.

When the ceremony was over and Papa had paid the fee, they
had coffee with the Judge and his wife, and then rode again. By

the time they reached the wagon yard, where Papa turned in the sidesaddle and the mare, it was already light in the east.

Papa did not carry Mama across any kind of threshold. He did, instead, a far more significant thing. He kissed her, and lifted her possessively and fondly to the seat of a Studebaker wagon. Then he climbed up to unwrap the reins from the brake handle and shake them over the backs of his horses.

That was when the wagon wheels began turning.

Five

*T*his brand-new day started as theirs alone, as if it had been especially created for such blessed new beginnings. Everybody else slept. Mama had known the Hallettsville town square only when it was busy with wagons and ox carts on market days, or was ranged with more important buggies and surreys when the Tenth Judicial District Court was in session, and people watched the courthouse with speculative interest or dire misgivings. She knew it on Saturday nights when dance music filled the halls of justice: then the livery rigs and the saddle horses waited until the fiddlers finally struck up the air of "Home, Sweet Home."

But now the square was forlorn and empty, lying vast in the half-light and the silence, without even a wind to wake the wheel-powdered dust. In the mild chill of October dawn, the town wore an air of age and decay, and fortunes gone downhill. There was the bandstand: patriots had rallied there, and recruiters had made resounding pleas for the Confederacy before Mama was born; now, in a few short years, the knives of idle whittlers had all but cut the railing down, and the initials carved on the balustrade by lovers were not significant.

Daylight broke full as the wagon rumbled across the Lavaca River bridge. Mama always remembered that she looked down at the swirl of brown water, and was giddied by height and motion. She had been too excited to eat during all the previous day; now hunger overtook that intensified excitement, and everything—last night's dance, the elopement, the marriage ceremony—seemed a dream. Fiddle music lingered in her memory; she heard a dance tune in the sounds of harness creak and wheel rattle, and all at once she was tired. Her thoughts raced down the road to Grandma Hester Ann's house; she wondered how her mother and her stepfather would take the news. Mama had always been very close to Grandma Hester Ann.

She glanced sidewise at her young husband. He was handsome in a very masculine way, bold and perhaps a little arrogant, and there was stubbornness in his jaw. He did not look at Mama now; she would learn that when Papa was handling a team of horses, she did not exist. He watched the road for mudholes and stretches of deep sand, and talked only when talk was necessary. He wore buckskin gauntlets with red stars printed on the flaring cuffs, and handled the reins in a way that was both caress and command, and Mama remembered how tenderly he had held her hand when they danced. There was strength in his hands, but they were small and slender, and almost as soft as a woman's; they looked as if he never had worked. Mama used to say that they could have been the hands of a gambler, but Papa neither played cards nor drank. He had no special cronies among the other young bloods who showed up at the dances, but was remembered as a man who traveled alone. He was quiet and introspective, and maybe dangerous.

It occurred to Mama then—as it was to occur to her many times afterward—that she really did not know very much about young Woodie Bosworth.

Looking back, now, and trying to understand the enigma Papa was, I know there was a great deal of the poet in him. He *lived* his poetry, which is more satisfying than trying to write it. He was not given to repeated protestations of his love for Mama. He had told her in the beginning, and that sufficed. Papa was tender and passionate, and sometimes insanely jealous, but he did not say,

"I love you," more than two or three times in all his years with Mama, which is another proof that he did not understand women. She could have used more of that, because she was warm and possessive and needed to be told that she was wanted. In their basic needs and desires these two were almost exact opposites; they were inescapably at war from the start, although in the first sweet seasons neither realized that hostilities had commenced. And they did kindle some lovely fires. Papa could produce the spark—he was flint and steel. Mama was rawhide, soft and strong, pliable and enduring. Rawhide never wears out.

In her old age, when I had heard many stories of Papa's endless peregrinations, I asked Mama why she had gone along with them as far as she did, and she gave me a thoughtfully oblique answer:

"Well," she said after a moment's pause, "your papa never used a smutty word in all his life, and he never even looked at another woman. Besides, there were the children . . ."

When she spoke of him in those later years, he was always *"your papa,"* as if she had long before written disclaimer to all his works. And Papa had long before fallen into the habit of jerking his thumb over his shoulder and referring to Mama as *"she."*

It takes a lot of sadness to make personal pronouns become so impersonal.

II

The sun rose, bright with promise. It was going to be one of those blue and gold October days, lovely in Texas, with a few fleecy Gulf clouds lazing across the sky. Mama's spirits rose. It wasn't a dream, after all: she was really married, and this wagon road ran straight into all her tomorrows. The horses splashed into the shallow ford at Smeather's Creek. Papa let the reins go slack so his team could drink, and spoke for the first time since leaving the wagon yard.

He planned, he said, to head for Goliad, because it was kind of like new country down there—not so settled, not so fenced up. His folks would know if there was any land left where they could take up a squat. Anyway, they could rent a farm and put in a cotton crop. There was a sight of money in a good crop of cotton.

When he said "Goliad," he meant the county, not the town. The Bosworths had never been townspeople. They had chased good cotton land all across Mississippi; they sought it now in Texas. It was, indeed, the money crop of the day. But modern fertilizers had not been developed, and successive crops of cotton depleted and devastated the soil. This had caused the Bosworths to move, in the past. Papa, who was never a big or even successful cotton planter, found his own reasons. And now, in Texas, he was facing a changing economy. If a man had enough grass, he could make more money out of cattle than out of cotton. Papa knew this. *If a man could find open range, and didn't have to fight barbed wire fence.*

Mama knew very little about the actual cultivation of cotton— Grandma Hester Ann's cotton crops had always been planted and chopped and saved by Negro labor. Many of the same people who had belonged to her as slaves, before the war, still worked for her. Mama had watched them from a distance as they moved across the field with effortless grace to cut the jimson weeds that threatened to shade out the cotton plants. This was an ancient enemy; Mama didn't know that the original name was "Jamestown weed." And when she walked out wearing her sunbonnet, she knew nothing of the blinding sweat and aching back that went with cotton picking; her soft hands had always been soft and smooth, never blistered by a hoe handle or cut by hard, dry cotton bolls.

The horses drank and tossed their heads, rolling the bits over their tongues and slobbering silvery streams of water back into the creek. Papa looked behind to make sure the led horse had enough tether for drinking. He removed one gauntlet, and squeezed Mama's hand affectionately. His palm was sweating.

"You'll like it in Goliad," he assured her hopefully. "You'll get to see some new country."

"New country" was a catchphrase, a theme song. It would ring down the years until it became almost unbearably repetitive, until the phrase had only empty meaning, until Mama realized that "new country" was any country lying beyond the western hills.

For some reason, Papa had never gone up the Long Trail with

cattle—probably because he didn't want to be tied up, or committed, for months at a time. But he had helped to drive herds along the coastal plains, and to the tallying point at Sweet Home; he knew how exciting it was to hit the saddle when dawn was breaking, and how a man felt astride a good cutting horse. He knew the special freedom that went with a cowboy's job, even when he was working for wages: he rode out and did some roping, and built some fires and did some branding, and there was never anybody to tell him how much work he should do in a day. He had the sun on his shoulders and the wind in his face, and all the wide world of Texas to ride over and up and down.

There had been little in Papa's life that was actually his own. He had been raised in a rather confused fashion, with an older half-brother and half-sister of an age to take the spotlight. Mama was his first real possession, except for a horse or two. He was going to take her away from everything; he would have her just for himself, to cherish, to care for, to love. Papa's solitary nature was asserting itself here. He wanted nobody else around.

III

Mama always fondly recalled the arrival at Little Grandma's house at Sweet Home that day. She loved this place—a roomy and rambling one-story structure set back from the road, with a long front gallery and a yard shaded by moss-hung liveoaks. But now she saw it as she had seen the older buildings around the Hallettsville square earlier that morning: it needed paint, and new shutters. It had declined, along with Hester Ann's fortunes. When she married Thomas Carpenter, it could hardly have been with the idea of repairing these: he had children of his own and only modest holdings. The Reconstruction was over, but the years kept nibbling at Little Grandma's inheritance; the times kept challenging her way of life. . . .

The sound of wagons going by on the road was nothing unusual. Nobody was in sight. Papa swung his team up by the yard gate, and shouted, "Hello, the house!"

Thomas Carpenter came out on the gallery. In many ways, he was a very remarkable man. He was now seventy-four, but he had the vigor and appearance of a man nearer fifty. For a few seconds he stared, open-mouthed, recognizing the couple of the wagon seat but not quite understanding why they were there. Then he knew. This was no ordinary return from a dance—the wagon had a more established air than a livery stable rig. He yelled, "Well, howdy! Light and unhitch!" and went spryly into the house to fetch Hester Ann.

Papa helped Mama down from the wagon seat. He was beginning to sweat under the arms, because this would be women's territory. Little Grandma came out wearing a blue wrapper, her auburn hair still in curlers.

"I declare to goodness!" she exclaimed. "You young'uns have been out all night! What kind of mischief have you been up to?"

Mama ran sobbing into her arms, and Little Grandma instantly knew the nature of the mischief. They had their cry together, and it made Papa feel even more the stranger, the raider, the criminal. He took off his gauntlets and shook hands with Thomas Carpenter; he put them back on again, and watched Mama and Little Grandma. Papa always regarded woman's tears as an unfair weapon—a man had absolutely no defense against them. Besides, what call did anybody have to cry? Wasn't this supposed to be a happy occasion?

Papa and Mama stayed at Sweet Home for two days. It required most of that time to pack and load the things Mama wanted to take with her. Papa was fondly indulgent about these, but he could see no need for some of the items that were being put into his wagon. The big gilt-framed looking glass—where, on God's green earth, would she ever use a thing like that, even if it survived the first trip without being broken? Little Grandma quickly solved the latter problem by giving Mama four featherbeds and a dozen homemade quilts, along with pillows and sheets, and the looking glass was laid flat between the featherbeds. She wanted Mama to have a set of china, and the monogrammed silver that had been made from melted coin dollars; she brought out a cut-glass butter dish with a domed cover, and told Mama that it was an heirloom. Papa agreed that all these things were nice, but maybe a little bit fancy for camp use.

"Bettie Ivanhoe," Grandma Hester Ann said then, "you remember your little rocking chair—the one Bob made for you a year or two after the slaves were freed? You can have Woodie take off the rockers, and then you can use it as a high chair for your first baby."

Mama blushed to the roots of her auburn hair. Little Grandma smiled, and pulled her old leather-bound trunk out from beneath the high bed. It contained the books Thomas Rucker had loved.

"But you'll want to keep those!" Mama protested. "They're all Papa left you."

The other Thomas was not around when Little Grandma took the books out of the trunk, handling each one with a caress. She said, "No, these are for your children, too. Tell them about their Grandpa Rucker, and how smart he was—tell them to read good books and get the kind of education he had."

The Waverley novels, some of the works of Cooper and Washington Irving, the Greek and Latin grammars, and texts on astronomy and botany all went into the wagon.

Papa was anxious to get moving. He busied himself currying the horses while Mama visited with her mother; he removed the wagon wheels, and greased them, and he went over the harness. Thomas Carpenter went out of his way to be friendly and hospitable, but he got the impression that Papa was a very strange young man. Papa was restless and nervous. He couldn't sit still, and he conversed only in monosyllables. Carpenter wondered if he was in such an all-fired hurry to travel because he had gotten into some sort of scrape around Hallettsville.

Thomas Carpenter did not suspect the real cause of Papa's daydreaming and his restiveness. Mama revealed it years later, when she was fond of talking about her marriage. She had already said that Papa kissed her when he lifted her to the seat of the wagon, but now she seemingly contradicted herself:

"When your Papa and I got married," she said, "it was three days before I would let him kiss me."

I remember the Victorian primness with which Mama always recounted this, as if deploring a laxness in modern marriage mores.

Shotgun weddings, and babies born "prematurely" with full heads of hair and fingernails shocked her terribly. But, when she talked about her own marriage, she smoothed her starched gingham dress and began rocking; a wistful and tender look always softened her face into beauty that had no resemblance to the stern Victorian mold. Even in my earliest teens, I understood the difference between that kiss at the wagon yard after the wedding, and the one Mama withheld for three days.

The shortest route to Goliad would have been through Cuero and the old town of Clinton, in DeWitt County. Cuero was booming—it had become a railroad terminus five years before. Clinton, just across the Guadalupe River, had lost the county seat and was rapidly declining.

But Papa gave all DeWitt a wide berth, and never explained why he took the long way around. He may have been worried about the Sutton-Taylor feud, in which some of the Bosworths were reportedly at least mildly involved—a man had only to dispute a cattle brand with one of the Taylor henchmen, and he was in on the fringes of the vendetta. At this moment the case of one of the bloodiest killings—that of a Dr. Brazell and his son—was on the docket of the criminal court in San Antonio, and either way the verdict went, new shootings might break out. Whatever his fears or his reasons, Papa drove by way of Victoria instead. Here Mama spent her first night in a wagon yard—she thought it was a novel thing to get a lodging place for ten or fifteen cents, so long as you brought your own wagon.

Before they left Victoria next day, they went to a photographer's studio and had separate tintype portraits made.

It was many years before Mama ever had another picture taken.

I have the tintypes today. Mama looks like the child she must have been, as a fifteen-year-old bride. Yet, the portrait shows something else. I think Mama had to grow up fast, and that she did; I think I know why Papa never looked at another woman for as long as they were married. Mama's kisses were worth waiting for, and she was woman enough for any man.

IV

As they drove up to Grandpa Henry Bosworth's three-room log house in Goliad County, Mama thought surely they must be arriving at another wagon yard. Wagons stood by the barn and the corral and beside the house; wagons were under the liveoak trees. Mama counted seven of them. Then people began swarming out of the house to greet the newlyweds, and Papa explained. His older half-brother, Gus, was there from Lavaca with his wife and five children, and they had a wagon. Mama knew Gus and his wife, Josephine, who was Thomas Carpenter's daughter. Papa's younger sister, Docia, had recently married Nick Rogers—a ramrod-straight and blue-eyed young man from Waxahachie. Nick owned a wagon. Grandpa Henry still had four heavy wagons left from his days of hauling freight for the Confederacy, and he had acquired a lighter one for farm work.

Papa unhitched his team from the Studebaker amid this imposing array of wheels. There were enough Bosworth wagons to throw into a circle and stave off an Indian attack. And there were enough Bosworth men to defend the camp.

Wagons and journeyings were in the restless talk at mealtime and on the front gallery of afternoons when the breeze rustled the summer's dead morning glory vines. Uncle Nick and Aunt Docia were about to pull out for the western counties; he had a little capital and he aimed to go into sheep ranching. Papa said, *"Sheep?* Good God, man, why?" and Uncle Nick became violently enthusiastic on the subject. With cattle, he reminded Papa, you raised only meat and hides; with sheep, in the mild Texas climate, you could shear two wool clips a year, and still sell lambs and mutton. Besides, he argued, a man didn't have to go riding hell-for-leather after sheep, like he did when handling longhorns, and sheep would find forage on range so poor that cows would starve.

"They stink!" Papa grunted, and did not say that he had always enjoyed that riding hell-for-leather business, because it made a man feel free. The argument was to be continued, at intervals, twenty counties westward and twenty years later.

Papa's younger brothers, Will and Bob, drifted in and out of the family gathering and alarmed Mama more than a little. They were the kind of young men she had seen driving the longhorn herds through Sweet Home—the kind that got into shooting scrapes on Saturday nights. Will and Bob wore spurs, and carried sixshooters, although Grandpa Henry made them take off their guns before they came into the house. He also had laid down the law about wearing a gun to town. He said nobody but a coward would shoot an unarmed man, and as far as he knew there were not many cowards around. Texas, he said, had weeded them out.

Grandpa Henry and Grandma Martha Bounds Bosworth—Big Grandma—were also talking about moving west. They were only renting the place in Goliad. There was not enough pasture for cattle and the cotton crop had been disappointing, and the house would not shelter all the people who had come there in this mild October weather. Most of the guests, including Papa and Mama, had to sleep in their wagons.

Papa's older sister, Frances Elizabeth, had been married to Dr. George W. Jones—a Confederate surgeon—for more than ten years. They were living either in Lampasas or Comanche at that time, and Aunt Fanny had been writing enthusiastic letters to her parents about the new country.

It was easy for Big Grandma to catch the wanderlust. She was very susceptible, having been a Bounds. In two or three generations, her family had come from the Carolinas to Mississippi, then to Louisiana and Texas, always chasing better and cheaper and less worn-out cotton land.

"Woodie," she told Papa, "you and Bettie Ivanhoe ought to light out west. Go to Lampasas or Brown, or Comanche. Frances says you can still take up squats around there. It's a drier country and there's not any ague or fever."

The sallow light of the coal-oil lamp showed the struggle on Papa's face. Mama didn't say anything in this discussion between her husband and her in-laws. Until her marriage, she had never been away from her mother for one night in all her fifteen years. Lavaca was her world, populated by various Hanna cousins and Maulding connections in a rather confusing family group: the divorces and intermarriages of those two temptestuous clans made lines of kinship hard to follow. But everybody was friendly. Sometimes the elders had talked, a little wistfully, about Louisiana and Mississippi—places far away in time and distance, and therefore romantic. But all Mama had heard about West Texas was blended in her memory with tales of Comanche raids, Mexican fights, and desert hardships. She was ten when the last Indian battle of consequence was fought on Texas soil—the Second Battle of Adobe Walls—and she could remember reading about that in the Galveston *News*.

She thought it strange that the Bosworths were so fascinated by the western land and talked so matter-of-factly about going there. Never had the name of Sweet Home been so meaningful as now, with the warmth and security she had known there. Still, she told herself, she was a married woman now. She loved Woodie Bosworth. These were his people, and this seemed to be their way.

Somewhere out of her early training the stirringly beautiful passage from the Book of Ruth—spoken, she remembered, to a mother-in-law—came to mind:

Whither thou goest, I will go; and where thou lodgest, I will lodge: thy people shall be my people, and thy God my God . . .

Then Mama believed with all her heart that this was as things should be, and she was comforted. The words of Ruth sang in her mind and heart with their terrible beauty, and she heard Papa saying, maybe almost apologetically, that he aimed to try to make a crop of cotton, first, and right here in Goliad. She heard him say that Bettie would need to see her mother now and then, and not get too far away, right at the start.

V

This was the fall of the year, and, fortunately for Papa's peace of mind, trail herds were not gathered in the fall. Nevertheless, a lot of branding and tallying went on in preparation for the spring drives, and if a man listened with half an ear he could hear the jingle of spurs.

Papa tried valiantly. He shut his ears to all the seductive sounds of journeyings; he remembered that he was a married man, and a settled sort. He had turned farmer. He rented or leased a hundred acres with a two-room log house, and bought a one-horse Georgia Stock plough, cruelly bright as to blade.

Mama was happy, although she knew now that her idea of a cotton plantation, with Negro help, was a false one. This came pretty near to being a one-man farm. She boiled a vast quantity of water, and scalded the walls and the puncheon floors of the log house to kill the chinch bugs she felt sure were lurking there; the place, she thought, had been left scandalously dirty. None of the possessions were moved from the wagon until she had finished this eradication campaign.

That winter was remarkably mild in South Texas, and the far northwestern section had a severe drought. She and Papa read the Victoria *Advocate,* and there were certain published signs and portents. In Washington County, a well drilled a hundred and fifty-two feet deep did not strike water at all. Instead, it began discharging an inflammable gas, which was being piped in a small way for cooking purposes.

This foreshadow of Spindletop and other immeasurable oil riches did not impress Papa. He felt sorry for the man who had drilled for water for his cows and had found gas instead.

Papa liked the climate and the rolling prairie scenery. But he complained that Goliad was getting "too much settled." (It had approximately five thousand people at that time, or six to the square mile. In the 1960 Census, eighty years after Papa moved out, it had 5,429 people.)

Papa really wanted to raise cattle, or rather to gather them without the trouble of fences, but he realized that such an operation required control of big pastures. And the big pastures were already controlled. Cotton was the next best money crop.

He put in long hours of backbreaking toil to get the seed into the ground; he wore out successive pairs of Red Star buckskin gauntlets, and still developed calluses. His horses had never pulled a plough before and had to be taught. If Papa felt that ploughing was a demeaning labor both to man and beast, he said nothing, but went right along treating his horses as he always treated them: a horse was purely utilitarian, expected to perform any manner of service its master wished. Papa fed his horses well, on most occasions, but to him this was like refueling or greasing a car or tractor—it was to keep the horses in working order. Papa would fight a man for kicking a dog: a dog was a different thing, not expected to work. At times, he lost his notably short temper and beat his horses unmercifully, until Mama had to beg him to stop.

To make things worse about the ploughing Papa did, a prosperous neighbor began stringing barbed-wire fence around his fields and pastures. Papa regarded this as something of a personal affront when the wire came by his lease; he had seen horses pretty badly cut by barbed wire. He rested his plough at the end of the furrow, wiped the sweat from his eyes, and watched the new posts going into the ground, and the march of slender staves supporting and spacing the three-strand fence.

It was all the more frustrating because there was nothing Papa could do about it. "The world," he growled to Mama that evening, "has been shaved by a drunken barber!"

He always came home to the log house at dinnertime and before suppertime. Mama was there to comfort him. She brought him jugs of cold well water on hot spring mornings when he was chopping the weeds out of his cotton rows. Around this time, she began suffering attacks of morning nausea, and Papa knew—with some misgivings—that he had sowed other seed. This was when he looked with longing toward his saddle horse, grown fat and lazy, or at his wagon.

The wagon stood idle, except for infrequent trips into town for supplies. The steel tires rusted a little during the winter, but a few miles of running would make them bright again. In spring, Papa went through the ritual of greasing the wheel hubs again; he treated the tarp with linseed oil, and wrapped slender rawhide around a splitting hickory bow.

His saddle had been hanging by its horn from a rawhide string, gathering dust in the barn. Papa took it down and went over it with neat's-foot oil. The roundups were on again; he could hear their siren sounds. A few trail herds went by, raising dust, the riders cursing the same barbed wire Papa cursed. The sounds of their passage stirred him as much as the wild northward honking of wild geese.

Papa did not complain. He merely became more introspective and more monosyllabic. He looked at Mama in the yellow lamplight, when he was tired, and loved her dearly and possessively. And, still, he had been trapped. He was fenced in by the barbs of responsibility and was no longer his own man. His saddle hung on the wall, and his spurs were silent.

In April, a green and fruitful month in that part of Texas, Mama had a miscarriage. It scared Papa half to death. When the pains and the bleeding began, he got down the home remedy book of which he was most proud—it was written by the same Dr. Pierce who sold Golden Medical Discovery and Favorite Prescription. It told what to do in case of sprain or nosebleed, insect bite or measles, but said nothing about what Mama was enduring now. Papa caught up the saddle horse and sweated him out fearfully in a ride for a doctor in Goliad. It was all over when they got back to the log cabin. Mama cried a little, and blamed herself; she whispered, "I'm so sorry, Woodie—I wanted him!" And then she drifted off to sleep, and the doctor took a chew of tobacco and said she would be all right.

With daylight, Papa went out and looked at his cotton. It was a foot high, green and thriving. But it had lost all charm for him. He cursed bitterly, and tore off his hat and dashed it to the ground. He was through.

A month later, he aborted the cotton crop by selling it in the ground for a rather trivial sum. This was, in a way, an act of self-immolation, and Papa had never felt happier. Let the other man worry, now, about weeds; let him contend with the ubiquitous boll weevil and cope with the squat labor of crawling along to drag a ten-foot sack at picking time. Let him handle the business of hauling and ginning and sweating out what a bale of cotton would bring that fall. The scales had fallen from Papa's eyes. He was suddenly free as a bird, with a small capital gain in hand. It would buy corn for the horses, and grub for the chuckbox, and a few gallons of coal oil.

What else did a man need?

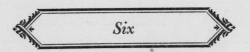

Six

*"The life of one man spanned the rise and complete
transformation of the ranch; it spanned the rise and fall
of the cattle kingdom."* —WALTER PRESCOTT WEBB,
The Great Plains

*P*apa was that man. He was born
out of time for the kind of life he would have loved living: he would
have made a good mountain man, along with Jim Bridger and Kit
Carson and Jedediah Smith, because for them there was always "new
country" over the hills, and they were the first white men to see it.
For them, the grass grew tall, and the streams ran clear, and the game
was plentiful.

Yet even the mountain men lived to see river canyons trapped
out, and farmers making their way west of the fur trader's town of
St. Louis. The march of America was inexorable.

The new country had already really gone when Papa was born,
in 1856. That was the year in which the first steam locomotive
puffed across the Mississippi at Rock Island, Illinois, and its cow-
catcher was pointed straight toward a West that had pretty well been
won. But Papa did see the transformation of the ranch, and the rise
and fall of the cattle kingdom. He was an active witness to these

when he and Mama hitched up the horse and drove northwestward June, 1880, with the Texas summer already hot and strong.

There had been more letters from Aunt Fanny and Uncle George. There had been letters from Aunt Docia—she and Uncle Nick had been to Lampasas and were pushing even farther westward. And now Mama's half-brother, Ed Maulding, was in Comanche and writing Mama that she ought to move that way.

Perhaps it was a sort of disease. A lot of people were writing letters like that. Brown County, which was where Papa and Mama let the wheels stop rolling, had only 544 people in the 1870 Census. In 1880, it had nearly 8,500.

Papa drove through the postoak country and the red clay hills; he came out on the prairies and could see the rimrocks of the Balcones Escarpment on the far horizon. And by now he was beginning to be disturbed. He and Mama were never really alone. There was always another wagon or two in sight along the road, and when they camped at night he could see five or six campfires along the prairie. It seemed to him that he had been too late again—everybody was headed the same way.

Besides, he did not seem to be getting away from barbed wire. Some of the road to Brown had been laned with it, and wherever he looked it was shining in the sun and singing in the wind, all the long way from Goliad.

Still, Brown County was new country, of a sort. Papa established a base camp near the river, about six miles from the town of Brownwood, and he and Mama first spent some time visiting their kinfolk in the area. And then Papa started looking for a job.

He would have preferred, again, to be in the saddle, working with the longhorned cows—but only under the old conditions. Papa had known cattlemen of the old open-range school—"free grass" men, they were called—and he had ridden for some of them in his early teens. It is doubtful that any cowboy's life was ever romantic, but if this was ever true, it must have been then. Most able-bodied Texans went off to fight somebody, somewhere, during the Civil War; the untended cattle stayed home in the brush and multiplied amazingly. For the next ten years, and longer, fortunes were made from scratch by roping and branding them and driving them to Kansas markets opened by the railroads.

Papa had a small hand in that, when ranching was a way of life, increasingly competitive in an active outdoors fashion, but never methodical in the bookkeeping sense, and never mechanical.

The railroads came even to Texas, after a time. Fences and windmills were there before. Things changed.

Papa worked, before his marriage, for some of the "big pasture" men. These were individuals who hated any kind of fence as much as Papa did, but were astute enough to go along with the changing times. They had settled, originally, on creeks where their cows could drink; they owned only small tracts of land there, but could let their cattle graze far back on the open range, on State land. However, smaller operators began filing claims to the State land, denying the rancher access to grazing, and sometimes even shutting him off from the water of the creek. It became apparent that a cattleman would have to own or lease his entire range—and then it became obvious that he would have to fence it.

The first Texas fences had been made of boards, but this was in the piney woods where lumber abounded. Westward, on the prairies, they planted fences of *bois d'arc,* which was the osage orange, or of roses. Papa might have endured such fences as these—they did not cut the hides of horse and cattle to ribbons. But five years before he and Mama were married, a man named Joseph Farwell Glidden, living near De Kalb, Illinois, came out with the definitive patent on barbed wire.

Mr. Glidden made a pile of money out of this. Papa, conversely, grew poorer, and his life was never the same.

There had already been hundreds of patents on fencing, because the problem was acute throughout all the Plains country where there was no timber. Glidden's discovery that barbs could be inserted between twistetd strands of smooth wire was a simple thing, but it led to that transformation of the ranch. It changed the economics and the customs of the West, and even put a different look on the face

of the land. At a glance across a hillside, anyone could see that
sheep or goats had been pastured on one side of the barbed wire,
and cattle on the other.

Most of all, it changed Texas, which already had more than its
share of barbs on the mesquite and cactus. And it infuriated Papa
beyond all reason, since he owned neither an acre of land nor a
blade of grass. He could not see that a revolution was taking place.

Barbed wire, in fact, became a huge industry before Papa knew
what was going on. John Warne Gates—later to become famous as
"Bet-You-a-Million" Gates—put on a piece of razzle-dazzle show-
manship in San Antonio to promote barbed wire. Barn posters advertised it. Cattle kings such as Shanghai Pierce saw the light, and
then began buying it by the carload. Papa was working, then, for
Shanghai Pierce's arch-enemy, Bob Stafford. The first thing he knew,
Stafford was ordering barbed wire, too.

All Papa knew was that he had no traffic with barbed wire, but he
was being fenced in. Every time he wanted to pull off the road to
camp in a likely liveoak motte, every time he tried to water his horses
at a waterhole, he ran into barbed wire.

This was when his one-man war with barbed wire began. He waged
the war carefully, and was never caught; he must have known from
the beginning that he could not win. But he got in some good licks.

Papa had archaic ideas about such bounties of nature as creeks
and waterholes and salt deposits. He felt that such things were not
really owned by any man, any more than an individual could lay
claim to a sunset or moonrise, or the dew that freshened the grass.
Who put them there? How was it that the buffalo and deer and lesser
creatures had been enjoying them for hundreds of thousands of years,
and the Indians for a long time afterward?

This was Papa's religion. It was simpler, and much broader, than
anything written in the books. He believed in it, and he practiced it
as much as the times would permit.

He was disappointed, now, with what he found in Brown County.
Papa had expected this land to be a real frontier, and he had run

into a land boom—a population explosion of sorts. It was a big county, and there really was room in it, but not enough room for Papa. He was already looking over the line into Coleman, to the westward and not so settled.

But now Mama was pregnant again and starry-eyed at the coming of her first baby. Papa hemmed and hawed, and then humored her in every way. She filled out, and was more beautiful than before, and he loved her.

He rented some land and meant to put a crop in the ground, but meanwhile he began working for day wages as a carpenter. The population gain called for a lot of new houses, and Papa helped build them. He was busy, and he earned money, but he was not happy. His saddle was collecting dust again. He heard that a big Coleman rancher was in town, hiring hands, and went to see him at the hotel.

The rancher was a large man, with a heavy gold watch chain on his vest, and he sat handy to a spittoon while he chewed tobacco. "Need some hands, all right," he admitted, as Papa later recounted the conversation. "Pay you a dollar and a half a day, and beans, to help me fence ten sections of pasture over at my place."

Papa stiffened. "You mean build fence?"

"That's right, son. I'm puttin' that ten sections under three strands of bull-proof barbed wire."

"Well, by God, sir!" Papa said, rising, "I don't need a job that bad! I'll see you in hell with your back broke before I'll stoop to stringing your goddamned barbed wire!"

He turned to go. "Now, hold your horses, son!" the ranchman said mildly. "I reckon I can get all the hands I need. But I'd just like to tell you that I feel the same way you do. Except, goddamnit, there's a difference. *You* ain't got any land to fence, and I by god damn well *have* to fence mine!"

II

Papa was now rising twenty-five years old. Before coming to Brown, he had been at best only a jackleg carpenter. He was not fond of carpentry, any more than he had been fond of farming, but now he

[74]

learned some of its skills and became able to build a frame house all by himself. He got away from his labors as often as he could: at the slightest excuse, he and Mama threw some bedding into the wagon and went off for visits of several days with Uncle George and Aunt Fanny Jones in Comanche, or with Ed Maulding and his family in Lampasas. The word went up and down the creeks that Bettie and Woodie had come to visit, and all the clan within wagon distance turned out to camp under the liveoak trees and have an old-fashioned barbecue, and sleep on the ground in good summer weather.

"Now, you come back, hear?" Aunt Fanny would call when they finally started for home. "We haven't got much, but we can always put the big pot in the little one."

Coming back meant that Papa could get the wagon on the road, for a little while at least. Driving to Comanche for another visit late in the fall, they passed a country store that displayed a basket of red apples. Mama was seized with a sudden craving for apples.

Papa smiled at her fondly. "It's a wonder you didn't up and decide you just had to have something like strawberries or oysters," he teased as he got down from the wagon. "You want to be careful, Bettie."

My oldest brother, Dee, was born on March 27, 1881. There was a small red birthmark on his lip, but it disappeared within a few weeks and left him without a blemish, much to Mama's relief.

"It was a perfect little red apple," she said. "I just know I touched my lip that time when I wanted the apples so bad. . . ."

The baby took up all of Mama's time, and she was lonely no longer when Papa was away at work. She seemed always busy, now, with Dee, and this fed Papa's restlessness. He talked, that summer, about pushing farther west; he might go down to Tom Green, he said, where Nick and Docia were. He got down his rifle and cleaned and oiled it, and drew imaginary beads on buck deer and maverick cattle. But meat wouldn't keep in the hot weather, and he ate bacon instead, and waited until the first cool day of autumn. . . .

A north wind was blowing, not strong enough to be called a norther, but just enough to put a hint of fall in the air. Pecans were falling along the creek bottoms, and at night he could hear wild geese honking on their way south. It did Papa a world of good to catch up the horses as if he really intended going somewhere. He tied the saddle horse behind the wagon, and left early, whistling softly to himself. The road he took was not recorded, but it was one he had observed previously—it ran alongside a large open pasture.

Papa went five or six miles farther away from town, and then turned out into the pasture and left the wagon pretty well concealed in a hackberry motte. He took the saddle horse, with his rifle in its boot under his left leg. There was a scatter of half-wild cattle grazing across the rolling prairie, all headed down wind. It took Papa only a few minutes to find the beef he wanted.

This was a maverick red bull, rising two years old, not yet big enough to assert his maleness against the surly and quarrelsome older bulls, and not yet so big as to be tough when dressed down as meat for the frying pan. He had somehow escaped the indignities of branding, earmarking and castration; he was grazing along the bank of a draw, between thick clumps of liveoak and hackberry and wild walnut trees. Papa stayed in the saddle—nothing excited the range cattle more than the curious spectacle of a man on foot. He rode warily around to get down wind from the red bull and shot him just behind the left shoulder. The two-year-old fell in his tracks.

Now came the business that Papa always found distasteful. He would have to get his rope over a limb, hoist the carcass clear of the ground, cut the jugular vein to bleed his kill while it was still warm, slit the hide down the belly and along all four legs, and skin it off the back. He would have to rip open the belly and stand back to keep the steaming convoluted mass of bowels from falling on his feet. He would of necessity be bloody to his elbows, and the blowflies would be swarming around him.

Still, it had to be done. Papa was looking for a suitable limb, rope in hand, when he heard horses coming through the brush.

He swung back into his saddle and listened for a moment. Yes, they were coming down the draw, on the same side. At least two of them.

Papa rode slowly and silently across the dry draw bed, and took up a position in the thick motte on the farther bank, where he watched.

There were two riders, all right, both about his own age. And they did not act like the owners of the pasture or any of the cattle grazing there; they did not even act as though they worked for the outfit. They came into the open, and saw the inert red bull, and knew by the blood that he had been freshly killed. Then they looked all around them, furtively. Seeing nothing, they glanced at each other.

The shorter man slapped his leather leggings with his hand and laughed. "Somebody shore got his wind up, didn't he?" he rejoiced. "Well—finders keepers!"

The other spat tobacco juice. "Saves a cartridge," he said laconically.

He got down off his horse and put a loop on the red bull's hind hocks. He tossed the end of the rope to his partner, who took a *dar la vuelta* around his saddlehorn with it and started dragging the carcass toward a likely-looking liveoak.

Papa went quietly and happily away from there, taking out his watch to note the time. Hour and a half to two hours for two men, he figured, depending on how adept they were with their skinning blades. With the blowflies buzzing, and gnats getting in their eyes, and the buzzards beginning to circle overhead. And when they had finished, anybody who saw them would know what they'd been up to, because it was impossible to butcher a cow without being liberally spattered with gore.

He found a stretch where the grass was good and the sun was warm against an outcropping of rock. He took the headstall off his horse and loosened the cinch, and let the animal graze. Papa cut himself a chew of tobacco and sprawled against the sun-warmed rock, out of the wind, where he relaxed in calm contemplation and poetic ease.

After nearly two hours, he rode back across the draw and came up through the brush to take a cautious look. His timing had been good. The two men had the carcass dressed, with the hide spread hair down on the grass to receive liver and heart and lights; they were now about to quarter the beef.

Papa hit spurs quite suddenly to his horse, and tore into the open with a great popping and crashing of underbrush, his saddle gun held high.

"What the hell?" he shouted angrily. "What do you mean, beefing *my* cattle?"

The two did not reply at all. They leaped for their saddles and joined the birds, not even taking off in the same direction. One of them dropped a fine bone-handled IXL Barlow knife, which Papa kept and used for a long time; the other left a fairly new rope. Papa waited a little while before he stuck his saddle gun back into its boot, to make sure they were long gone. Then he went back to get his wagon, and drive it under the tree. He was still chuckling happily to himself.

He put a wagon tarp over the meat, went on down the draw a little way, and then turned right to get back into the road. But he had come farther into the pasture than he realized. The road must have turned off to the right to aim for a pass in the low hills. It was nearly three miles before Papa found it—and when he did, he ran smack into a brand-new barbed-wire fence.

Papa drew rein and cursed; he swung around and backtracked for half a mile, and then decided that the whole damned place had been put under wire. He was leaving wagon tracks in the pasture—he had to get back on the county road to be safe. Back up the wire he went, expecting to find the end of it, or at least a gate. The fence was still there, and there was no gate. (Governor Ireland called a special session of the Texas Legislature three years later and put through a law. It made fence cutting a felony, but it also required a gate every three miles.)

Just then, Papa heard the sound of hammering just over the next rise. He looked at the posts. They were new, and the earth around the postholes was still fresh and damp. Somebody was building fence until hell wouldn't have it—just over the hill.

[78]

"Dad-blamed sons-of-bitches!" Papa fumed. "What right have they got to fence me off the road? I'll show 'em!"

He got down with his wire cutters in hand. Each of the tautly strung strands made a beautiful twanging noise, something like a parted banjo string. Each whipped and coiled away from the post. Wire flying that way could cut a man's throat if he didn't watch out.

Now the way was open to the claybank road, and Papa started to get back on his wagon seat when that hammering assailed his ears again. It seemed to travel down the wire with a telephonic effect. It mocked him. There were several men, just over the hill, driving staples into cedar posts. Cinching down the thorned wire, so that it would cut the hides of cattle and horses, and tear men's britches when they went through.

"Dad-blamed dirty sons-of-bitches!"

Papa crossed over to the road, where any man had the right to drive upon his lawful occasions, but where he would leave no individual tracks. He drove very slowly, very leisurely, along the string of new fence: he traveled at about the rate the fence builders were unrolling their spools of wire.

At regularly spaced intervals—every four or five posts—Papa wrapped his reins around the brake handle, got down with his wire cutters, and clipped three strands of wire. He was a hill and a hollow behind the fence crew for a couple of miles.

Then he tired of the sport, took note of the sun lowering in the sky, and turned the wagon around to head for home. There was no justification for what may seem to have been a piece of sophomoric vandalism, but this many years afterward I can attempt to rationalize. Papa was suddenly fed up with his hated enemy; he had just staged a one-man rebellion against a thing many men disliked. It was, as he admitted later, "something I had to get out of my craw. . . ."

There was much more beef than he and Mama could use, even when he cut a lot of it into thin, lean strips and sun-dried it into jerky, after the Indian-Mexican fashion. He carried more than half of it around to neighbors within a radius of several miles and presented it to them, using the language that had become something of a code among the maverickers: "I thought maybe you folks could use a little rabbit meat."

One quarter of the beef he hung on the outside north wall of the house, in the shade, and high enough that varmints couldn't reach it. Mama cut steaks from this, and cooked them the only way she knew, short of having a barbecue out under the trees. She rolled the steaks in flour, and fried them in deep fat, and then made thickening gravy from the grease.

It may honestly be said that Mama was never really a very good cook. She had not needed to learn as a girl in Little Grandma's house; they still had a Negro cook even after the slaves were freed. She had no oven that really worked, and had to depend upon the skillet. There was a saying, a little later, that the frying pan had killed more Texans than the Comanches ever did, and there was truth in this.

But Papa was not the kind of man to get ulcers from fried food, or anything else. He took things as calmly as he could, up to a certain point, and then—as in the case of the wire cutting—he exploded cleanly and with immense satisfaction.

He chuckled as he ate steak from the two-year-old maverick bull, and enjoyed it immensely, and never mind how it was cooked.

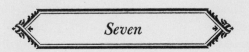

Seven

"Well, we sure-enough traveled, them days. Seems like Papa made up his mind all of a sudden—he might come in at night and not say a word, but next morning we'd be on the road. But I don't exactly know where we went when I was just a kid. Like the feller says, we back-tracked so many times I am all jumbled up." —DEE

*I*n this year, his eighty-first, my oldest brother's memory is actually phenomenal. He remembers most names, and can summon up sights and sounds and smells out of the long past; his gentle Texas drawl breathes life into the few faded words I found on yellowed paper, and gives them meaning. He remains a tall man with long arms and sloping, powerful shoulders, with a walk shaped early by the saddle; his eyesight has failed, but he goes every day for the mail in the small West Texas town where he has lived for forty years. The people he passes on the street he cannot see, but they know him, and they call out, "Howdy, Mr. Dee!" The Mexicans who make up half the town's population, say more softly, *"Buenos días, Señor Di,"* and it pleases them greatly that he answers in their own tongue and speaks it as fluently and as musically as they do while he rummages in his pockets for the chewing gum he always carries for their children.

Many of the Mexicans worked for him, over the years. Mr. Dee built nearly all the windmills in Terrell County, a high and rocky land that spreads across 2,388 square miles of semidesert ranch country without even a garden patch to suggest agriculture. The ranchmen of Terrell will never forget that Mr. Dee helped them get water deep out of the thirsty ground, and the windmills spinning like bright dimes in the sunshine of far-off divides will stand as his monuments.

But I wonder what Papa would think now, if he knew that one of his sons had stayed in a single Texas county for forty years? And what would he say about the windmills? A few of them were being erected in Brown County when Dee was a baby, and Papa was of two minds concerning them. A windmill was an admirable thing to Papa when the water keg was rattling in its rack on the side of the wagon, or when his horses were thirsty, or when tires began wobbling on shrinking wheels. But very probably Papa would not have built a windmill, any more than he would string barbed wire. The two did much to make each other necessary, and profitable; they actively conspired to kill the open range.

Papa had already been in Brown County longer than he would remain in most places, in the future. Apparently he tried, very earnestly, to settle down. But new people kept coming in, crowding him. Dee was about a year old and does not remember when they went to Coleman, but we both can recall the wistful note in Mama's voice when she told about the morning-glories.

Aunt Fanny had given her some morning-glory seed on one of the visits to Comanche. Mama planted this at the south end of the small front gallery of their rented cabin on one of those warm February days in Texas, when the sheepherder's noon siesta is troubled by the knowledge that the ewes may begin dropping their lambs at any moment, when the bloom is soft and fragrant on the catclaw, and there are other unmistakable but deceptive signs of spring. Using Papa's clawhammer, and string patiently unraveled from flour sacks,

Mama constructed a latticework all the way up to the eaves of the gallery.

The urge to plant something in the springtime is universal but Mama's small effort had deeper significance. It was a sort of prayer for permanency. Gypsies and circus roustabouts, fruit pickers and other migratory workers never plant anything. Mama wanted to see something of her very own take root, much more than she wanted summer shade or the brief matutinal beauty of the flowers. The symbolism could be carried farther, but it would be only coincidental that what she planted was a vine—a thing soft and clinging, needing strength and permanency upon which to climb. Coincidental, too, that morning-glories grow swiftly and bloom prodigiously in spring and early summer. In August they close their blossoms into a false and belated spinsterhood of tight, dried rolls, inviolate to butterfly and bee, while they nurture the seed for a new generation of growth. The broad, heart-shaped leaves turn brown on wiry yellow vines; they cling tenaciously to what is left of their life, and rustle in the wind until winter comes. . . .

The morning-glories had climbed high on the strings when Papa rode home one evening and announced that they were going to move. He had found some new country—over in Coleman. Not far away, he said, as if that made a difference. Maybe fifty miles, and they could make it in three days' driving.

"It's not so settled up, over there," Papa said. He hung his wide-brimmed hat on a nail, and swung a chair around so he could straddle it, facing the back: the way he got on the chair was the way he would have mounted a horse. All at once he was in a great good humor, as pleased as a child with a new play pretty. "Maybe," he said, "we can take up a squat of land."

Mama sighed. "We could have bought this place," she reminded him. "I thought you liked it well enough here."

"Did," Papa said. "Until so many folks kept coming in."

"Or you could build us a new house, Woodie. Having a new house would be mighty nice."

"Couldn't afford enough land," Papa said. "You don't want to be cooped up on some little two-by-four piece of land with a paling fence around it."

Mama had seen some pretty paling fences, painted white, with roses climbing over them.

"We've got to think about the future," Papa went on. "Got to think about the long haul."

Dee woke suddenly and began threshing around in his crib. He started bawling. Mama hastened to lift him and see if he was dry. "You want some supper, don't you, honey boy?" she crooned. All of Mama's boys were always "honey boys"; she talked baby talk to them until they were in long pants. "There, there—Mama will give you some supper!"

"Trouble is," Papa said, "there are too many people in this country. Makes land prices go sky-west and crooked. I tell you, Brown is ruined—just plumb ruined!"

He felt that Mama was no longer listening. She was in her armless rocking chair, cradling the baby, nourishing him at her breast. Papa's face softened as he watched, and he shook his head with an admiration he never lost. Some women would have had to put their babies on Eagle Brand condensed milk before now; Mama never did. She nursed each of her children until they were well over a year old; she weaned some of them only because a new baby was coming, never because she had run out of milk. Papa, intending no disrespect at all, used to laugh and say proudly, "I swear, Bettie, you just beat any Jersey I ever saw!"

After supper, he began loading the wagon.

They went to Coleman, traveling through the postoak country of the West Cross Timbers and coming out on the mesquite-green rolling prairie. The wagon rolled through the shadow of rimrocked Santa Anna Mountain, the highest hill Mama had ever seen. When she admired this, Papa laughed exultingly, and said, "I told you you'd like this country. Look how open it is. Man can see for miles!"

It was different enough to take Mama's mind off the morning-glories that would bloom for somebody else, or die for want of water. And maybe a man could see too far, there, without finding the will-o'-the-wisp he pursued—although now Papa was haunted by less ghostly lights. The leading cattle trail went squarely through Coleman County in that spring and summer of 1882: it pointed for Buffalo Gap, to the north in Taylor County, and went on across the singing rivers with the singing names, it passed Fort Phantom Hill, crossed the Wichita and the Pease where the bones of the buffalo lay whitening, and came to Doan's Crossing on the Red. Considerably more than a quarter of a million longhorns were trailed up to Kansas that year, and a great bawling lot of them went through Coleman County. The trail was moving westward a little every year—it, too, was being crowded by the barbed wire.

The herds came up from the south, hanging their banners of dust in the sky; the lead steer walked proudly, with a half-wild grace, and their horns gleamed like sun-tipped bayonets. But Papa was on the sidelines of the march, and sometimes in the reviewing stand, not even getting a salute. The riders were busy; they had no time for a man up on the roof of a new house, driving shingle nails. Besides, he was probably another farmer—a nester—and he'd be fencing the place this time next year. . . .

Papa laid few shingles when a herd was going by. He listened to the far-off murmur until it became music, and then turned into a tumult of bawls and bellows; he heard the shouts of cowboys riding point and flank and swing, and even envied those who rode in the dusty drag with their bandannas pulled up over mouth and nose to keep from being suffocated. He spat out a mouthful of shingle nails and swore.

Fenced in, he told himself. Here he was, right on the Western Trail, and by God fenced in just as plain as if he had four strands of barbed wire around him, hog tight, horse high and bull strong! Oh, it amounted to that. If he just had enough money ahead for six months —enough to take care of Mama and the baby until he got back— he'd hit the saddle so fast it would make your head swim.

But he didn't have the money ahead for six months. And now Mama told him, rather shyly, that she was going to have another baby.

"What?" Papa exclaimed, and then patted her hand and said, "That's just wonderful, Bettie—*you're* just wonderful!" Then he had to get outside the four walls of the tent before they closed in upon him completely, and he reached for his hat and went out to grain-feed and curry his horses. They were frisky and full of oats. "Stand still, damn you!" Papa swore. "Stand still, I said!"

II

It helped that Papa moved his camp several times that year, and that he got away from carpenter work now and then to hire out for day wages on some of the ranches. The herds went by well up through the summer, making their restless music, leaving behind their exciting scents: burned mesquite and smoldering cowchip campfire smoke, trampled grass, Fish Brand slicker smell, and the aroma of coffee boiled, and boiled again, in blackened old tin pots. Two herds bedded down a few miles apart stampeded one night in a lightning storm and ran so near the tent that Mama was terrified with the fear that they would be trampled. Papa moved the wagon up closer to serve as a bulwark, and the thunder went by harmlessly enough. Next morning he got a couple of days' work in the saddle, because nearly four thousand cattle wearing several brands were mixed, as he said, "until hell wouldn't have 'em." And there were a score of dead steers along a broken stretch of barbed wire some five miles to the south of where the cattle had started running.

Men began muttering about the wire, complaining that big operators had fenced in public lands, shutting off public water. Many a trail driver saw no reason why he should go twenty miles out of his way to get around a fence.

It began in a small way, on nights when the moon was dark; it blazed spectacularly, that year, into the Fence Cutter's War. There were a few shootings. The sheriff of Coleman telegraphed Austin, and Texas Rangers rode that way in the laconic and frugal manner in which Rangers were always assigned—which is to say Coleman County got maybe two Rangers. They wore no uniform, and a man didn't know one from Adam, but they were always quiet, soft-spoken men, very deliberate and very knowing, and all that made them twice as dangerous.

They came around and asked Papa some pointed questions, and he answered in monosyllables. I have reluctantly rejected a temptation to fictionize here and say that Papa had been riding with the fence cutters—I cannot prove that he did. There are some records of the affair, which was rather drawn out: a young Ranger named Ira Aten came that way and made friends with some of the young bloods of the area; he and a comrade established a very creditable intelligence organization and began to learn whose wire was going to be cut, and when. Aten wrote some engaging reports to Austin, describing an ingenious idea he had developed for a dynamite "boom" (bomb) which would go off when anybody tampered with the wire and blow the cutter (or maybe the ranchman) to Kingdom Come. Ranger Aten, far ahead of his time in the science of weapons development, had something that would have called for the fence cutters to organize and train demolition teams. But Austin, alarmed, ordered him to slow down. . . .

And Papa, who never liked Rangers—although he respected them greatly—got out of Coleman fast, and under cover of darkness. He went as if somebody had built a fire under the tails of his horses.

Not far, actually, in that first jump, but far enough. He was back-tracking, now, in the manner that confused Dee in the years of his early memory: he went to Lampasas County, and pitched his camp near the small town of Centerfitt, which is no longer on the map or in the atlases.

My oldest sister was born there on July 18, 1883. They named her Norah Hetty. The middle name was an affectionate diminutive for Hester, and it revealed, poignantly, just how very homesick Mama had become for Sweet Home and for Little Grandma Hester Ann.

I do not know how long the family stayed in Lampasas that time.

Perhaps it was as much as a year. But once anybody suggested to Papa that it was time to go somewhere, he was ready to hitch up and go—even if it meant backtracking into the eastern counties where he hated the population expansion. I only have the family Bible to go on, at this period before Dee and Norah began to be aware of where they were and where the wagon rolled.

But Lampasas County got embroiled in the Fence Cutter's War, too, and perhaps Papa turned a more sensitive and willing ear to Mama's wistfully expressed desire to visit her mother. They went down to Lavaca somewhere around 1884, and it was no weekend jaunt in those days—it involved some two hundred miles of travel, and there were immense stretches of sandy land and black waxy loam in which a wagon did well to make ten miles in a day.

They enjoyed a long visit with Little Grandma, who adored the children. Thomas Carpenter thought Norah was about the cutest child he had ever seen. There was that about the old man: he didn't have much use for the boys but he loved all the girls from the toddling stage on. Little Grandma was still living off her land, and there was not much of it left.

Papa had to make a living, and now he heard of work to be had in Karnes County, where they were building the San Antonio and Aransas Pass Railroad. Once again, Mama said good-bye to Little Grandma . . . once again the wagon rolled. They went across DeWitt to Helena, in Karnes, and Mama was quite happy. She was back in the coastal plains country she loved; she was not too far from Sweet Home. And Papa got a job as a teamster, driving horses pulling a scraper to pile earth for the right-of-way and the embankment where ties and rails would be laid.

He liked handling horses, but he did not care for this job of earth moving. If there was any romance about "the end of steel" and all that sort of thing associated with the building of pioneer railroads, then it came later: it was not around when Papa was there. He knew only dusty, hard work, and swarms of gnats in his face in the sultry afternoons, and arm muscles aching from the tug of the scraper handles as the blade bit into stubborn soil. And if anybody had told him he was helping to build the West, he would have said, "Helping to build it? By God, I'm helping to *ruin* it!"

A scar on the earth's face was a scar, to Papa, whether made by a scraper blade or a ploughshare.

The tent was in a liveoak motte, not far from the place where the right-of-way construction gang worked; it moved several times, as the embankment crawled in the direction of San Antonio.

"The men used to come over to our camp after work and bring me candy," Norah remembers. "They would tell me if I would give them a kiss they would give me a sack of candy. I was nearly four years old then.

"I would look at Mama, and she would shake her head. Then I would go a few steps toward the man with the candy, and look at her again, and the men would laugh and say, 'Come on, honey—I've got some candy for you!' I just knew Mama would whip me, but I couldn't resist the candy. So I always walked up and kissed the man, and after he left Mama always gave me a good whipping with a switch and I couldn't sit down for several days. . . ."

The first of these occasions found Papa cast in the rather unusual role of defender of his children. He saw Mama reach for the switch and lost his temper.

"Leave the child alone, Bettie!" he roared. "I swear—what's eating you? What's she done wrong?"

"Now you just keep out of this!" Mama warned him. "I'm going to see that she has a good raising. I won't have her thinking it's all right to kiss every Tom, Dick, and Harry that comes along!"

"I said leave her alone! Some of these boys got young'uns of their own back home, and they get lonesome for 'em. They don't mean anything when they ask Norah for a little hug or kiss. The way you act you'd think she was practically grown up!"

He was no match for Mama in an argument. When it reached a certain degree of heat, Papa always grunted and retreated into his shell. He sulked for several days, eating his meals in silence, suffering when the salt or sugar was not passed to him, stalking outside afterward to sit and brood and feed his many frustrations like so many crawling leeches.

It is obvious that the quarrels were always patched up, and that it was sweet to forgive and make up, although Papa's nature was such that he would never admit that he had been in the wrong. He was willing to be generous and noble about it—and things fell into a pattern that repeated itself, very regularly, about every two years. The family was growing. My second-oldest brother, J. T., was born September 11, 1885. He had only the set of initials for his name, and Mama had to explain, many times, that they didn't stand for John Thomas or anything else. He was always known as Jay.

Claudia Ivanhoe, born September 22, 1887, came off better where names were concerned. Upon being introduced to her, people would roll the richness of "Claudia Ivanhoe Bosworth" over their tongues, and ask Mama if she got the name out of a novel, or a play. (As a child, I always thought it was a curious thing that Ivanhoe married a man—her cousin—with the completely uninspiring name of Willie Jones. But that's what love can do sometimes.)

The pattern of birth was a neat one, and satisfied everybody: a boy and a girl, a boy and a girl. It was the frequency of the pattern that appalled Papa. He looked at the children, growing out of their clothes, Dee already as high as a fencepost. *They're like that—like fenceposts, fencing me in!*

And the scraper work for the railroad wore him out physically, and beat down upon his thoughts and his very vision. It was a tedious, crawling job, this adding his anonymous molehill to the mountain of earth needed for embankment or fill. It offered no change of horizons. Sometimes it was weeks before Papa, wiping the sweat from his eyes, could see over the next prairie swell.

On a hot morning when his frustrations were piled higher than the embankment and the gnats were especially bad, his horses balked at pulling the scraper upgrade. Papa swore, and doubled the slack of his reins and laid it hard across their rumps, making the sweat fly and leaving an impressionistic design of broad crisscrossed stripes on the hides of the team. The construction boss, a burly New Jersey Irishman unlearned in the ways of Texans, came over with a piece of rope in his hand.

Papa stepped back, transferring his wrath to the foreman. "You hit my horses, damn you, and I'll kill you!" he warned.

The foreman stared, and choked on a swallow of tobacco juice. He was a hard man in a fight; he wasn't afraid of Papa, but he was confused.

"Well, what the hell?" he asked. "You're whippin' 'em, ain't you?"

"I'll whip 'em any time I damn well please! But nobody else does —*sabe?* Now, goddamn you, just give me my time!"

The railroad went on, without Papa's assistance, and finally reached San Antonio. But it took a long time.

III

Papa rented a small farm while he had some of his wages left, but it was late summer, and no time, thank God, to put a crop into the ground. He needed a wagon trip after all that scraper work. He loaded the wagon with bedding and the camping outfit; he put Dee and Norah and Jay in the back and helped Mama to the wagon seat with the baby, Ivanhoe, in her arms. They were going to Sweet Home to visit Little Grandma.

Nothing went right for Papa that year. On the first night away from the newly rented place, he made camp among the tall pecan trees in the San Antonio River bottom. It had been a hot, oppressive day, and by sundown the thunderheads were piled around the southeastern rim of the world, and there was wind in them. It came up with darkness, striking with a sudden savage fury that threatened to rip the tarp from the wagon bows. Norah began to cry, and Mama, nursing the baby, tried to comfort her. Papa had already unhitched the team.

He always used care in selecting camping sites, but now it began to look as if this one was unsafe. The wind bent the tall pecans, and a heavy limb raked across the wagon sheet, splintering a hickory bow.

"We've got to get out of here, Bettie!" Papa said. "I saw a house just across the field, over yonder. We'll have to run for it. You carry the baby, and I'll carry Jay. Norah! You stop crying. You and Dee stick with us."

Rain came in sheets as they climbed out of the swaying wagon, and the wind nearly blew them down. Lightning flashes showed the way the furrows ran in the field, already gleaming pale with ankle-deep water. Lightning showed the house ahead of them—an unpainted frame structure standing on blocks high enough off the ground that dogs could take shelter underneath, high enough that a cooling breeze could blow under the floor in summertime. The dogs would not come out in that kind of weather for any man, and Papa hammered on the door until the owner opened it, holding a coal-oil lantern.

"Goda'mighty!" he exclaimed. "Come in before you drown! Mary, get your shoes on—we got company. It's the folks you seen drive up in the wagon."

Mary brought out a chair and put it in the middle of the room.

"Set here," she told Mama. "We ain't got much, but you're shore welcome. Listen to that wind!"

Papa was surveying the house with his carpenter's eye. It was new and had only one room. There was a bed at one end, and a table and wood-burning cook stove at the other. Rain blew down the stove pipe and hissed into the remnants of the supper fire.

"Built her myself," the man said, seeing Papa's glance. "Lucky I done a good job of shinglin'. Ain't seen any leaks yet."

The children clustered around Mama's chair. The woman of the house pulled up the only other chair she had, and sat near Mama, her face pale. The wind was increasing; the two women tried to talk, and could not hear each other. The door was still open, and Papa stood there with his host, watching the rain slant past in the lantern light. He saw the farmer's lips moving.

"How's that?" Papa asked.

"Said I ain't seen it blow so hard since the Indianola hurricane, in

[92]

'75!" the man shouted. "Lucky I built her good and tight. She'll ride it out, I reckon."

At that instant, the house lurched and came up off its blocks. Papa and the other man obeyed a very natural impulse without taking time to consider their actions. They leaped out the door together, landed in the mud and water, and ducked low as the house sailed over their heads.

Mama remembered, later, that she was praying. She tried to put her free arm around Dee and Norah and Jay, while the other arm held the baby. She stayed in the chair as if glued to its bottom.

The house was airborne for several seconds. It traveled more than fifty yards, and then settled to earth with a crash that broke some of Mary's dishes, but did not topple Mama's chair. The wind had spent itself in that last climactic gust, and now Papa and the farmer came scrambling through the door, the latter still clutching his lantern. Their faces were white under a spatter of mud.

"My God, Bettie—are you all right—are you all right?" Papa implored. "I didn't mean to leave you—I didn't mean to spook that way! Honestly, Bettie! I just don't know what happened!"

A sob caught in Mama's throat. "Don't talk so loud!" she said fiercely. "You'll wake the baby!"

One of the many reasons Papa was never successful at farming was his habit of emulating old Israel Putnam, of Revolutionary War fame —he was always going off leaving his plough at the end of a furrow. Papa did this simply because he was tired of ploughing; he had no high-sounding cause for the history books, owned no red-coated enemies for his countrymen to hate, and heard no fife-and-drum music to speed the rolling of his wheels. Still, in his own peculiar way, he was as much of a rebel as General Putnam ever was. Papa fought the drably uniformed forces of a growing conservatism; he shattered lances on the shield of inexorable time; he fumed against shrinking space. One of his most maddening frustrations was that he had never been the first man anywhere. If he could have driven his wagon to the top of a rise and looked down upon a wilderness untouched by man, and large enough to accommodate his desires, he might have been content to end his travels.

Nothing like that was left. Cattlemen had already pushed into the Texas Panhandle, and now even farmers were going there. Herds and flocks had crossed the Pecos; some of them were even down in the remote mountain fastnesses of the Big Bend. The Big Bend of the Rio Grande always held a fascination for Papa. He was to be a long time getting there, and it would be the only country Papa never left.

Like Miniver Cheevy, Papa had been born too late.

In the years of 1887, 1888 and 1889, Papa moved a great deal, but never traveled far. He shuttled restlessly back and forth from Karnes to Lavaca to Wharton counties, putting crops into the ground and then selling them there. He traded one crop of cotton for a horse, feeling that he was short of horses at the moment. Dee remembers that this was not a very good horse, but Papa pointed out that even a horse that was getting "long in the tooth" (his words for age) was better than a cottonfield full of boll weevils.

They went to Lavaca many times to see Grandma Hester Ann; they lived for a rent-free period with her at Sweet Home, and Dee developed a child's passionate hatred for Thomas Carpenter. He and Norah got into some kind of dispute while they were playing in the sand; the old man came out to take Norah's side, and accidentally stepped on Dee's thumb with his heavy boot.

But they always went back to Karnes. Papa liked it there. It was a place where the frontier lingered long and died hard: the county seat of Helena had once boasted proudly that it was "the toughest town in the world." They lived for a while near Runge—that was where Uncle Lee Maulding had the store with the music box—and Mama papered the bare walls of a log cabin with old copies of the Galveston *News*. Again, they were in Kenedy Junction, so that Dee could go to school, and here they rented part of a livery stable.

Mama scrubbed and scalded to kill the chinch bugs she said dirty people left behind. There was a wagon yard adjoining. Wagon teams came and went, campfires burned all night, and coffee being boiled in the open smelled better to Papa than the coffee that was brewing on the wood-burning stove; the wanderlust stirred in his blood. Dee did not get much schooling—four months this time, and later another month or two at times caught on the fly. The school bully in Kenedy thrashed him regularly until Papa took down a razor strap and told his eldest son that unless he licked the bully he would get a bigger licking at home. Dee came out victorious in the next encounter, and after that the two boys were pals.

Papa said, "See? You could have done it all the time!" He knew what confidence was worth in others; he never had a great deal of it in himself.

When school was out, Papa moved to another farm and made one memorable crop of cotton. It was so high that it concealed Papa and Mama—and a man they had hired—when they picked it. Dee was big enough to drag a cotton sack along the rows; Norah stayed in the house to take care of the baby, and to summon Mama when the baby needed feeding.

When the crop was laid by, Dee got another month of school. Mama took the other children to visit a neighbor one day, and returned to find that vandals had entered her unlocked door, helped themselves to the freshly-churned butter, and then had shattered Grandma Hester Ann's heirloom butter dish against a tree in the yard. Mama wept.

Things were being broken up in Little Grandma's house at Sweet Home too at this time. She went into her bedroom to get a sunbonnet needed for her garden work and surprised Thomas Carpenter on his hands and knees, delving into the trunk he had pulled out from beneath the four-poster bed.

Hester Ann's wrath was magnificent. She leaped astride the back of her aging husband, and rode him out the door on his all-fours. He never had a chance to rise: she was in the saddle, topping him free style without bridle or hackamore, slapping his face like a bronco buster dusting the ears of a mustang with his hat. Carpenter finally threw her near the front gate, but Little Grandma bounced to her feet instantly, and he was no match for her red-haired temper. She pointed to the gate and told him to go through it, and to keep going.

He came back later for his things, and she threw them into the yard where he could pick them up. Papa and Mama were in Lavaca not long after this; Dee remembers seeing the gaunt old man coming over the prairie rise, hat in hand, to beg Hester Ann to take him back.

She was adamant. At the end of her fortunes, she was disillusioned and done with men. One way or another—through murder and bigamy, through untimely death and by nibbling at her sustenance—all men had betrayed her.

It was not very long after this that Little Grandma died in her garden. She was far from being an old woman, but it may have been best so. The end came quietly, and came before she had lost everything; it saved her from having to adjust to a very different way of life.

Her only daughter was already living in that very different way, and was beginning to see little hope for improvement. Papa had made a little money on that cotton crop—enough to buy a small piece of land—enough to buy lumber so that he could build a house.

Papa was not one to invest his money in an area that was settling up so fast. He bought, instead, a spanking new Studebaker wagon.

Eight

'*E*ighty-nine was a fruitful year in all respects. Mama's fifth child, a girl named Maude Ella, was born in November, around the time Papa got the new wagon. Papa was a very inconsistent man: he railed against the population increase, but continued, steadily, to contribute more than his share to the mounting census figures.

Dee was at school. Norah was minding Ivanhoe, and watching the new baby. Out in the yard, where Papa was sawing and hammering something, Jay played with a cigar-box wagon that had spools for wheels and two whiskey bottles hitched to it with string harness for horses. Mama sat before her cherished looking glass, brushing her waist-long hair and asking the mirror the eternal questions of a woman's vanity. She was a few months past twenty-five. She had been married ten years and had borne five children.

The mirror told her that her wealth of hair was still a rich, glossy auburn, with a natural curl, and that her face was not quite the little-girl's face of her tintype portrait, but was still unlined. She had taken care of her complexion: she always wore a sunbonnet when riding the wagon, and used whatever cold cream she could find, and powdered her face with prepared chalk. Her hands were roughened from opening cotton bolls, but they were still shapely. She stood and turned all the way around, studying her reflection critically.

"You're mighty pretty, Mama!" Norah said.

And Mama gave her stock reply, even though a child's compliment could make her blush with pride. "Pretty, my foot!" she said.

Her hips had widened, and her waist was understandably thicker than it had been at fifteen. But she still had a figure, and to a man's eye—she knew this by the way Papa looked at her—the fuller dimensions were more pleasing.

If she gave any thought at all to the number of children she had borne, she must have remembered that fertility ran high on both sides of the house. All the Hannas had raised large families. Grandpa Henry Bosworth had sired ten children, and the oldest of them—Papa's half-brother Gus—was well along toward producing an even dozen of his own.

It is unlikely, however, that Mama even considered the matter of children, and certainly she did not mourn the fact that she already had five. She loved babies. Two of her three daughters raised large numbers of offspring, and when they said anything about the children's getting underfoot, Mama chided them dramatically.

"Bless Patty, you ought to love having them step on your feet!" she said more than once. "When they grow up and start treading on your heartstrings—that's what hurts!"

This must have been a quote lifted from one of Mrs. Southworth's novels. Perhaps Papa trod on Mama's heartstrings more than once— he may even have driven his horses and wagon over them. The children never grieved her at all. The girls stayed out of trouble and went to their marriages starry-eyed and intact. The boys worried her at times with certain reckless adventurings, and teased her with highly detailed schemes to rob the Southern Pacific and turn outlaws, but Mama was secretly proud of their maleness, and finally learned to know when she was being teased.

Papa came in and put away his tools. "Got to get some more lumber tomorrow," he said.

"What on earth are you making, Woodie?" Mama asked. "I declare, I thought all that hammering was going to wake the baby! Are you building a house?"

Papa poured water into a tin basin, and washed his hands. "Bettie," he said, looking very pleased with himself, "I'm going to make a pile of money. Me and Sam Ezell. We're going into partners."

"Doing what?" Mama asked suspiciously.

"Look," Papa said, pointing out the window. "See that? It's a quail trap. I'll have a dozen of them finished by tomorrow night. Sam ain't much help building the traps, with his one arm, but he's standing the price of the lumber. And he can run the trapline as good as anybody. We'll trap bobwhites, and Mexican blues—the brush is plumb full of them. Ought to catch maybe a couple of dozen a day as easy as falling off a log. Ought to sell them to the hotel in Kenedy Junction for two–three dollars a dozen." He looked at Mama triumphantly, as if success had already come his way. "Money in it, I tell you!"

"I sure hate to see the pretty little things killed!" Mama said. "Don't you ask me to wring their necks, because—"

"Oh, we won't kill them, Bettie! No, we'll run the trapline every morning early and bring the birds back in tow sacks. We'll keep them in a pen—with feed and water, of course—till we've got a whole slew, and then we'll take 'em to Kenedy. Alive."

"It still seems like a shame," Mama said doubtfully. She set about fixing supper, and it occurred to her that the partnership with Sam Ezell was a new departure—even a kind of business venture. She felt sorry for the quail, but many of them would be shot by hunters anyway. And if this thing did work out, maybe Papa would stop talking about going up to Comanche County. The restlessness had fevered him of late. The last time they had been visiting in Lavaca, Gus's wife Josephine had laughed and said that in all her life she had never seen a man as fiddle-footed as Woodie Bosworth.

The quail-trapping enterprise had been Sam Ezell's idea. He was a man of ideas, all along, perhaps forced to imaginative schemes because he had left an arm on some Confederate battlefield. Twelve or fifteen years older than Papa, he had a family to support, and his children ran mostly to girls who were not much help on the farm. He made a joke of this. "Seems like," he told Papa, "that we have always been livin' in the dry creek bottoms. Or maybe every time my wife had a baby it was a bad drought. Anyway, when they was born, they split."

But Mama knew the Ezells for respectable people, honest and clean. And there were no game laws to protect quail with closed seasons; the trapping would be entirely legitimate. Papa saddled up and rode to Kenedy Junction to talk with the people at the hotel. He came back humming a tune, and made his spurs jingle into the house. The hotel owner figured he could use mighty near all the quail they could catch.

"He sure is going to do it up fancy!" Papa said. "You know that blackboard in the dining room? Said he'd write it up there as 'Partridge on Toast.' I never heard it called that, before."

Mama had never seen the blackboard menu, either; she couldn't remember eating out. But it pleased her that Papa was in such high spirits the rest of that week. He and Sam Ezell took the traps out in the wagon. Each was a slatted wooden box, one end of which was propped on an upright pine controlled by a horizontal trigger. If a bird pecked at a piece of cracked corn placed on the trigger arm, or even jostled it while feeding on grain scattered on the ground, the snare would fall. It was, Papa said, an old Indian device. The traps were big enough to catch eight or ten or even a dozen birds at one springing of the trigger.

They took a sack of cracked corn with them, and set the traps along two or three miles of brush-dotted prairie, in the edges of the brush so they would not be knocked over by cattle. Next morning, by prearrangement, they rode out at six o'clock, when dew or frost was still on the grass, taking along a new supply of bait tied to their saddlehorns.

That first day, they brought back more than twenty birds to put into the pen Papa had made of fine-mesh chicken wire that covered top and sides. The second day, they trapped thirty-two, and the third running of the trapline was almost as successful.

Mama refused to go out and look at the quail. Papa went there to freshen the pan of water and see about the feed. The birds fluttered into a far corner of their prison, and beat heads and wings against the wire. They tried to rise in explosive, whirring flight, but there was not enough room. The haunting desperation of all caged wild creatures glittered in their beady eyes.

"Poor little devils!" Papa heard himself saying. "Poor little devils—fenced in!"

Next morning, he told Sam Ezell that the cooped birds didn't seem to be feeding very well. Might lose weight, he said, unless they were taken to Kenedy right away. "Now I got a carpenter job to do," he went on. "But if you could run 'em in to the hotel, you're welcome to drive my team."

"Do it tomorrow," Sam grunted. "Kind of tied up today, myself. . . ."

So they rode the trapline together at six o'clock the next morning. Ezell was dumbfounded. Papa took off his wide-brimmed hat and scratched his head in a good show of perplexity.

Not one of the traps had been sprung. The catch was zero.

"Goda'mighty damn!" Ezell exploded. "What happened? You figger somebody else has got the idea? Somebody else settin' traps?"

Papa shook his head. "Haven't seen any signs. Must be that we have just cleaned them out. Wasn't as many as we thought. Not a quail left in the brush."

A hundred yards away, in the chaparral, a Mexican blue cock gave the lie to him at that propitious moment. *"Tostón!"* it called, either as a danger signal or to summon the harem of hens. *"Tostón, Tostón!"*

"Brush is full of the little bastards!" Sam Ezell said. He spat tobacco juice at a tarantula making its hairy-legged way along a cow trail, and missed. "Better luck tomorrow, maybe," he said.

When they rode back home, it was to find that their business fortunes had fallen even lower. The door to the wire pen was open. The birds had flown the coop.

Ezell threw his hat on the ground. "Goda'mighty good goddamn!" he roared. "Who done this? One of your young'uns, maybe?"

"Hell, no!" Papa said coldly. "They wouldn't fool around with this pen. Could have been a coon, maybe."

"Yeah—some two-legged coon!" Sam said. He bit viciously into a plug of tobacco. "Well, we have to start all over again, damn it. And I'm goin' to get a padlock and chain for this here door. And I'll see you in the mornin' at six."

"*Adiós,*" Papa said.

At six the following morning there was frost to silver the grass, indicating a rather hard winter, but the traps were utterly devoid of quail. They were empty, too, on the three successive mornings. The Great Southwestern Texas Game Farm died an incipient death without ever turning a penny of profit, and Papa not only breathed more easily, but he also began catching up on his sleep.

He was to be associated with Sam Ezell, several years later, in an enterprise slightly more profitable and infinitely more dangerous. He liked Sam a whole lot. Sam, he said, was a man "you could ride the river with."

But Sam Ezell just never would have understood why Papa was getting up at five o'clock every morning to ride the trapline and turn all the birds loose before resetting the traps and scattering a little cracked corn under them to make it appear no quail had ever been there.

Nor would Sam have ever understood what drove Papa to open the door of the big pen to let fifteen or twenty dollars fly away.

When you came right down to it, Papa didn't understand it either. All he knew was the quail had a trapped look in their eyes, and they were beating their heads against the wire, and he couldn't bear to see anything fenced in.

II

So they went to Comanche after all. They went late in the winter, when the unpredictable northers blasted across the treeless Panhandle and shrieked over the rest of Texas. They were facing the wind, and it blustered into the pucker of the wagon tarp and almost blew it off the hooped hickory bows.

"It was mighty cold on the wagon seat," Mama said. "It just seemed like there wasn't anything between us and the North Pole but a barbed-wire fence. . . ."

The children were under the wagon sheet, huddled in the warmth of featherbeds and quilts and their own body heat. Papa tucked a quilt and a piece of tarp over the seat for a lap robe, and put a lighted coal-oil lantern on the floor of the wagon box. He and Mama were snug—up to their waists. Above that zone, even though they bundled up in all the clothing they had, they froze.

Sleet stung their faces, and cold rain, and always the cutting wind. The roads were bad: Papa warmed himself into a sweat on more than one occasion when he got down to curse the horses and whip them through the deep mud, and some days they only made five or six miles. They knew hungry nights, when cold rain hissed into the campfire and drowned it before anything could be cooked; the children ate biscuits that were nothing but warmed dough, and bacon still raw. They managed a wagon yard or two, and woke the night man, and Mama cooked whole meals on one-lidded potbellied stoves, with it pouring rain outside. . . .

The wagon yards are gone now, and long gone, and with them a way of travel nobody remembers. The rutted roads have been bound tightly with pavement, and motels have their snide and competitive lures: free TV, swimming pools, cracked ice and air conditioning, Beautyrest mattresses, and what-not. But the motels can never produce anybody to compare with the night man at the livery stable and wagon yard. He was fixture and character. He was always a small man of uncertain age, as leathery as the harness he handled; so far as anyone knew, he had neither relatives nor ties of any kind, and nobody asked where he came from. Late at night, he would come out of the tack room where he slept, carrying a lantern and taking a fresh chew of tobacco. The hospitality he dispensed was laconical and free—hell, what could anybody do to a wagon yard as long as they didn't set the hay afire? He spat tobacco juice into the stove, and told the lady of the wagon that she was welcome to fry up a meal on it. The night man at the wagon yard was a "loner," and something between him and Papa always made them immediate friends and *compañeros*. . . .

The journey to Comanche took more than two weeks. Before she made it, Mama hated all wagon yards and disliked having to stay in them. Just after her marriage there had been a sort of unpolished novelty about them, but she came early to the conclusion that a prairie camp was much more private, and that wagon yards were ordinarily frequented by a class of people with which she did not wish to be identified. Their unwashed, scabby-kneed children ran whooping all over the lot, and came up to peer, impolitely, into what the family was having for supper—until Mama suspected that they were hungry. One night, in a wagon yard, she had seen silhouettes on a lantern-yellowed wagon tarp of a man and woman embracing before they blew out the light and went to bed. Papa laughed, and said well, it was their home; Mama thought the dumb show indicated a shocking lack of manners and breeding.

But on the trip to Comanche, with her cheeks frostbitten and her teeth chattering in the rhythm of the wind-whipped wagon sheet slapping the bows, she was forced to a new appraisal. By comparison with an open camp on the prairie, a wagon yard was a hostel, a haven—even an inn on the wilderness road. It offered warmth and security. Wagon yards, at least, had dry firewood.

It is absurd, perhaps, to attach larger significance to Papa's actions in those days now distant. But something happened when he freed the quail. It was an unconsciously symbolical act, perhaps; no psychologists and no psychiatrists were there to probe Papa's dreams and suppressed desires and hidden motivations. Both he and Mama leaned more toward the cures and palliatives of Dr. Pierce, whose name adorned many a barn. But, when Papa turned the quail loose, he freed his own wild spirit from all its encompassing fences and let it soar.

Never again did he put his hand to the plough. He picked cotton for other people—yes. It was a way of making a little money; it had nothing to do, essentially, with the epic drama of seed and harvest, and it did not bind him. He could weigh his sack, collect his money, and go.

Never again did he stay anywhere as long as he had remained in Karnes. When the imprisoned quail took wing, so did Papa, and with something of the same wild surprise. Little Grandma Hester Ann was dead, and Mama had no ties closer than her two half-brothers. The road was open for travel.

Papa never had any ties at all. He had been reared under the old, individualistic frontier code which early severed the umbilical cord. They told it, on the old Texas frontier: "Son, here's a rock. Now you go out and throw it and kill your own breakfast. . . ."

There is something of Papa in all of his children. I have made my own way since I was thirteen and big enough to throw my own rock. We are individuals, as Papa was, and do not feed upon each other. I have not seen my brother Jay for forty-three years.

III

There was another succession of camps, in houses where Mama poured her boiling water in cracks and crevices to kill the bugs, in a place where Papa built a lean-to arbor on the house and Mama planted balsam vines and morning-glories and saw them mature, for once. She carried white sand from the creek, and scoured her floors with it; she had, always, that passion for cleanliness.

Norah ran up and down the gallery singing "Skip to My Lou," and:

> *Charlie, he is a nice young man,*
> *Charlie, he is a dandy . . .*

and then Mama would come out to ask what people would think of the family if they heard such songs? It was all right, Mama said, to sing things like "Home, Sweet Home," or "My Old Kentucky Home," or "Gentle Annie." Snap, she said, was not a decent game; she would not allow her children to play it.

They moved into another place where a ranchman paid Papa fifteen dollars a month, with room and board for the family, just to see that the Mexican *vaqueros* did their work. There were no expenses that were not absorbed by the feudal system: even the laundry was done, and Norah remembers that her dresses were starched so stiffly that she could not sit down in them. The ranch had a woman cook, with so many people to feed "it was like she was cooking for a hotel," and the food was good.

Considering everything, this was probably the best job Papa ever had. His fifteen dollars a month was clear money. He had acquired a dozen head of cows and calves of his own, and the benevolent ranch owner—one of the last of the feudal lords—let him graze them free of charge.

This was the chance for a man to build up his own herd and establish his own brand. Many a Texas cowman got his start that way. But there was trouble: the owner of the ranch was *too* benevolent, with a soft spot in his heart for little children. Maude was just beginning to walk, and to communicate her wants. She had a passion for brown sugar, which she called "num."

"Please don't give her any more!" Mama told the ranchman.

But little Maude beat on the pantry door. "Num!" she cried. "Num, num, num!" And the ranch owner said, "Well there, there, of course my little baby will have some num!" And he gave her so much brown sugar that she ate nothing else and developed dysentery.

There was a family consultation and Mama was distraught. "I told him!" she said. "I keep telling him not to give her sugar. And she cries, and he keeps on giving it to her. What will we do?"

She was ill herself. She didn't know it, but Papa saw that she was at the end of her tether. He said, "Well, Mr. Choate is a mighty fine man, but we'll just have to move. No other way out of it."

Thus he talked himself into what he wanted all the time, and lifted

Mama to the wagon seat. He sold his cattle to Mr. Choate, and the wagon wheels rolled again. "We couldn't stay there," Papa said later. "Old Man Choate was feeding Maude too much brown sugar."

After a few days on the wagon, Maude and Mama and everybody else were all right. The roads ran free.

They went farther into Comanche County to stay awhile with Aunt Fanny and her husband, Dr. George Jones. There was a high old time with a log-rolling and a quilting bee: the men rolled logs and put them into place for a new house, and after just so much of this arduous work all of them repaired to a wagon that had a jug in it. The women had already prepared a picnic dinner, and meanwhile attended to their quilting and dipped a little snuff. In the afternoon, things turned loud and hilarious and there was *a cappella* singing of all the old songs. Meanwhile, Maude toddled into the yard and put a hard and spiny grassbur into her mouth. She tried to swallow it, and it stuck in her throat.

This ruined the party. A Texas grassbur is one of the things most inedible in all the world. Mama tried reaching it with her fingers, and only succeeded in pushing it farther down the throat of the choking child. Fortunately, Uncle George came driving up in his buggy at that moment. He may not have been a great physician, but he was a good man in emergencies such as this one. He promptly seized a spoon and used its handle to depress Maude's tongue, then he went after the grassbur with a pair of forceps—the same pair, he said, that he had used to take a Minié ball out of a man's shoulder in the War. Maude turned blue in the face and went limp; Uncle George brought out the grassbur, clotted with blood. Norah was sick, watching.

Uncle George spanked Maude as if she were a newborn baby, and she resumed her screaming. He gave her an extra whack. "That," he said, "is for eating grassburs! Even goats don't eat grassburs!"

Mama breathed again, too. But the log-rolling and the quilting bee had lost their charm.

Not long after this, Papa caught up the horses. "New country!" he said, and the wagon rolled southwest into Tom Green County, and into a cold winter. The trip took two weeks. The tent Papa usually carried had been worn out and discarded; now the bedding was put down on a wagon sheet spread on the ground and folded back over the featherbeds and blankets to provide extra protection from the wind. But when it rained everybody had to get up and crowd into the wagon, where they slept as best they could.

Mama slept sitting up, and wondered if she would ever have a roof to call her own.

Nine

"It seemed like the older Papa got, the worse his temper was: he would just fly off the handle, and want to break something, or maybe take it out on the horses. I reckon he would have shot that bossy woman in Tom Green County, that time, if Mama hadn't taken the gun away from him. But she couldn't argue with him any more than with a fence post. He'd just sull, like an old 'possum, and wouldn't say a word for a week. . . ." —NORAH

*I*t is a long way, even today, from Sweet Home to San Angelo; it was a longer distance in that winter of 1890-91, and farther still from the realization of any of Mama's dreams. At the time, she thought she had come to the "jumping-off place."

The western portion of Tom Green County had been parceled out not long before to create several other counties; even so, it was a bigger piece of Texas real estate than it is now, and it came about as near to being a part of the frontier as Papa would find for a long time. He could look at a town, driving through it, and tell you what kind of country was around it, and he liked San Angelo.

He didn't see any carriages around, and not even a fringe-topped surrey. Ranch wagons outnumbered the buggies, and there were freight outfits with twelve-horse teams. Cowboys rode festively down Chadbourne Street; the hitching rails in front of the pleasure palaces on East Concho were crowded with horses. The temper of the town put Papa into a high-stepping mood, and he wrapped his reins around the brake handle and said he thought he would get out and rattle his hocks a little. Not being a drinking man, he did nothing but buy provisions and ask for directions to the sheep camp of Uncle Nick and Aunt Docia Rogers.

He remembered snuff for Mama, and brought a sack of candy for the children. Sitting on the wagon seat, Mama had been counting saloons—there were two or three to every block in the business district, and that seemed a lot for a town of only four or five thousand people. San Angelo was the cowboy and sheepherder capital of West Texas, and it remained so for a long time.

Papa's money was all gone now; he didn't even have enough to camp at a wagon yard. He drove out past Fort Concho just to see the place, which had not been garrisoned with troops since the Indians gave up their hopeless struggle, and then he crossed the river and turned south on the old stage road. Off to the west a few miles was an intriguing topographical formation: two small rock-crowned buttes rose from the prairie in a totally unexplainable fashion. There were no other hills around.

"Look there, Bettie!" Papa said. "Feller who gave me the directions said they call 'em Twin Mountains now, but on the old surveys they used to be known as the Breasts of Cleopatra and the Teats of Venus."

"Woodie!" Mama reproved him. "The children can hear you!"

"Nothing wrong with those names," Papa chuckled.

Neither he nor Mama had any idea, then, that some ten years later their tent on the McGill ranch would stand squarely between those mammillate mountains, and that I would be born there. If Mama believed that prenatal influence could mark Dee's lip with a red apple, she might have given some sober reflection to what such surroundings could (and did) do to her youngest son.

Papa admired the landscape and drove on, overwhelmed for a while by the bounties of nature. He went down past the conjunction of the south and middle forks of the three-pronged Concho River, but he was too smart to camp on the low ground. Ruined foundations there recalled the flood that had destroyed Ben Ficklin's Stage Station eight years before.

(You must remember that we not only covered Texas up and down and sideways, but that Papa backtracked many times, and we backtracked after Papa was no longer in the driver's seat. All of this journey was to be repeated when I was four years old, and we came dangerously near to being wiped out by another flood in the same place.)

Papa camped on high ground. Chill came with dusk. A wind rose to flap the wagon tarp and blow showers of sparks from the campfire. The afterglow of sunset hung long in the western sky, as it does in semidesert country, and bullbats whizzed overhead. Coyotes began howling, and Mama would not have been surprised at an Indian attack. She was glad when daylight came.

There was not enough wood left near the camp to cook breakfast, and for the first time Mama had to burn dried cowchips for her fire. She nursed Maude on the wagon seat, and watched the horizons widen into a limitless expanse of level plain. The wagon was now like a ship at sea, crawling across infinity. These were the Lipan Flats: a fabled place, forbidding and fascinating, but the fascination was Papa's alone. In the centuries of the Plains Indians it had been a grassland rivaling those high steppes where the Tartars rode, but with a more kindly climate. The Lipans were an Apache tribe, and warlike, but no match for the Comanche horsemen who came down out of the north to push them westward across the Pecos, and southward over the Rio Grande. The Indians burned the high grass on occasion, and with it the mesquites, until the latter growth had tremendous roots underground and was hardly more than shrubbery above. The first white men came with the notion of getting rich quick on the good pastures—and overstocked and sheeped off the grass. The flocks moved on to seek better forage; they left the land to the lonesome wind, to the jackrabbits and wild coyotes, and to the wilder lobo wolves.

The grass always came back in that miracle of resurrection that is the way of grass, and smaller operators, like my Uncle Nick Rogers, moved in.

The dogs barked, and Uncle Nick came out of the dust-stained tent where a stovepipe sent a wreath of mesquite-scented smoke into the evening air. Papa couldn't understand how a man working with sheep could stay so square-shouldered and arrow straight.

"Docia! Docia!" he called over his shoulder. "It's Bettie and Woodie! Well, I'll be dadgummed! I don't see how you found us, forty miles away to God and hell and gone from Nowhere! Get down and rest your team."

Mama sniffed a little at this greeting. She always suspected that Uncle Nick was not a very religious man. I know that Abel was a sheep man and Cain ran cattle (the pattern of violence between the two rival camps was set that early), and I know about the shepherds watching their flocks by night, and some of the other Biblical references to sheep. But I never blamed Uncle Nick for being not a very religious man. Anybody who has ever herded sheep, or dipped them, or sheared them, or tried to protect them from their own ingrained and colossal stupidities, should be forgiven occasional lapses into blasphemy.

Uncle Nick and Aunt Docia now had two children of their own, and the camp was crowded. The family stayed there two weeks, while Papa rode out to look for a house and a job. He found both, but they were not in the same place. The house was twenty-five miles away, on the old government road that ran between Fort McKavett and Fort Concho; the job was twenty miles from the Rogers camp, in the opposite direction, where a rancher wanted Papa to build him a small frame dwelling.

He told Mama it was not a time when he could afford to be choosy. They drove all day to reach the house, and it was long after dark when they arrived. By lantern light, Mama swept out the two small, cheerless rooms, and put pieces of oilcloth over the broken windowpanes. With daylight she saw that the house stood in the middle of the endless flats, with a fenced horse trap and a big dirt tank at its back. In front—only thirty feet away—was the road, with freight wagons going by.

Papa saddled his horse early, with forty-five miles to ride. "I'll be back in two weeks," he said. "Just as soon as I get the house done."

He had never been away overnight. Mama's heart sank as she looked at the empty horizons and heard the lonesome wind.

"I haven't got any money, Woodie," she reminded him. "And there's not much grub . . ."

"Just two weeks," he repeated. "No place to spend any money anyway. You'll be all right, and when I get back we'll find another place."

He left her there with the five small children clustered around her skirts, and rode away into the wind. They could see him a long time before the horse carried him over the horizon.

That night Mama was afraid for the first time in her life. She hung quilts over the four windows, and threw the flimsy thumb latches on the doors; she kept the lantern burning, and she and the children slept in one room. A couple of freight-wagon outfits went by, traveling late; Mama imagined that there were tramps walking the road, and she heard the coyotes howling until sunrise. With Dee to help, she managed to set up her cookstove; she unloaded the sewing machine and hung her looking glass from a nail on the wall. Then she heated water, which the children carried from the dirt tank, and began scrubbing the floors.

She marked off the days on a calendar advertising a San Angelo hardware store, and she watched the food supply dwindle. On the fourteenth day the food was nearly all gone, and Papa did not return. On the fifteenth, Mama and Dee went out to try to catch the horses when they came to the tank to drink.

The horses were doing fine on the curly brown mesquite grass. They were in a playful mood. They let Mama and Dee come within a few feet of them with the headstalls, and then they kicked up their heels and ran away. They ran away again on the sixteenth day, and on the seventeenth.

Papa still did not come home. Next day there was only a handful of food left in the chuckbox.

On the morning of the nineteenth day, Mama put corn in her dishpan and went with Dee into the horse trap. They walked a mile, to the far corner of the pasture, and found the horses grazing there. Mama shook the corn in the pan and the team came up near enough for Dee to get a rope around their necks.

The things went back into the wagon, and Mama hitched up. She drove the twenty-five miles to Uncle Nick's camp in a fast trot and got there just as darkness fell. Next morning, Uncle Nick rode to the other ranch, and Papa came back with him.

"I'll just say, Bettie!" he declared. "You sure went to a lot of trouble. I'd have been home tomorrow."

"Tomorrow, my foot!" Mama retorted angrily. "The children wouldn't have had anything to eat *today!* And I can tell you right now—this is the last time you're ever going off and leave us alone like that. You can just put that in your pipe and smoke it!"

Papa turned red, but said nothing. Instead, he took the attitude that it was he who had been wronged, and sulked for three days.

Then he got a job as rider and windmill fixer for a ranchman named Berry.

II

Mr. Berry and his wife had two small children. They also had money, and spent it freely, but with no outward show—at the time, they were living in two stove-heated tents, and breaking the ice on the trough to drink with the horses. They were gambling on the chancy price of beef, and betting everything on the weather. Two or three dry years in a row could always ruin a Texas cattleman; good fall rains could make him rich. There was a saying that if it rains in Texas in September it just don't make a damn who's in the White House.

This was one of Papa's "permanent" camps. He removed the wagon box and put it on blocks; Mr. Berry gave him a second wagon box which was similarly mounted. The family of seven lived in these two narrow shelters during that winter, but Mama had to cook outside, even in rain and snow. Mr. Berry told her to bring the children and come over to the two tents just any old time they wanted to get warm, or felt like visiting. When Christmas was near, Mr. Berry drove to San Angelo and brought back a big wooden box crammed with toys and nuts and candies. The old-time Texas notion that any celebration should be noisy also made that Christmas sound like the Fourth of July—there was another box loaded with firecrackers, roman candles and skyrockets. New Year's Day was ushered in, of course, by the custom of stepping outside at daybreak and emptying a good-sized sixshooter into the air.

It was a good job, but Papa was already finding something with which he could not live. Mrs. Berry was a friendly woman, but inclined to take the bit in her teeth now and then, and (as Papa put it) "run away with the whole damned ranch." There was this about Papa: he was completely male, and wore the pants in his own household, and expected other men to do the same. He could not remotely conceive of any situation in which a woman told a man what to do.

Perhaps Mrs. Berry was simply trying to be a good manager and a good helpmeet. She wasn't at all uppity about it, but she saw no reason why she shouldn't stop by the two wagon boxes when she had been out for a horseback ride, and tell Woodie Bosworth that the windmill in the south pasture was creaking as if it had a dry bearing. The first time this happened, Papa grumbled a little, but he rode down to grease the windmill. The next time, it was a break in the barbed wire that enclosed the horse trap.

"I'm going to tell Berry to keep that woman away from here!" Papa threatened. "I won't have her sticking her nose into my business!"

"You'll do nothing of the kind!" Mama said. "After all, I guess this is as much her place as it is his."

Papa brooded. He wouldn't talk to Mrs. Berry. At first he grunted very impolitely when she mentioned that she had seen a wormy steer in some part of the pasture. Then he refused to talk to her at all. After that, it began to seem as if she took a particular delight in trying to find things she could tell him to do . . . and the war was on.

Mama's own special enemy was the wind. It was long before the days of the Dust Bowl, but the winds of West Texas have always had a high soil content. They picked up sand and gravel and hurled them against the two wagon tarps with a dry and harsh whisper that said, "Go—go!" and there was no answer. The wind blew a fine, tooth-edging grit into pots and pans and supper plates. Dry northers shrieked down over the unprotected Lipan Flats; cattle and horses and sheep suffered from sore-eye, and humans shared this common affliction. Lips chapped and split and bled. Noses ran eternally, and Mama discovered another patent medicine in which she soon had boundless faith. This was Doctor Sage's Catarrh Remedy.

"Shucks!" Papa said. "I'll bet you that stuff is nothing but salt water. Tastes just like the Gulf did, down around Port Lavaca."

"I want you to get two or three more bottles the first time you go to Angelo," Mama said firmly. "You, children! Time for you to gargle your medicine, and snuff some of it up your noses!"

I wonder what ever happened to catarrh? It was a pretty popular ailment in the days when nobody in that part of the country had ever heard of sinuses.

Life was rough on the Lipan Flats. Mama had not been consulted about moving there, nor would it have done her any good to vote against the move. Independent action was out of the question. She had no money; she had no place to go. And she had her pride.

Besides, as she pointed out later, there were the children. They were her only reason for living. There were always the children, and more coming, and the battle lines became more sharply drawn, with Papa on one side and Mama and her children on the other.

She still loved Papa, but it was becoming a hopeless and despairing love.

The battle went on, sporadically, but with increasingly shorter periods of armistice. It was the age-old conflict between the woman's desire for security and the man's yearning for adventure. There is no telling what a good psychiatrist could have done for Papa— or what one might have learned from him. Certainly the case history would have been most interesting.

There were no psychiatrists, no marriage counselors, and not even a newspaper column to give advice to the lovelorn. It would have helped if Papa would have argued, because then perhaps they could have talked things out in a reasonably mature fashion. As it was, in that winter on the Lipan Flats, they were not nearly halfway through their wanderings, but they were almost midway in their marriage, and danger signals were flying.

Neither recognized them.

III

Mr. Berry, for all his generosity and hospitality, must have had a particular enemy of his own—somebody who fancied he had branded the wrong yearling, or resented his fence line or thought he had committed the cardinal sin of leaving a gate open. Because one moonlight night when the March winds were blowing and the coyotes were howling in the chaparral, somebody stole one of Mr. Berry's windmills.

This is not an easy thing to do, and it has been noted that men often turn thieves because they are essentially opposed to any form of labor. Nor would the theft of a windmill enrich anyone, to any great extent. To benefit at all from the larceny, a man would have to have a well drilled, and he certainly would have needed a plausible explanation of how it came about that he was erecting a second-hand windmill over it. Dee was in the windmill business for many years, and he never heard of second-hand windmills.

Nor could he ever explain just what happened to Mr. Berry's mill. The theft was either an act of revenge, or it was one of the most difficult pieces of frontier humor that had yet been perpetrated.

Papa first heard about it from Mrs. Berry. She came riding up to the wagon-box camp early in the morning.

"Somebody's stolen the south windmill!" she yelled.

Papa was saddling up and slinging a bottle of screw-worm killer on the saddlehorn. Fly time comes early in that part of Texas.

The intelligence was so startling that he forgot he wasn't speaking to Mrs. Berry.

"Did what?" he asked.

"Stole the south windmill! I want you to ride out and see if you can follow the tracks. I want you to drop everything, and—"

"Are you crazy?" Papa asked. "People don't steal windmills!"

"Don't you call me crazy! You just go down there and look. It's gone, and I want you to look for it, and don't be slow about it, either!"

She wheeled her horse and put him in a lope toward the ranch tents. Apparently Mr. Berry had not yet heard the news.

"Damn crazy woman!" Papa muttered as she rode off. "Never heard of such a thing."

Then he began to get mad. He went into the wagon box where Mama was brushing her hair before her looking glass. "Thinks she can send me off on a wild-goose chase like that, she's *loco*," he said. "I'm not a greenhorn kid! Berry didn't get me with Arbuckle stamps!"

"What on earth are you talking about?" Mama demanded.

"That damn fool woman! She rode up and told me somebody stole the south windmill last night. Ordered me to go look for it. That's the limit!"

Norah came in just then. "Papa," she said, "here comes Mrs. Berry."

Papa's face went white. "I'll kill that goddamn woman!" he said, and picked up the saddle gun that leaned against the sideboards.

"Woodie!" Mama called in alarm. *"Woodie!* Put down that gun!"

Papa pushed Norah out of the narrow way, and started for the tarp-hung entrance. He could see the rancher's wife now, only a hundred yards away, coming to ask why he hadn't got moving, coming to give him another order. "She does that," he muttered, "and I'll kill her, sure as hell!"

Norah began to cry. Mama moved fast down the floor of the wagon box. She came up behind Papa and grabbed his arm just as he was about to step outside with the gun. She spun him around and got both hands on the rifle, and managed to wrest it from Papa's grasp.

"You sit down and cool off!" she told him, and gave him a push toward a hidebottomed chair.

Papa sat down, still white-faced as a Hereford steer, and shaking all over. Mama went outside and hurriedly put the gun down at the side of the wagon box.

"Where's Woodie?" Mrs. Berry began. "I told him I wanted him to go track down those windmill thieves. I told him—"

"Woodie's kind of sick," Mama said softly. "I think you'd better leave him alone today, Mrs. Berry. I'm sorry."

She went back in, and Mrs. Berry sat for a moment with her mouth open, and then rode away.

"Well," Mama said, "I guess we'd better start packing and loading the things. . . ."

They hitched up the horses and left early the next morning. They drove back down through the prairie and postoak country—all the way back to Karnes County, and then on to Lavaca to visit Uncle Gus and his family. Mama saw Sweet Home again, and the gray house behind the spreading liveoaks. She cried a little as they went by: someone with a large number of barefoot children was living there now, and the place looked rundown.

But now they could make a new start. The children could go to school next fall. There had been no school in twenty miles, out on the Lipan Flats.

An education for her children was all Mama wanted now. She had long before stopped dreaming of someday owning a big plantation, with hired help to pick the cotton that would make them rich. A lot of other Texans had stopped dreaming that too. There were no plantations left.

The new word was "ranch," and it was a more democratic word, but one that suggested sweat and saddle leather and barbed wire; it meant dusty winds and a long, hard pull. Mama thought about the Berrys, who had money enough to make the gamble, and still had far to go. She knew, by now, that Papa had to have something quicker, something acquired all at once; he would never get rich by the long pull.

This was when the enthusiastic letters began coming from the older of her half-brothers, Uncle Ed Maulding, who was still up in Comanche. He told Papa that another piece of land was going to be thrown open in the Cherokee Strip, in Oklahoma Territory. It was new country, he said; a man would be a fool not to take advantage of the opportunity.

It was that "new country" that intrigued Papa. He knew about the original opening of the Cherokee lands, back in April of 1889, when twenty thousand people were lined up to make the race, and the "Sooners" jumped the gun. Twenty thousand people were more than Papa wanted to see in any place; he was glad he hadn't gone. But maybe the big rush was over now, and maybe the thing to do was to get on the ground early.

The spark was kindled. Other letters came from Uncle Ed, who had announced his own intention of joining the forthcoming run. Papa caught fire.

It would be the longest wagon trip Mama had ever made, and things were falling into their customary pattern. She had just discovered that she was pregnant again.

Meanwhile, far out in Tom Green County, the Berrys had found their windmill a day or two after Papa drove off the job. It had been partly dismantled and was hidden in the mesquites a few miles away, with the wooden tower lying on its side.

"I don't recollect, for sure," Dee told me, "but I reckon it must have rained that night, and washed out the tracks. It wasn't a very big windmill, compared to what you see now. There are places in that country where you get water at a pretty shallow depth, and you don't need a big mill to lift the rods—not the way the wind blows on the Lipan Flats. Probably two or three men with a wagon could have done the job."

I laughed, remembering Papa and the wire cutting. "You don't think Papa hauled it away to get even with Mrs. Berry, do you?"

"Papa? He never would have done that much hard work."

"Do you believe he really would have shot her?"

"Well, you never could tell what was going on in Papa's mind. I didn't see that little fracas—I was out hunting rabbits, or something. Norah always claimed he was so mad he was plumb clean out of his head, and I know that he couldn't stand bossy women. But I don't figure he would have shot her. You know he never raised his hand to Mama, and he never had many fights. He was always the one who got out of town just before there was a killing."

We decided that Papa only intended to scare the pants off Mrs. Berry, because he didn't think she should have been wearing them, and that he put on quite a good act.

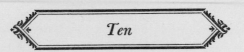

Ten

*P*apa told Uncle Gus and Aunt Jo—who had called him "fiddle-footed"—that his roving days were over. Just no two ways about it, he said: the move to Oklahoma Territory was going to be his last. (Papa usually called it the "Indian Territory," as a holdover from the old days.)

This, he said, was what he had always wanted: a chance to take up free land in a new country, to settle down and work to prove up his claim, and then acquire some of the land adjoining. He didn't want any little puny two-bit outfit. He'd soon have his own help—Dee was ten, and growing out of his britches mighty fast, and Jay would soon be seven. Norah was eight, and could already cook for the whole family when Mama was ill, or was confined with a new baby.

"How much land will you get free?" Uncle Gus asked. "You going to farm, or raise cows?"

Papa wasn't sure about the size of the tract. Some people said it would be 160 acres—a quarter section. Others insisted a man with a family could get a whole section.

"But I'll go far enough out that I can buy land around me for maybe four bits an acre," Papa said. "And I ain't going to farm.

That was all buffalo range up there, you know—ought to have grass on it teat-high to a tall cow. No, sir—I'll ranch!"

He saw that Mama looked a little worried at his statement that he intended to go far out. "Of course, we'll probably have to live in the tent until I can get a house built," he told her almost apologetically. "Lots of folks start out up there with dugouts and sod roofs. But we've got the tent for summertime, and I can finish a house before winter."

Mama dreaded the long trip, but the mention of a house of her own made her eyes shine. The next baby was coming in January. None of the other five children had been born in her very own house. "What about schools?" she asked. "As long as there's a school close enough—"

"Oh, there'll be schools!" Papa assured her. "This is Government land. They've even got schools for the Indians."

He aimed to make this final trip in high style. He had taken most of the heavier household possessions to the freight depot at Victoria, and was having them shipped by rail, all the way to Vernon, and the family would travel only with the camping outfit. Vernon was far up in Wilbarger County, almost to the Red River.

Papa was studying a railroad map of Texas. It showed the railroad playing out just the other side of Wichita Falls, but it was an old map; the freight agent had told him that the line reached Vernon all right.

"We'll head for Alleyton," Papa said, "and cross the Colorado River there, and we'll get over the Brazos at Pitt's Bridge—that's up here in Burleson County. Then we'll go through Waco, and Fort Worth—both of them are pretty big towns now. Oh, you'll see a lot of new country this trip!"

Mama sighed. She had seen all the new country she wanted to see; she was weary of hearing the words. But the children caught Papa's excitement, and crowded around to watch him trace the route on the map. Texas was a pale yellow, the color of mesquite grass that has been sun-cured in a dry year; what there was of Oklahoma Territory was pink, and Norah began to picture it as a land of flowers. Papa was in such a happy mood that he even joked with the children, and that was a very rare thing.

"We'll be going right up the top of the map," he pointed out. "Now, of course, that's going to be uphill all the way, and you might have to get out and push, now and then. If you drove south, it would be downhill."

They believed him, and wanted to know if you just fell off when you got to the edge of the map, and Papa laughed and said you got a new map before that happened. But he had spoken more truth than he knew. The roads were bad that spring; the wagon traversed an uncommon amount of sticky gumbo mud and deep sand, and the family went up through a large part of Texas with only Papa on the wagon. Mama and the children were not actually pushing, but sometimes they were strung out for a quarter of a mile behind the wagon, walking through difficult stretches to lighten the horses' load. Some days they walked farther than they rode. But Texas was deep in springtime; the weather was soft, and hearts were high. This was the biggest of all their adventures.

Texas was growing, stretching, fermenting, bubbling over. Wagons came down the laned roads, headed the other way, following some Papa had already dreamed and forgotten. There was none of today's mad hurrying, with eyes only for the stripe on the pavement and the reassuring highway number. Papa prided himself on being the first to turn out so the other driver could pass, although at times he met travelers equally polite. Drawing abreast, the two wagons always stopped, and it was something like whaling ships holding a gam at sea.

"Howdy, stranger!"

"Howdy, yourself! Travelin' far?"

"Right smart piece. All the way up to Indian Territory."

"That so? Say . . . could I borrow a chew of tobacco from you? I'm plumb out. . . . Much obliged. Well, now, I had a brother-in-law that went up there in '89. Ain't heard from him, so I reckon he's doin' all right. You figure on takin' up some land?"

"If it looks good. Mighty nice-lookin' team of horses you got there." '

"Well, they just been eatin' their heads off all winter. Won't be so frisky time we get down to Goliad. How's the road farther on?"

"Muddy in spots, but I don't reckon you'll have any trouble with them bays. What's it like between here and Waco?"

"You want to watch out for a sandy stretch up yonder about three miles. Stay in the middle, or you'll be up to your hubs. About a half mile of it."

"Well, much obliged for telling me. *Adiós!*"

"Good luck to you, stranger."

They came always, at evening time, to the gypsy charm of the wagon camp, to woodsmoke and flickering firelight and the good empty-belly smells of coffee boiling, and bacon frying, and hot bread rising in the skillet. Sometimes Papa could buy fresh tomatoes or a dozen roasting ears from a farmer who might take a dime and say, "You just pick your own." Everybody was hungry, and everybody was comfortably tired at the long day's ending: the featherbeds and home-made quilts and tarp covers felt good after Papa had stepped out of the firelight to look at the sky and pronounce his forecast. He would say whether or not it was going to rain, and would decide who slept in the wagon and who could sleep on the ground. He gave the horses corn; the children could hear them munching and blowing in the *morrals,* as drowsiness came, and later Papa would remove the feed bags and either hobble or stake the horses where they could graze.

It seemed only minutes later that the last stars were winking out in the sky, and it was red in the east. Papa was out to get the horses; Mama was already putting wood on the fire, and leaning her greased skillet lid toward the coals. The bed tarps were always damp; the bent grass was drenched with dew, and the whole world wore the fragrance of dawn. A new day—a strange road—and nobody knew what adventures might unfold. On a day beginning like this, the children saw Papa pull rein at a village crossroads, and get down from the wagon seat to walk over to where a man was kicking a bony yellow dog. Papa said nothing at all; he simply hauled off and knocked the man up against a piece of wooden sidewalk, and the man lay there, bleeding a little at the corner of his mouth.

Papa suddenly seemed seven feet tall. He glared around him at several onlookers.

"Any of you sons-of-bitches got anything to say?" he asked.

Nobody had anything to say. Papa had enlivened their afternoon, and they would talk about it later. Nothing much ever happened at that place.

Papa dusted his hands with a fine dramatic gesture. He mounted the wagon seat again, and the children admired him.

A strange man, my father. Toward evening of the same day, his horses rebelled at a hard piece of road, and it is remembered that he beat them unmercifully. Mama reproached him, and he withdrew into a shell of silence. She set about preparing supper; it was the time of day when she was boss of the camp. And it was becoming increasingly difficult for her to stoop over her campfire pots and pans as her pregnancy advanced.

Mama never told me whether or not she had ever heard the saying that Texas was all right for men and dogs, but hell on women and horses. She didn't need to hear that wry philosophy put into words. In one day—and through many other days—she had actually lived it.

II

I have been working with a Texas railroad map of circa 1882, and have reason to believe this is the same one by which Papa charted his personal Northwest Passage. There is no place on it where I can draw a line and say, "This is where disillusionment began." The very nature of disillusionment precludes a line of demarcation on a map, or in the recounting of events; it is not usually a sudden thing, but vague and subtle in its beginnings. Papa was still in reasonably high spirits when the family reached Fort Worth. It was quite the largest town they had ever seen, and somehow Papa got confused and found himself going through the town twice before he could get out on the road. This made him extremely angry.

He managed to hold his temper, however. On the road up to Wichita Falls, he began meeting a new breed of the "Howdy, stranger!" travelers. They looked like men who had been through an experience, at least, if not an ordeal. Papa was still unfailingly polite: he pulled out to give them wheel room, or held open a pasture gate for five minutes when he saw another wagon coming over a far prairie rise. He noticed that the conversations had taken a different turn:

"Howdy, stranger! Where you headed?"

"Well, we're pointin' for the Indian Territory. Aim to take up a squat of land up there, if it looks good."

Attitudes had changed in the last hundred and fifty miles. Now there was a slow, ominous shake of the head. A thoughtful and considered squirt of tobacco juice, carefully aimed according to the wind.

"Mighty hard country, stranger!"

Papa was not one to give up a dream easily. "That so? What's wrong about it?"

"Well, weather—for one thing. I had a brother-in-law that went up there with the Sooners, back in '89. Got lost and froze to death last year, just trying to go to the privy—excuse me, ma'am. I'm bringin' his widow back to Texas. It's plumb hard country...."

Papa pressed on, but a little more slowly, because he had never liked cold weather. He was thoughtful now, and he carried no Excelsior banners through the villages of the high northern plains.

"Yes, sir—that country's mighty tough! I built me a dugout, and there was a stampede this spring, and we had ourselves a long-horned steer right in the livin' room! Fell through the roof. If you can't afford to fence, you can't afford to own the land...."

"Comes one of them cyclones, and the only place to be is in a hole in the ground. I seen one pick up a house and barn and carry them four miles away...."

"Well, you got troubles with the Gover'ment. It shore ought to stay out of private business, but it don't. You don't make your improvements, and you lose your claim. . . ."

"There was good grass, but I didn't like the water. It always had red mud in it, and didn't taste good. . . ."

It got to where Papa didn't want to tell people where he was going. He invented a brother-in-law of his own. He was just taking a little *pasear,* he said; he was going to visit a brother-in-law who lived in Vernon.

"Tough town," they told him. "That big Waggoner ranch owns the whole shootin' match—if you ain't with the Waggoners, you ain't nobody. And if you go on across Red River at Doan's Crossin', watch out for them rises when the snow is meltin' up in New Mexico. Knew a man that got drownded there last year."

All this pessimism drove Papa into one of his uncommunicative moods. He got to Vernon, all right; he went on through the town and got as far as Doan's Crossing. A whole cluster of buildings had sprung up here from the one store that had begun business with walls made of buffalo hides. Papa must have felt a sort of satisfaction at having reached the place: if he had ridden the Western Cattle Trail a dozen years earlier, he would have thrown the lead steers into the river at this spot, and Doan's Store would have been his supply point, his post office, and the only place in a hundred miles where a man could sit on the counter and eat a can of sardines or greengage plums.

Now he drove out far enough to look upon the Red. It was like a broad pink ribbon in the sunshine. Now and then a cottonwood tree floated down the current, twisting and turning, heavy enough to smash a wagon's sideboards or drown a team.

That was Oklahoma Territory on the other side. As far as Papa could see, it looked no different. On the map, it was pink, and a man had the right to expect a change when he crossed an important boundary such as the Red River.

"Hell!" Papa exclaimed.

Mama didn't say anything. The children, behind the wagon seat, gazed wide-eyed upon the alien ground, but they kept quiet. This was the moment of decision.

Papa suddenly swung the horses around, and drove back to Vernon. He was in one of his silent moods which the children classified as, "Hush—Papa's thinking!" and he said nothing to anybody. He drove straight to the freight depot. The summer sun distilled a pungence from the creosote-treated ties; the rails reached out, narrowing into infinity; a telegraph key chattered mysteriously into a tobacco can—it used to seem that all old tobacco cans ended up being used as echo chambers for the Morse Code.

The family waited in the wagon. Papa went to the window of the freight depot, and asked if they had a shipment consigned to W. E. Bosworth.

They said yes, they had it.

Papa paid the bill, and uncrated his things right on the platform, while one of the two daily trains went by. It took a little doing to make room for the things in the wagon. They added weight, and crowded everybody a little, but Mama was glad to get her looking glass back unbroken. And the children rejoiced at seeing familiar items of furniture again, and said it would be all right, because now they would be going downhill on the map. . . .

That evening, Papa camped a little way out of Vernon, and then he pressed on, as eager to get south as he had been to drive northward. About a week later, he got mixed up with Fort Worth again.

"I can't figure out what happened," Dee told me. "But we went through Fort Worth five times on that trip. It could have been the roads, but I don't think it was that—I think Papa had trouble making up his mind which way to head."

It must have been the latter. There were no clover-leaf confusions in those days, and milestones were good, solid, honest rocks at the side of the road. Papa finally got out of town and headed southeast, following the Brazos River again. At times he shuddered, remembering his narrow escape. In the words of the old Texians he had come *purty nelly* (or pretty nearly) to leaving Texas.

In sober afterthought, this seemed a terrible thing, comparable to voting the Republican ticket, and the idea that it is unthinkable still persists. I am the only member of Papa's family who has ever lived outside the boundaries of Texas. Some ten or twelve years ago the now defunct *Collier's* magazine carried an article on the Big Bend National Park, and quoted a relative of mine by marriage, Boy (or Boyce) Babb, who had owned quite a ranch in the area until the Park Service bought him out.

"Mr. Babb," the article writer asked, "have you ever been East?"

"Yep—far as you can go without gettin' clear out of the country," he said.

"You mean New York, Mr. Babb?"

"Why, hell no, son—I mean Corpus Christi . . ."

III

Fall was in the air, and other wagon outfits were headed south just like the migratory birds. One of these fell into common company with Papa's party, something in the manner of ships coming together on the same course at sea, and before long Papa had struck up a rather close friendship with the driver of the other wagon.

This was a man named Joe Wilkins. He had yellow hair, yellow eyebrows, and a yellow mustache stained brown in its middle by an incessant chewing of borrowed tobacco. His overalls looked more lived in than worn, and were out at the knees. His wife, a dumpy woman shaped like a sack of corn meal tied loosely somewhere near the middle, was probably a first cousin to him. She had the same ripe cornshuck-colored hair, and freckles, and the same unkempt and un-washed look. So did their five children, and these shocked Mama. They were incredibly dirty.

Mama had strict rules for traveling. Once a week she made Papa camp for a day while she boiled the children's clothes and the sheets and pillow cases and towels in lye water, and suds made with strong yellow soap. She ran everything through a rinse, and then through bluing water; she dried them in the sun. The bedding and everything else had that clean, sweet fragrance of wind and sunshine. And if the children did not bathe on any other day, they were scrubbed thoroughly on wash days.

The Wilkins outfit had no such regimen. Joe Wilkins always came over after the two wagons had stopped for the night; he swapped stories with Papa, and borrowed cuts of chewing tobacco. Mrs. Wilkins sent one of the unwashed children over nearly every evening, to "borry the loan" of a cup of sugar and a few dips of Garrett's snuff. The family stayed over on Mama's wash days, but did no washing of their own.

"I declare to goodness!" Mama said. "Did you see that young'un? Her dress was just black! It was shiny and sticky with molasses and gravy and tallow drippings, and her hair hadn't been combed for a month!" Then, raising her voice, "You children! I won't have you playing with those Wilkins kids—hear me? I never saw such poor white trash!"

Papa was more tolerant. He said, "Well, Bettie, that's how they were raised. They're Rawhiders."

"I don't care what they are," Mama retorted. "I won't let my children associate with them!"

She put her nose high in the air, and lost a chance to make a sociological study of a rather strange class of people. It was highly unusual that Joe Wilkins and his family were traveling alone: Rawhiders customarily banded together like gypsies, and Mama could have been afflicted with five or six wagons of them. She didn't know exactly what was meant by the term "Rawhiders"—if Papa had said they were Methodists or Campbellites, her answer would have been the same: "Well, bless Patty, I don't care *what* they are—they're plain dirty!"

The people called Rawhiders had come out of Tennessee and the Carolinas before and during the Civil War. That conflict uprooted them, if they had roots at all; none of them had ever owned land or slaves, and they had always made their living by trapping and hunting and fishing. Many fled conscription, having no stake in the Confederacy, and got their name because they used rawhide in so many ways:

it repaired their wagons and their harness, it made their chairs and stools and buckets. The clannish groups were all related by blood and intermarriage, and half the growing boys would be named "John Wesley." All the women dipped snuff; all the men chewed tobacco. Perhaps there was a strain of gypsy in them despite their coloring: there was apt to be fiddle music and singing around their campfires, and dallyings that would mean further intermarriages in the course of time.

Joe Wilkins was a lanky, slab-sided, drawling man. He wanted to swap horses and wagons. Papa refused to trade, because the Studebaker was comparatively new. It came out that Joe Wilkins' wife had decided their Shuttler wagon was plumb unhealthy: she blamed it for measles and mumps and chicken pox. Bain wagons were equally unhealthy for some people, she told Mama.

Mama flinched and blamed Mrs. Wilkins instead of the wagon. "I just don't see why you travel with that outfit!" she told Papa.

Papa grunted something about the road being free, and the old Shuttler wagon was always just far enough behind to stay out of the Studebaker's dust. When Papa turned out to make camp, so did Joe Wilkins. Mama began to suspect that there were more than five children hiding in the Shuttler. Either that, she said, or the frowzy Mrs. Wilkins deliberately saw to it that the young'uns assumed successive disguises of dirt before she sent them over to "borry the loan" of another cup of something.

On one of Mama's wash days, Joe Wilkins went fishing in the Brazos River, and repaid some of the loans, in part, by bringing Papa a fine mess of catfish. Nobody could find out just where the family was traveling; Wilkins was vague on that point, and Papa concluded—with something of envy—that they weren' t going anywhere in particular.

Mama grew more and more indignant. She never understood why Papa liked the yellow-haired, rawboned man. Nor could Papa have explained. But Joe Wilkins had achieved absolute freedom, and therefore was to be admired. He owned nothing but the wagon and his horses, he owed nobody (except for countless small charities disguised as loans), and he made no pretense of being or looking respectable. He appeared to be fond of his children, but was not responsible to or for them. He would fall in, somewhere, with other Rawhiders, and wander farther south and west with them; rawhide would patch the harness and hold the old wagon together; the Wilkins family would grow, and would always get by.

Papa had less than a dollar in his pocket, and now he finally got rid of Joe Wilkins by announcing that he was going to stop in Robertson County and go to work picking cotton. Wilkins nodded, borrowed a chew of tobacco, and said, "Well, it's been right nice travelin' with you folks. Good luck!"

And he splashed the rump of his off horse with a squirt of amber juice, shook his reins, and was gone down the road under the same swarm of blue-bottle flies that had followed him all the way down from Fort Worth. Mama shook her head and sighed. After a few more rootless years, would the Bosworth family look like that?

Papa laughed, and said of course they wouldn't. He said they'd pull on into Robertson County, where cotton pickers were reported to be getting two bits for a hundred pounds. The family would stay there quite a while, and rest up (dragging cotton sacks along the rows), and would make a stake.

He did not want to talk about Oklahoma Territory, or the time wasted on the long trip. He did not know that up in Montague County, not very far from where he had reached the Red River, there was a place called Nocona, named for a wandering Comanche tribe. It is rather well known today for the manufacture of cowboy boots and other leather goods.

Nocona means "Those-Who-Turn-Back-Before-They-Get-There."

Eleven

*R*obertson County would never
have been Papa's choice as a place to rest his horses, except for the
immediate crisis in the chuckbox and that immutable expectancy of
the baby in January. Driving down through the sandy hills on the
north, he saw at once that it wasn't his kind of country. Entirely too
much farming was going on to suit his tastes, and he watched both
sides of the road in vain for a big pasture that might hold some
maverick beef. In ranch country the larder would never have
dropped so low.

It was one of those days when minor irritations swarm around
a man like gnats. Papa lost the road and had to turn back. Maude
was crying with the stomach ache, and the paregoric wasn't handy
in the chuckbox this time; they had to stop and move the household
goods in the wagon before they found it. One of the horses threw a
shoe and was limping before Papa knew it; he had to call another
halt and do a temporary blacksmithing job. He remarked that more
than half the wagons that passed were driven by Negroes, and when
they reached Hearne he saw an uncommon number of colored people
on the street, and grew morbidly pessimistic about his chances for

economic survival. He doubted that white folks picked cotton here at all, with so much cheap labor available.

Hearne was a railroad junction, and prospering; it had rows of new frame houses adorned with the framework cornices that had lately become the fashion. This gingerbread offended the carpenter in Papa—probably because a vast amount of skilled and patient hand labor appeared to have been involved.

"I swear, I wouldn't be caught dead in a house like that!" he complained, pointing to an exceptionally gaudy dwelling. "Just like fancying up a privy with stars and crescents!"

"Woodie, you hush!" Mama said. "I won't have the children using that word!"

(Mama always called a privy a "closet." This equally Elizabethan term was quite safe, even when guests were unfamiliar both with the word and the premises. No house Mama ever lived in had clothes closets.)

The streets of the town were wide, and busy with wagons hauling cotton to the gins, and bales to the warehouse or freight depot. Negroes drove many of these with a proprietary air, and Papa muttered that the world had been shaved by a drunken barber.

He pulled up in front of a grocery and feed store, and broke his last four-bit piece to buy Mama a dime can of snuff and a sack of jawbreakers for the children. "I don't suppose the farmers around here hire white folks to pick cotton, do they?" he asked the proprietor.

"Why, shore they do, neighbor!" the man said in surprise. He walked to the front of the store, and pointed. "Take that road yonder, and go west to the river bottom, and you won't have no trouble a'tall. Big crop this year. Town's a-boomin'!"

Four Negroes came down the wooden sidewalk, peered furtively into the store's flyspecked windows, and went on. "All right, don't trade here!" the merchant said bitterly. Then, to Papa: "Tenant farmers. Some of 'em work land where their daddies was slaves. Raise their own cotton. But they have to buy their grub from the plantation commissary, and they git skinned regular." He snapped the elastic bands that held his black sleeve guards, and studied Papa and the wagon. "Aimin' to settle here, neighbor?" he asked in a Chamber of Commerce tone. "Fastest-growin' county in this part of Texas. More'n twenty-six thousand people in the last census."

Being called "neighbor" irritated Papa, too. The thought of being cooped up in a single county with so much humanity was just too much.

"How many?" he asked the storekeeper.

"More'n twenty-six thousand. I forget the exact number."

"Then about half of 'em ought to pack up and by God leave!" Papa snapped. "It's getting to where there ain't any room left!"

He turned on his heel without even a "much obliged." Mama was watching from the wagon seat, where she held Maude on her lap; the older children peered out under the rolled-up tarp, and everybody wondered what Papa was so mad about. The storekeeper stood slack-jawed, wondering too.

So far as I know, nobody ever heeded any advice Papa may have given them, and certainly he was without honor as a prophet in his own and every other country. But this time he had called the turn: there came a day when cotton was no longer king, and when oil fields and aircraft factories and chemical plants took their toll, and so did the booming cities.

Robertson County has only fifteen thousand population now. Papa would have regarded this as real civic progress.

II

The wagon turned around the corner of a brown, wind-rustled cornfield, and came suddenly upon a weathered wooden gate in a barbed-wire fence. This was where the cotton began.

"My lands!" Mama exclaimed. "Just look at that cotton! It would be almost a pleasure to pick cotton like that!"

Papa sat up straight on the wagon seat and licked his lips, his resolve weakening under an unaccustomed surge of ambition. *One crop of cotton like that, and a man would be on Easy Street for a*

*year. Two or three good years in a row, and all hell couldn't hold
him.*

"Woodie," Mama said, picking at his sleeve, "why couldn't *we*
stay here and put in a crop next spring?"

"No," Papa said, steeling himself against temptation. "No, you
can't count on rain . . . and the boll weevils would come in . . . and
this is bottom land—high rent land. No. And besides, what you just
said—cotton picking ain't a pleasure anywhere. Some of it is just
tougher than others."

Dee got down to open the gate, and they saw that the cotton was
higher than his head. The rows ran straight across the black land;
the slanting sun of a late October afternoon limned their green and
white glister, and struck reds and yellows from trees that marked
the river bank beyond. Papa began feeling more nearly content as
he drove on: the sight and sound of a river have especial charm at
the end of a hard day's journey.

He found a spot on the shelving bank where the stream made a
wide and lazy bend, and notched his brake handle there. Rain had
leached the ashes of successive campfires at the edge of the trees.
A scatter of empty whiskey bottles, faded soda-cracker boxes, and
cans that had contained greengage plums showed that fishermen
favored the spot; several dried and whiskered heads of sizable catfish hanging from the trees where they had been skinned proved
that some of the campers had been lucky. The children piled out of
the wagon, loud and shrill with the excitement of arrival, and everybody went to look at the river. A long sandbar curved down the near
side of the bend, beckoning invitingly to bare feet, and bullfrogs
leaped noisily into a lily-padded slough that ran between a sandbar
and the grassy bank. Somewhere back in the trees a woodpecker
made one final staccato attack on a dead pecan limb and then put
down his hammer for the day. The light was failing, tarnishing the
molten silver of the water, lingering longest on the pale sand. Killdees
landed there on swift-running feet, shrilled their plaintive laments,
and took wing again in mid-cry like departing spirits.

Papa untied the led horse and unhitched the team, giving them *morrals* of corn before staking them out to graze. He propped the wagon tongue with the singletree, and hung the sweaty horse collars and the harness on it. The children threw flat stones to make them sail and skip across the river, and waded tentatively in the sandbar shallows until Mama called them to "rustle" her some wood. Dee set a trotline, baiting the hooks with scraps of bacon rind. Maude was crying again, this time with hunger; Mama made a sugar tit to sustain her until supper.

The evening was cool, but a few hardy mosquitoes came around the campfire, and Norah told the younger children to listen to them humming "Cousin, cousin!" Papa put green cowchips on the fire after all the cooking was done, and made an effective smudge that was only a little more endurable than the mosquitoes. Everybody felt relaxed and sleepy, and was happy to be done with traveling for a little while. There had been enough food, the fire spread its warmth, and the river made soft music going by. Papa stepped out to look at the stars, and said everybody could sleep on the ground. He had seen the light of a farmhouse about a half mile away.

Tomorrow he would put up the tent and unload some of the things. Tomorrow, if there were jobs to be had in the cotton fields, the family would go to work.

"When I make some money, could I get me a pair of leather knee pads?" Dee asked.

Mama said probably he could—that is, after they had bought some grub. She said everybody could use tow sacks for knee pads, to start with, if they needed them. With the cotton that high, maybe they could pick it standing flat-footed.

When Papa shut his eyes that night, he could still see the split-ripe bolls bending the five-foot cotton, and it was a disturbingly pretty sight. He lay listening, knowing where the horses moved around their stake pins, thinking that the croaking bullfrogs sounded big enough to provide a mess of fried legs, missing—now that he thought about it—the howling of coyotes. Too many people here, and too much ploughed land; the coyotes liked it unfenced and wild, and they had moved westward. Then a wedge of wild geese went arrow-straight and high over the river, and Papa sat up and listened to their tameless clamor until it was only a whisper in the southern sky.

Hunger came close to the camp on the Brazos. Most women would have worried, but Mama had been inured to varying degrees of hardship and privation by the twelve years of her marriage, and if she worried she kept it to herself. She told the children they would manage, until they had money, by "putting the big pot in the little one." The common danger did something, momentarily, to strengthen family unity: Mama and Norah picked wild greens, Dee caught catfish for two meals, and Papa shot a cottontail, a brace of squirrels, and a mallard duck. The lard and coffee held out one day after the flour and beans were all gone.

But Papa was collecting cotton money every day after weighing in, and on Friday they drove to Hearne and bought enough staples to last a month. The storekeeper kept calling Papa "neighbor," but he threw in a bag of hoarhound candy for the children.

"*Lagniappe,* they call it over in Louisiana," he said. "Means kind of like somethin'-for-nothin'."

"The Mexicans call it *pilón,*" Papa said, warming up to the man a little. "Much obliged to you."

He had provided for his family—with, of course, some assistance on their part. He had bought grain for his horses too, and he was in a good humor as they started back to camp. Then they passed a school on the edge of the town, just when the children were getting out and starting home with their books.

Papa glanced guiltily at Mama. Her nose was turning red, and that was a sure sign she was about to cry.

"Now, damn it, Bettie, we're doing the best we can!" he told her. "We've got to make a little stake, so we can get back to Karnes. They'll be in school next year."

"It's always next year!" Mama sobbed. "Next year—next year!"

"But I'll give you my word—we'll get back to Karnes, and I'll get a job, and they'll go to school. In Kenedy Junction."

Mama blew her nose. "Dee and Norah and Jay ought to be in school right now! They don't belong in a cotton patch! *I'll* help you pick cotton—I'll pick my fingers to the bone to keep them in school!"

Papa looked at her almost tenderly. "You've got no business picking cotton more than a few weeks longer, and you know it," he said. "And it's not the money they make—it's just that we can't live close to a school and pick cotton too."

"Well then, why don't we move to town? You could get some carpenter work."

"Building that kind of house—like that one there? No, sir! I'd just as soon be building—"

"Woodie!"

"Well, you heard me promise. Next year."

They drove on back to camp in silence, and with a space between them on the wagon seat. That space, and those silences, were steadily growing wider and longer.

There may have been a time, in plantation days, when Negroes sang their contentment across the sun-warmed cotton fields. Perhaps they still sing, in the South, out of the music born in them as a race, and out of what little is left to them of another characteristic which is fast diminishing as this century grows older—a blessed, natural ability to find happiness in simple things. But I do not believe that the singing of any group of people, engaged in concerted labor, necessarily means that they are happy, or that they like the work they are doing. A chorused song imparts rhythm to muscular movement, makes the work mechanical, and helps pass the time. Fo'c'sle hands walked the capstan around in freezing wind and rain and in tropical heat, bellowing sea chanteys; the voyageurs and the Erie Canalmen roared lustily at paddle and winch; a song sometimes helps soldiers on the march—and a soldier on a long hike *hates* his job, the sergeant, and the Department of the Army. When working alone, men may hum or whistle; they seldom sing loudly enough for anybody to hear them. The cowboy on night herd was an exception, and he sang with a purpose and not because he was happy. The sound of his voice reassured the cattle, saved him further work, and helped him keep awake.

Papa had sung songs while riding around a bedded-down herd at night, but he never lifted his voice in the cotton rows. Neither did any of his children.

Cotton is always picked when the weather is either too hot or too cold. The picking begins early on crisp fall mornings when frost glistens on the fluff and the bolls are stiff and sharp-spiked; chapped fingers ache so much with the cold that one seldom notices the cuts until blood begins to dye the cotton long before it reaches the mills. The sun climbs, and coats and sweaters are left at the beginning of a row that has no end. The sun begins to blister the back of the neck. Snakes thaw out and become limber enough to bite. Clouds of gnats torture the vision with a bilious shimmer; individual gnats sting before committing suicide in streams of sweat. Cotton plants are inevitably too high to reach kneeling, and too low to strip standing erect. Cotton stuffed by the pitiful handful into a ten-foot sack is so light it cannot possibly increase the dragging weight—but it does. Before long, the sack weighs two hundred pounds as it is being pulled; it snags on roots and will not drag straight along the row, which is always uphill. The shoulder strap twists and cuts and rubs blisters. When the picker wearily plods up to the wagon where the scales are, his burden weighs only fifty pounds.

Fleece-lined leather knee pads or not, everybody winds up with sore knees and a stiff, aching back.

Modern cotton-picking machines, used in big cultivation areas, may have thrown a lot of cotton pickers out of work. If so, they are one of the greatest boons mankind has ever known.

The baby was coming in January, and as she pulled her sack down the cotton rows Mama knew she had lost another dream. It would not be born in her own house, or in any other house. It would be born in the tent on the Brazos bottoms.

She picked cotton right up to the end of November; after that she was still cooking for the family and doing her weekly washing at the campfire. When the cotton season was over, it was too late to move: she could no longer climb to the seat of the wagon. Papa found a little carpenter work (building unadorned barns) and then it began to rain as if it were going to rain all winter. Papa found solace in the rain as he sat idle in the crowded tent, with five restless children underfoot. He was actually waiting for the baby to arrive before starting for Karnes County, but the drone of the rain on the canvas reminded him that the roads were so bad he couldn't travel anyway.

Then the river rose high enough to cover the sandbar, and there was work to do. Papa moved the wagon about three hundred yards up the slope and out of flood danger, and set up the tent there. It was a difficult task in the mud, and the horses knew his temper before it was finished.

The sun came out again, and the tent canvas steamed, and wet wood smoked on the campfire. The cotton farmer came down to look anxiously at the widening brown torrent and speculate how much of his rich black soil would be washed to the Gulf; he told Papa that folks in town said the river hadn't crested yet—Fort Worth and other places up toward the headwaters were still catching it. Papa walked with the farmer to where the catfish heads hung under the trees; they had to shout, there, against the sullen roar that came from mid-channel. The bend swung the turbulent flow toward the near shore, and then outward again to create a backlash and a large, noisy whirlpool. Even while they talked, the brown water crept higher along the shelf. Driftwood and uprooted saplings spun by, caught in the eddy for a little while before straightening out in the main current.

The farmer went back home, discouraged and afraid. Nobody could do any work, and the whole family watched the flood waters, now bearing the handiwork of man, and pieces of his goods and chattels. Fence rails and planks from hog pens went by, with occasional bloated carcasses of livestock. A privy with its door latched shut was sucked into the maelstrom and circled there long enough for the children to giggle and wonder if anybody had been caught inside.

The day the river crested, Papa had decided he could wait no longer to ride to Hearne for supplies he could carry on the saddle, and to find out where the nearest doctor lived. He had just saddled the horse when Dee and Norah and Jay came running frantically up the muddy slope, shrill with excitement.

"A house!" Dee was shouting, in the lead. "Look, Papa—look! Here comes a *house!*"

III

The stage was set for Papa's most splendid hour, and for the epic deed that later would make him a living, breathing, towering Paul Bunyan (or, more appropriately, a Pecos Bill) in my eyes. This was to form the basis, in my own tender and imaginative years, for the beginnings of a legend and a folklore without which Papa would not have existed for me at all—not, at any rate, for a long time.

What he did that day on the eastern shore of the flooded Brazos was not only a decisive and dramatic thing, but also one accomplished completely within character.

Here came a house, sweeping around the upper reaches of the bend and bearing down upon the watching family as majestically as a river steamboat standing in for a landing. It was a one-story frame dwelling with new white paint. It yawed and turned in the clutch of the river, having neither helm nor rudder, but it rode high and buoyantly, like a tight and seaworthy craft, and glistened in the midday sun. Papa saw from afar that it was a fairly new house, because a strip of gingerbread cornice ran around the eaves; a full revolution showed him that a small front gallery had carried away in the flood, leaving several two-by-four rafters projecting nakedly from the wall.

The children jumped up and down and yelled gleefully. They saw the house lurch into the eddying backwash and spin crazily inshore, where the sandbar had been; it steadied there, momentarily, and floated toward the trees.

Papa toed his stirrup and swung suddenly into his saddle, alive and alert. "Dee," he yelled over his shoulder, "bring me that rope out of the wagon!"

He was already getting his plaited horsehide *riata* off the saddle; he was already riding toward the river, pointing a little downstream; everybody guessed, now, what he was going to try to do, and the whole family held its breath.

The horse splashed into the brown water, hock-deep, knee-deep, belly-deep under the farther trees, where overhanging branches leaned down to trail their fingers in the flood. Mama's hand was at her mouth; she called, "Woodie! You be careful!" and nobody heard her. The derelict dwelling twisted out of the whirlpool and caromed against the springy green branches of a liveoak. A window shattered, glass and sash alike splintering; nobody heard the sound above the roar of the river. Then Papa rose in his stirrups, swung his loop out at his side in that short and quick way of a *vaquero* accustomed to roping cattle in the hindering brush, and made his cast.

It was a small loop, and it went cleanly over the end of one of the projecting two-by-fours. Papa's horse had not forgotten working with cattle: it sat back on its hindquarters, braced to take the shock of a running steer when the slack was spent, and Papa made his *dar la vuelta* around the saddlehorn.

Mama expected to see the girth strap break, and saddle, Papa, and all go flying over the horse's ears into the water. But the liveoak limb took the shock again, and then Papa got the *riata* around a solid tree trunk.

He turned his horse and met Dee, who was wading waist-deep in the water to bring the coil of Manila rope. It was Papa's pride, now, that he handled the rest of the job without dismounting or otherwise getting wet. He secured the extra rope to another two-by-four, and ran this to a second tree. The liveoak limb that had broken the window was scratching a great deal of paint off the wall, but the house was cinched down as tightly as a pair of team ropers can hold a calf for branding.

Papa rode modestly back to the acclaim of his family, with Dee splashing proudly at his stirrup. "I declare!" Mama greeted him, laughing. "First time I ever saw anybody rope a house!"

"I've had worse trouble with an old mossyhorn steer," Papa said, and laughed too.

"Wonder how far it washed down the river?"

Papa shook his head soberly. "Just no telling. Maybe a few miles— maybe all the way from up around Waco, or even farther. Not anything inside, from what I could see through the windows. I reckon they figured they couldn't save the house, but they had time to get all the furniture out. Looks like about four rooms. Somebody was a damn fool to build a new house on low ground."

Dee and Norah and Jay were dancing around chanting, "Papa roped a house! Papa roped a house!" Ivanhoe joined in the chant, and Maude tried to dance and fell in the mud.

"You, Maude!" Mama scolded. "That'll be three dresses you've had on today!" But she was still glowing with pride. Papa had saved a home for somebody lucky enough to own one.

"You know," Papa said, slouching over to rest his forearms on the pommel of his saddle, "that house is kind of a maverick. In a way. Well . . . if I'm going to get that grub and find that doctor, I'd better ride."

The river began going down that night. Two days later, the house Papa had roped was settling on the flood-bent grass, slightly aslant, and the Brazos was steadily retreating to its accustomed channel. It would take a little while to build the sandbar again, and a little while for the wind to shake the driftwood out of the tree branches.

The wind was gathering its strength for that task. A cold norther had followed the rain.

Papa waded through the mud, then removed his boots at the door, and explored the house. He had been right about the furniture: even the stove was gone, although two joints of stovepipe still hung from their baling-wire support. There was a box of stovewood in the kitchen, and a few pieces of bric-a-brac, a dirty pillow case and one cotton sock on the floor in another room. In the living room were two pictures and a framed motto that said "God Bless Our Home." One of the pictures was a colored print showing two horses terribly frightened at a thunder-and-lightning storm just behind them and obviously coming closer every minute, crowding them against a railing of a fence. The other picture was an enlarged crayon reproduction of a tintype showing a woman sitting in an ornately carved chair, and a man standing stiffly at her shoulder. The man had frazzled mutton-chop whiskers, and small, close-set eyes.

This picture disturbed Papa. The man seemed to be watching him, everywhere he moved in the room. Finally he turned the portrait to the wall.

"Woodie," Mama asked him that evening after supper, "what are you going to do about the house? Are you going to try to find the owner?"

"I've been studying what to do," Papa said. He listened to the wind. It was rising, whistling around the tent, making the lantern light flutter and smoke.

"Maybe there would be something in the paper about it," Mama suggested.

Papa grunted.

Next day he went down to the house, and found that the wind was drying the ground around it. He decided it wouldn't be too much of a job to jack up the floor on the lower slope, and put some underpinning there to make it level. He had roped this house out of the flood, and it really was something of a maverick.

The weather turned colder in the first few days of January. Papa told himself that if *he* had lost a house, he'd have been out looking for it before now.

Neither the cotton farmer nor his wife could identify the house. Nobody in the town of Hearne (which is to say the neighborly store-keeper) had heard anything about a house being missing.

All this helped Papa study what to do—this, and the cold norther and the fact that a baby was coming. A week after he had roped the house out of the Brazos flood, Papa loaded the cookstove and sewing machine and Mama's looking glass into the wagon, struck the tent, drove down the slope, and moved in.

Mama's sixth child, a daughter named Lily May, was born in a house, after all, on January 17, 1892.

IV

Texas men have done strange things with ropes. They say a cowboy who had a few drinks once paced a Texas & Pacific locomotive as the train was leaving town, and threw his loop over the smokestack—a feat which caused saddle and horse to part company, in the vernacular of the spectators, *"pronto."*

I remember Halloweens which were considered incomplete until someone had ridden with a come-a-ti-yi-yippee past some privy—preferably a public convenience serving courthouse, hotel, or school—to swing a wide loop, dally the rope around a saddlehorn, and bring the structure crashing to the ground. This performance was eminently more satisfactory, of course, if the privy were occupied at the time.

So far as I know, however, Papa was the only man who ever roped a house. This knowledge sustained me in my childhood, when Papa was not around—when, in fact, he had become only a misty legend to me. It fended off any feelings of insecurity I may have had: at least I do not remember ever having a sense of insecurity. Other boys had fathers in residence, yes, and I did not. I studied these male parents all the more closely, and observed that many of them were short and bald and had pot bellies, some went around the house on Sundays wearing their undershirts; they scratched, and read Eugene V. Debs's *Appeal to Reason,* and shocked me with unpatriotic utterance at a time when I was reading things like *The Liberty Boys of* '76 and was sure nothing could be wrong with America. They did not impress me.

The father of one boy had reportedly Killed a Bear. This was no mean accomplishment in the hills of West Texas, where bears had always been in short supply. This boy was given to boasting about his father.

But a father in residence has certain drawbacks. I was well aware that this man—a windmill fixer—was afraid of his wife. When he spent an evening in the pool hall, he had to make it appear that he had been working overtime out on some lonely divide where a ranch windmill had ceased to pump. Leaving the pool hall, he would go by an old gasoline engine that had been used to saw stone for the new schoolhouse, and would smear himself liberally with grease. In that prying, spying way of small boys, I saw him do it more than once, and after that the account of his having Killed a Bear had no effect upon me.

"You think that's something? Anybody can kill a bear. You know what my father did, one time? My father—Papa—*he* Roped a House!"

The story had been handed down to me. It grew with the telling. By the time I was done with it, Papa had roped a Colonial mansion with immense white pillars and people sitting on the veranda sipping mint juleps. And Papa was eight feet tall.

At the time Papa actually roped the house, he had no idea, of course, that his act would make a conversation piece for one of his sons, yet unborn. He knew very well that a day of reckoning was bound to come, and he was growing increasingly nervous watching for it over his shoulder.

But, meanwhile, he had reason to be proud. He had provided shelter for his family during the worst of winter. Mama had gone through the period of her confinement in comfort. The house was tight and warm; Mama kept it clean, and the river sang at its door. Papa used his skill as a carpenter to repair the shattered sash and the broken windowpanes. He gave as much as he took.

The inevitable day came when a man rode up on a sorry-looking roan. He was following every crook and turn of the river, and had been fighting the brush. He had mutton-chop whiskers and close-set eyes.

"Howdy, stranger!" Papa greeted him from the living room door.

The rider went livid. "Jesus God, man!" he yelled. "What do you mean—livin' in *my* house? This here's *my* house! By God, I'll git the sheriff, and—"

"Now wait a minute!" Papa said. "If it hadn't been for me, you know where your house would've been? It would've been floatin' out in the Gulf of Mexico. It would have been busted on some beach. I *saved* this house for you, you ungrateful son-of-a-bitch!"

"Well . . . I—I want it back! I'll git the law!"

"Never said I aimed to keep it," Papa told him.

"But you're *livin'* in it! You're livin' in my house!"

It was several minutes before the shouting died down and Papa convinced the man that a favor had been done him. They made a deal then. Papa had three horses. The owner of the house would bring down three more, and between them they would haul the house back up the river to its original site, which was thirty miles upstream.

"What's the job worth to you?" Papa asked.

"Well, maybe twenty-five dollars."

"How come you waited all this time to start looking for it?"

"Had sickness in the family," the man said. "And at first I figured the house was plumb gone—lost—all the way to the Gulf. But my wife said I ought to look, anyway."

Papa nodded, remembering the face of the woman in the portrait. "Well," he said, "I'll take the job."

He moved everything back out of the house and once more set up the family in the tent. He spent several days of hard labor helping truck the house back upstream along inhospitable roads. Then he asked for his twenty-five dollars.

"Well, now," said the owner, and his eyes grew even more narrow, "I figure it this way. I owe you twenty-five dollars. You owe me six weeks' rent. It about evens up."

That was how the matter rested. Papa fumed. He lost his temper and called the man everything he knew, but to no avail. In the long run he was glad to be rid of the whole mess.

"We're too far east!" he told Mama. "These people back here would skin a flea for its hide and tallow—I don't want anything more to do with them! We're heading for Karnes."

Twelve

"Stafford and other big ranchers claimed the cattle even though they weren't branded and the country wasn't fenced much. It was just full of outlaws. There was a lot of mysterious riding at night, and we never knew whether Papa would come home or not. Uncle Gus's son Billy wasn't but seventeen when he and another boy were waylaid and killed. Then Papa went up to Wharton County and took up some land, but the trouble caught up with him . . ."

—NORAH

The trouble that caught up with Papa during those next two years left permanent scars upon his spirit. What little pride he had left was gone, and with it the spur-jingling *sang-froid* of his younger days; he was a beaten man, frightened by his responsibilities and bewildered by the conviction that the Fates had conspired to undo him. The trouble lost him the only piece of land he ever had a chance of proving up and owning; it caused his children to go hungry more than once, and perhaps it came near costing him his life. Still, these were only one man's troubles, and if it is true that misery loves company Papa could have found millions of companions throughout the nation at that time. For when he crossed the Brazos and moved back to Karnes County, he ran head on into the terrible panic of 1893.

Dr. Walter Prescott Webb (*The Great Plains*) points out that the cattle boom of the eighties and a corresponding invasion of farmers into the Great Plains area were "accompanied or preceded by the deceptive wet years," and quotes a U.S. Geological Survey as saying, "The height of the 'boom,' as well as its heaviest penalties and the end of it, was in 1893."

Even the weather was Papa's enemy.

It did not rain much in Texas that September, nor would September rain have changed things to any great degree: all at once Texans were discovering that it really *did* make a difference who was in the White House. The fact that they were dependent upon the rest of the United States came as something of a shock to Texans, and especially to older citizens who had been schooled in the Three R's of Republic, Rebellion, and Reconstruction. Many of these still thought of Texas as an independent country, and of Washington as a place—something like Austin—"back in the States."

Papa neither knew nor cared who was representing him on Capitol Hill. No Congressman ever sent him free garden seed; he did not stay in any one place long enough to pay poll taxes and vote. He did know, of course, that James Stephen Hogg had been elected governor —everybody knew that, not because Hogg had done a tremendously important service by correcting railroad land abuses, but because it was reported he had named his three daughters Ima, Ura, and Wera. Things like that get around without benefit of paid advertising. (This was only a third true. There was only Miss Ima—a grand lady who owned gold-plated bathroom fixtures.)

The rocky times were getting rockier as the Studebaker wagon rolled down to Runge, where Uncle Lee Maulding ran the country store and fascinated Dee with his music box. Fences were few— a man could still pull off the road and make camp wherever he found wood and water. But the grazing for his horses was poor that fall; the grass was parched and brittle, and dust hung in the wake of the wagon and filtered into Mama's bedclothes, and plagued her at her campfire cooking.

They seldom saw a newspaper when they were traveling. If Papa could have read the editorials, he would have known that the so-called "Billion Dollar Congress" of 1890 was now being blamed by the Democrats for bankrupting the country; its Civil War Pension Act was costing sixty-eight million dollars in the first three years, the Navy was embarked on a building program to raise it from twelfth to fifth place among the fleets of the world, and there were other vast expenditures not understandable to a man on a wagon with six kids to feed. The McKinley Tariff was still hotly debated in crossroads store and cow camp.

Papa did not understand tariffs either. He learned a little about them when Grover Cleveland abolished the tariff on wool, and Australian fleece poured into the country duty-free. Aunt Docia wrote from Tom Green County that she and Uncle Nick were broke—the sheep they owned were now worth only a dollar a head.

Wheat dropped to fifty cents a bushel, cotton hit six cents a pound, and unless a man had livestock to feed it was more profitable for him to burn corn for fuel on the treeless plains than to ship it to market.

"Recession" and "depression" are later terms, and much more kind. "Panic" is a word to stop the heart, suggesting blind, unreasoning fear. Its synonym in Texas was "stampede," in which brute fright spreads and herd instinct takes over, and there is nothing to do but run. The panic of 1893 was a stampede. It had a definite beginning, just after Cleveland's second inauguration. The Reading Railway collapsed, and nobody in Texas had ever heard of the Reading Railway, but this was a signal for other railroads to go into receivership, businesses to fail, and banks to close their doors. The Pullman Car Company's Chicago strike would touch off sympathy strikes in twenty-seven states and territories, Eugene V. Debs would be martyred in jail, and I would be listening to arguments out of his *Appeal to Reason* seventeen years later.

Before it was over, Coxey's ragged "army" would march on Washington—that place that was something like Austin, but without a dome so lofty. And hungry men would line up at soup kitchens.

Texas had no soup kitchens. Texas was still independent. If a

[153]

man went hungry there, everybody thought it was his own fault. There was plenty of maverick beef on the hoof, and every Texan had a gun and knew how to shoot.

II

Karnes County was full of kinfolk when the Bosworth family returned with tales of the Red River and the Brazos flood, and how Papa Roped a House.

They rolled up to Uncle Gus's house one evening, and went through the ritual. Papa shouted, "Hello, the house!" Somebody called back, "Hello, yourself!" and Papa said, "Call in your dogs, so we can come in!"

Uncle Gus Bosworth, Papa's half-brother and seventeen years his senior, was living on a farm near Runge. He was fifty that year, a settled man with a gray mustache and nine children still around the house, and a tenth on the way. If the Bosworth fields had ever been as fertile as their masters, this story would have been different. But they never were.

Papa drove up with his brood of six, and the result was bedlam, but everybody concerned was conditioned to bedlam. Papa and Mama camped out under the liveoak trees until the weather turned cold and the times grew rockier. Then they moved into the house with Uncle Gus and his family. I do not know how big this house was; I only know that it was thoroughly inhabited.

Papa looked for work, and found none. Mama worried, and ran out of snuff, but nobody complained. The whole pack of children whooped and hollered along the creek bottoms on frosty nights, hunting 'coons and 'possums. Even the older girls went along for the fun, and 'possums baked with with sweet potatoes that had their second-year growth and were so big they had to be split with an axe were a welcome addition to the menu. Uncle Gus's third son, Billy, was the ringleader in these forays. He was a tall, slender boy, at times filled with irreverent laughter and lusty horseplay, at times with something of Papa's brooding restlessness in his dark eyes.

At seventeen, he was too old to be a boy, and not old enough to take his place as a man: he wanted his own horse and rope, and Uncle Gus would not let him carry a pistol.

Fifteen growing children require a formidable amount of food. Uncle Gus had the drought that year, and had never been a very successful farmer. He was milking one cow, a brindled beast that did well to yield a gallon of milk a day. His older daughters strained this through flour sacks at night, and put it away to cool. Next morning, there was an unvarying dialogue:

AUNT JO: "I declare to goodness! The cat has got all the cream again!"

CHORUS: "Yes—a two-legged cat!"

Somebody was skimming the cream, and drinking it. They never found out who it was, because it wasn't really important—there wasn't enough milk to go around anyway, not with fifteen children. All other food was shared, and before long there was not enough of it. The sweet potatoes ran out. Mama used to sing a song that said: "Great big 'taters in sandy land . . ." but when they were gone, the fifteen children went on a cornbread and weak coffee diet, and had nothing else for days.

"Then Papa saddled up his horse and rode out one evening about dark," Norah told me. "Next morning he came back with a fat yearling across the forks of his saddle. Well, we were just as hungry as you can be! Dee couldn't wait for Mama to cook that meat— he took his pocket knife, and cut some strips of lean beef off the carcass, and we ate it raw."

She laughs about it now. In her seventies, with beautiful white, curly hair and voice soft as the wind along the willow *vegas* of the Rio Grande, where she lives, she tells the story with an infectious giggle that could come from a teen-ager. She is beautiful, my oldest sister.

But, at the time, nobody complained, she says. It was understood that in Texas you were apt to be caught between a rock and a hard place.

Only Mama was unhappy, and her unhappiness came from hunger of another kind. "Next year" had come, and the children were still not in school.

Papa flew into a frustrated rage. "Damn it, Bettie—first things come first!" he said. "Until the times get better, we're having enough trouble just getting enough to eat! We're doing the best we can."

He was trying. Dee and Norah remember how horsemen rode up to the house after dark, and made bird calls or other signals to add to the mystery. And how Papa saddled and rode with them, and how Mama kept a lamp burning, and waited and worried until the sky was gray with a new dawn.

Then hoof sound and spur jingle and saddle squeak outside, and the noise a restive horse makes fluttering his bit. Some guarded conversation, and the thump of a quarter of beef on the gallery floor, and the other men riding away.

Juicy calf ribs on the coals, floured steaks sizzling in the skillet, and thickening gravy made with the grease after the meat had been cooked to death. Sweet potatoes baked in the ashes until candy ran out of them, and cornbread hoecakes browning on the fire, and fifteen children to feed. A jug of strongly flavored blackstrap molasses, sometimes a little wild honey, sometimes the scrapings from a barrel of brown sugar.

Feast or famine. No refrigeration. Eat up the meat, or it would spoil.

They got through the winter somehow; they fed the children, although there were times when everybody went on the cornbread and weak coffee diet for several days at a stretch, and it became a sort of game—it was an adventure. The molasses jug was empty, and somebody had licked it. The cat got the cream again.

Uncle Gus did no night riding. He wore the mantle of respectability; he was a farmer, and had made no cotton that year. Papa was younger. Papa rode at night. *Never mind whether it's a maverick or not, shoot the sonofabitch!*

"Billy," said Uncle Gus on a day when the larder was full, "will you say grace?"

"Yes, sir," Billy said. He bowed his head. The other fourteen children, sitting at three separate tables, bowed their heads. So did Uncle Gus and Aunt Jo, Papa and Mama. And nobody saw the devil in Billy's black eyes as he began, solemnly enough:

"Bless the meat, and damn the skin—
Back your ears, and pitch in!"

"William!" roared Uncle Gus, but it was too late. Everybody was already eating. And even Mama, knowing her children had been hungry, enjoyed a laugh.

III

The winter came early, cold and dry. Northers whistled down across Texas, reddening the sky with dust, staining the clothes Mama hung out to dry; northers flapped the wagon sheet and twisted the last leaves from postoak and hackberry. Ill-nourished cattle drifted with the wind and were bogged down to perish in the mud of shrinking waterholes or died against some barbed-wire fence. Every pasture had its scatter of carcasses left to bloat and burst; there were too many for buzzards to handle, and they put their stench upon the land. Old-timers remembered other big "die-ups," and shook their heads because there was no preventive and no remedy.

Only the hides were worth money now, if a skinner found the carcasses before the smell became unbearable. A good cowhide was worth four bits.

The big ranchers claimed they owned the hides of even the unbranded cattle that died on their land, or the land they used for grazing. But regularly employed cowboys were too busy trying to save the live cattle, and besides, cowboys always hated skinning cattle as much as they did building fence. That left the skinning to the man who had no job—and in Karnes County, at the time of the Panic and the drought, there were plenty of these. They had always shot mavericks for beef; they saw no reason why good hides should be left on the prairie to stiffen and shrivel and rot after the maggots had gone.

Crudely lettered warnings were posted along roads and trails and fences, saying that skinners would be shot. Of course the law—what there was of it—was on the side of the big operators. But even if the sheriff stopped a wagon loaded with hides on the Cuero or Victoria road, nobody could prove where the hides had come from. The skinners had gone on the night shift.

Down around Uncle Ed Maulding's store at Runge, talk of violence and of reprisal drowned out the tunes in his music box. Some cold-eyed men chewed their tobacco and said nothing; nobody knew whether they were skinning cattle or not. Then there were a few minor shooting scrapes, and a fast horse—as always in Texas—was a good insurance policy. It was almost as if the Sutton-Taylor feud had been revived: the quarrel went down the line, pitting henchmen against smaller operators, and hired riders against the man who was only a meat hunter. The biggest owner in those parts was Stafford, and Papa had worked for him in younger days. Stafford had warred for a long time with the bigger Shanghai Pierce, but now his back was to the wall and he fought lesser foes.

One-armed Sam Ezell, Papa's partner again, was still doing the planning. Papa rode with him, and they shot fresh beef and skinned cows by moonlight, all that winter. Sometimes they came in empty-handed, and sometimes they were wary about approaching the house, as if fearing ambush there. But if they had close calls—if they had been shot at—Papa did not worry Mama with the details.

It was seventeen-year-old Billy who paid the penalty as he drove Uncle Gus's wagon back from Runge on a day in spring. Riding with him was a neighbor whose name has been lost: he was a little older, he had done some night riding, and he had bragged a bit at Uncle Lee's store where the cold-eyed men sat on the knife-scarred counter. They speared greengage plums out of a can with their skinning blades; they whittled pine sticks, and chewed tobacco, and said nothing.

The wagon came to a pasture gate—the only one between the store and Uncle Gus's house. It stopped there like all old wagons used to do, with a creaking of harness and a settling noise along the running gear, the trace chains slackened and silent and the horses fighting flies and rolling their bits and maybe taking advantage of the stop to empty their bladders. Billy was handling the reins. The other boy got down and swung the plank gate open, lifting it on its sagging strap hinges.

As he did this, two men rose from concealment in the brush and shot him down. His hands clutched at the gate, and then trailed down the weathered planking and found the dust.

Billy saw both of the men. He had seen them at the store; he knew them, and recognition was mutual. Uncle Gus had refused to let Billy carry a gun. A gun would not have done him much good now, because there was no time between him and eternity. The guns blasted again.

The horses took the bits in their teeth and broke into a frightened run. There was only one way for them to go without a hand on the reins; they kept to the road, ran two miles or more, and clattered into Uncle Gus's yard, under the liveoak trees. Having come to the yard fence, they halted, trembling.

The noise of arrival was not usual. Uncle Gus and Aunt Jo came out, and all the children erupted, and Mama watched white-faced from the gallery. From a distance, Billy looked all right. He was still sitting erect on the wagon seat. He didn't turn; he didn't speak.

Uncle Gus went nearer with faltering steps and saw the color of his boy's face, and the color of the splotch on his shirt at breast and belly. He drew a sobbing breath and climbed on the wagon to pry Billy's fingers from their ghastly grip on the seat rail. Uncle Gus was standing on a front wheel hub, awkwardly balanced; he was not prepared to cope with what happened. The boy's body toppled forward, still rigid, still bent in a sitting posture. It fell across the footrest. With an agonizing slowness it went on down to strike the wagon tongue and roll to the earth, and the horses heard the thumping sound, and trembled anew.

"It was Butler and Burrus—they did it!" Norah says out of her long memory, and others speak the same names. "They didn't have anything against Billy, you know, but they had to shoot him to keep him from testifying."

Nobody had anything against young Billy. He had been sacrificed to the era, to the time and the place and the troubled circumstances: he was a victim of the Panic of 1893, and the Texas Skinning War. Nobody actually ever knew what happened at the pasture gate; everybody knew there were two men, because Billy had two different calibers of bullets in him.

Mama cried that night, as much in fear as in grief. She had looked upon young Billy, whose expression in death was one of innocent surprise, and then upon Dee, her first-born. He was twelve years old. In a little while he would be doing a man's work, riding and handling a team, perhaps driving a wagon loaded with disputed hides.

"Woodie!" she said. "Please, Woodie—let's leave this country! Let's clear out before it happens again! Go anywhere—just anywhere!"

Both Papa and Uncle Gus were cleaning and oiling their saddle guns. All they needed was somebody to shoot at, somebody definite: if they had really known the killers, a bloody feud would have resulted. But they didn't know who had shot Billy. They were fighting shadows.

"Now, Bettie," Papa said, in the nearest thing he ever had to sweet talk. "Now, Bettie—don't you worry. You just settle down. Nobody's going to say they ran me out of the country."

Papa's pride was up, and there was that stubbornness about him. Mama said, "But you can't fight the big ranchers, and if you keep on . . . "

"I said don't worry!" Papa repeated. "Besides," he added more softly, "we can't move right now. We'll have to wait. I found out about that house across the road today. We can move into it next week."

They moved into a two-room house across the field from Uncle Gus's place just in time. The year turned over, 1894 came with no noticeable improvement on the economic front, and my brother Floyd was born in February.

The panic lingered. There were no jobs. Papa and Sam Ezell were still riding by night and making a bare living. If Papa got any work as a carpenter, he had to take pay in farm produce, or eggs or poultry. Nobody had any money.

There was nothing to keep Papa in Karnes County, except that stubbornness. Nobody was going to run him out. And Sam Ezell had the same hard streak.

The infant Floyd lay in his crib, a most unusual baby. Perhaps he was a product of that period of calculated risk and desperate uncertainty; that time of mysterious nocturnal expeditions. Something shaped him: he seems to have been born with an unseasonably advanced attitude toward life, and filled with resentments and hostilities. I do not think Floyd ever felt insecure; he knew, instead, an early self-reliance and was sure of his knowledge. "Floyd," Mama used to say, "was just born grown-up."

As a baby, she said, he never cried. Instead, he lay in his crib and studied Papa with black, unwinking, accusing eyes. He smiled at other people, the way babies do, but he never smiled at Papa, whom he strongly resembled.

This got on Papa's nerves. "I swear, Bettie!" Papa said. "Why does he look at me like that?"

"Like what?" Mama asked, giving Floyd her breast.

"Well, like he knows me, but doesn't like me."

"He ought to know you," Mama said. "Looks enough like you."

More violence occurred in Karnes County, some of it striking close. Papa and Sam Ezell came finally to the reluctant conclusion that their horses would not drink the water in that area. They loaded up their wagons and moved northward to Wharton County.

But nothing changed, essentially. Hard times continued, a man still had to ride at night to shoot maverick beef and skin cattle to make a little money. Back in the industrial centers of the nation, the Panic was easing a little, but Texas was a long time away.

Papa and Sam Ezell now delivered their hides to the town of Ganado. It was a new town, just over ten years old; the name Ganado meant "herd" or "livestock," and had been chosen because of the vast numbers of longhorns roaming the prairies in that vicinity. Not half of these were branded, but the Texas cattle kings were hard put upon in those years because of drought and the collapse of market prices.

A gang rode up to the house of a man Papa knew one night. They killed him. His wife and baby hid between the featherbeds, but the blood lust was aroused, and they too were pulled out and slaughtered.

The next night, the wagon came by with Sam Ezell lying on the wagon seat, only half conscious. He had been beaten nearly to death.

Papa did not say anything. He came into the house and looked around, and saw Floyd—now several months old—regarding him with that same challenging, accusing, unflinching stare.

"The bastards!" Papa said. "The dirty bastards! If it wasn't for the kids . . . "

"Woodie!" Mama begged. "Please . . . "

"I'll be damned if I'll leave here by night!" Papa swore.

So he didn't. He left in the daytime, but what had happened to Billy Bosworth, and the murdered family of three, and the beating-up of Sam Ezell had scared him: he did not take an open road, but drove the Studebaker wagon across the prairie.

"It had been raining," Norah says, "and the waist-high grass was as wet as it could be, and just as soon as we got across one creek we could see another. The saw grass cut our legs and feet because we had to walk behind the wagon. And all of us started coming down sick with the fever. Papa just kept going. He swore he was going to Old Mexico this time."

Thirteen

*F*or a Texan born a short twenty years after the fall of the Alamo and the bloody massacre at Goliad, and raised on stories told by veterans of the Battle of San Jacinto, Papa had always been inordinately fond of Mexico and the Mexicans. The land south of the Rio Grande was new country indeed, but surely he must have known that, in those days, going there without capital, he would be no better off than a *peon*. But a destination helped salve Papa's conscience when the urge to travel was upon him, and now Mexico was his goal. Besides, he understood and liked the *mañana* philosophy popularly attributed to Mexicans: tomorrow he would find the country that suited him, tomorrow all would be better, and he would send the children to school. Today would take care of itself, and sufficient to it was the evil thereof.

He should have followed a road and taken his chances, that day when the family left Wharton County. In choosing the untracked prairie, instead, he had to cross six or seven flooded creeks; the wagon bogged down several times. Mama rode, holding Floyd in her arms, but the bigger children had to walk most of the way, and were forced to put their shoulders to the wheels when the wagon was mired. When dusk thickened they had finally reached a road Papa felt would be safe, but they had covered only a few miles. The children were wet and muddy and bedraggled, their bare feet and legs bleeding from cuts made by the cruel saw grass.

Now mosquitoes settled over the camp like a swirling, singing fog, and their bites stung like sparks from the campfire falling on bare skin. Papa tried a smudge of green cowchips, and the smoke made everybody miserable except the mosquitoes. It was the worst night in camp anybody in the family could remember.

But the warmth of the morning sun and the feel of the reins in his hand put Papa into an exuberant and *Viva Mexico* mood. The wagon tarp steamed, the mud dried and fell from the wheel spokes as the road improved, and new horizons waited. Papa glanced back over his shoulder a few times, but the only thing that really annoyed him, after a good breakfast, was the way Floyd looked at him as he drove.

"I figure a man could make his pile on minerals, down in Mexico," Papa said. "The Mexicans are all too busy being *vaqueros* to pay much attention to mining. They're born riders, and what they can do with a rope! I remember working with a Mexican with the Stafford outfit. He could stand in the corral with a bunch of wild mustangs milling around him, and he'd catch any horse you pointed out by throwing a figure-eight loop."

Mama had no desire to go all the way to Mexico to watch somebody's artistry with the *riata*. How far into Mexico did Papa intend to go? What about settling down? What about schools?

"Why, we might go all the way to Mexico City, but the minerals I was telling you about are out in Chihuahua and Sonora, I expect. They've got some of the finest colleges in the world in Mexico City, you know. Costs money to send a boy there, of course. Well, I aim to make some money."

Papa meant it. He had seven children to feed, and less than ten dollars in his pocket. But he meant it for *mañana*.

Tomorrow was just over the hills, yonder; it was only a day beyond yesterday. All a man had to do was to keep his wagon wheels turning.

[164]

It was early fall. It was the season of the year in which Papa always felt safe in traveling, because there would be cotton to pick. Therefore, his route to Old Mexico was a leisurely one and winding; he avoided the cattle country that lay directly south, and went up through the German settlement of Schulenburg.

The fields were whitening there. "Mighty damn funny how a German can always make a crop!" Papa said resentfully. "Mighty damn funny how it rains for the Germans when it don't rain for anybody else!"

He stopped there for a week or two, and made a little money. But not much, because luck wasn't with him. Dee and Norah and Jay had suddenly come down with the ague—malarial chills and fever. Mama had to take care of them, as well as look after Floyd and Lily May and Maude and Ivanhoe. She dosed the whole family with quinine until their ears rang. Papa picked cotton alone, made just enough money to buy provisions and feed, and then he hitched the team and moved on. The children were having their chills on schedule, almost as if by alarm clock; they were actually as comfortable in the wagon as they would have been in camp.

The next stop was La Grange, in Fayette County. Here, it was Dee and Norah and Jay who did the cotton picking—Mama and Papa had fallen victims to the malaria. The three children could not pick much, and the farmers were still paying depression wages for six-cent cotton. The supplies in the chuckbox ran low again.

If Papa couldn't work, he could still travel, and he felt a compulsion to hit the road. He and Mama alternately burned with fever and shook until they rattled the wagon seat. Neither had ever been sick before, and Papa, feeling that his fortunes had hit rock bottom, lapsed into one of his silent moods. Sometimes he drove all day without speaking, except to grunt between chattering teeth; at supper he might sit and suffer, staring at the sugar until Mama read his mind and handed it to him.

He halted one evening after dark, just short of the town of Bastrop, raging inwardly because he had driven into the cul-de-sac of a lane fenced with his ancient enemy, barbed wire. It was too dark to go farther. He pulled out of the road and got down, and knew at once by the feeling of the ground under his boots that there was no grass for the horses.

Mama said nothing when he left the team in harness and the saddle horse tethered behind the wagon. She turned the baby over to Norah, had a little chill that left her perspiring and weak, and told the children to rustle her some wood so she could fix supper. But, when the meal was finished, she turned to Papa.

"Are you going on, Woodie?" she asked gently enough. "If you aren't, why don't you unhitch the horses?"

Silence. Papa sat on a box near the campfire. He had eaten supper with his hat on. Its broad brim put his face in shadow, and nobody knew what he was thinking.

"And you haven't fed them," Mama said, a little more accusingly. No answer. *Feed them with what?*

There was no corn in the wagon. The chuckbox was down to a little bacon, a few cups of corn meal and beans, enough coffee for a day or two, and a half jug of molasses.

Mama poured hot water in her dishpan, put it on the lid of the chuckbox, and looked at Papa through the steam.

"Woodie, the horses haven't had anything to eat all day. I always heard it said that the first thing a man does is take care of his team. What are you going to do about it?"

The silence was shattered. "Goddamn it, Bettie!" Papa roared. "What do you *expect* me to do about it?"

They were both sick and irritable, and more than that: Mama was a long way down the road from Sweet Home, and quite disenchanted. She had endured hardships for herself without a murmur; she had shared them, in her protective way, with the children. But she could not bear to see dumb animals suffer, and now she faced Papa with a burst of temper.

"Why, bless Patty, I expect you to feed the horses! And to unhitch them so they can rest—they worked hard all day! Why did you pick this camp? Why didn't you stop where there was grazing?"

"Stop picking on me! It got dark, didn't it? There's not a moon, is there? How did I know we'd be fenced in?"

"I'm not picking on you, Woodie. I'm just saying you've got to take care of the horses. Oh, you had *your* supper, all right—you filled *your* belly! But look at them—gant as gutted snowbirds!"

"All right—*all right!*" Papa yelled. He bounced up from the box, a goaded and misunderstood man. He rummaged in the wagon until he found an empty tow sack.

"Goddamn it!" he said feelingly, and tottered through the barbed wire and into a cornfield, making the most of his illness. Mama and the children could hear him out there in the darkness, swearing and rustling the dry cornstalks like a December norther.

Dee was past thirteen. "Mama," he asked solemnly, "ain't that stealing?"

Mama had Floyd at her breast. "You hush!" she said. "All you young'uns get to bed—hear me? Your Papa's not stealing. It's more like borrowing a little something we need. He can find the farmer in the morning, and settle with him. You get to bed, now."

When Papa returned with the sack bulging over his shoulder, no one was up to hear his grumbling threat to feed the damned horses until they foundered. Nobody would have understood that his complaint was not directed at the moment, nor at the incident: he had grievances against the larger times and conditions, against all manner of indignities heaped upon mankind, and against all those who ground the faces of the poor. The farmer, owning property, fell into the last category. Papa hated the farmer.

He sat alone in the last flicker of the campfire shelling corn into three *morrals,* making his hands sore. He would by God feed the horses so much corn they would founder, and that would show Mama. No woman was going to tell him what to do.

Finally he unhitched the horses and fed them, and brooded again in the darkness listening to them munch the corn and blow and slobber into the *morrals,* and it took them forever to finish. After that, he staked them out in the lane. The fire went out; the camp was still. It was a dry and starry night, and Mama had put their bed tarp on the ground. Papa groped his way to it, and sat down on the edge of the bed to undress. He folded his clothes and put them under the tarp to protect them from the dew; he removed his boots and socks, and from long habit dusted the soles of his feet together, as a man brushes his palms, so that no sand or wisp of dry grass would be tracked into the bed linen. Then he slipped into bed with Mama. Floyd was cradled in the crook of her arm. It was too dark to tell, but Papa imagined that Floyd was lying awake watching him.

Papa wasn't sleepy. He lay looking at the stars, and he backslid a great distance from his youthful Baptist camp-meeting conversion. It seemed to him that God was so busy moving the stars and watching the sparrow's fall that He sometimes neglected man.

"Bettie?" he said after a time.

No answer. Mama was asleep. She was soft and inviting.

"Bettie!"

"Yes?" she murmured.

"I fed the damned horses. I hope you're satisfied!"

Feeding the horses under such conditions deserved acclaim. It had been accomplished with difficulty, and attended by risk. But Mama had no praise.

"About time, bless Patty!" she said, and turned over to go to sleep again.

"Hell!" Papa muttered. "Damn it all to hell!"

Sleeping there, unacclaimed and unrewarded, was out of the question. He got up, after a while, to pull on his boots and get his saddle and slicker and saddle blanket out of the wagon. Then he bedded down alone, as he had done when he was a cowboy, and "looked at the stars in the sky."

II

Nobody remembers that Papa extended himself at all in trying to find the farmer the next morning—he was too anxious to get out of that barbed-wire lane. Just after sunrise, he hitched up and drove on through Bastrop. When he glanced sidewise at the baby on Mama's

[168]

lap, he saw that Floyd was studying him in an almost scornful way. "Hadn't he ought to be asleep?" Papa asked. "I swear, he gets on my nerves!"

"He's a good baby," Mama said. "He just never cries at all, and he's never any trouble." She rocked Floyd fondly, and crooned: "Yes, you're Mama's precious little man, aren't you, honey boy?"

And then two riders came up from behind, one on either side of the wagon. The white man rode a blaze-faced bay horse; the Negro dangled long legs over a barebacked brown mule, with a piece of old rope for a hackamore.

"Whoa!" Papa said. "Howdy!"

The Negro showed an excessive amount of the whites of his eyes. "That's him!" he said, pointing. "That's the white man stole my cawn—I seen the waggin when he pulled out this mawnin'! Stole my cawn!" he repeated, and Papa saw that his patched and faded overalls were held up by only one strap, and that his pinched and pockmarked face had been ground by poverty.

Papa looked at the white man, whose expression showed infinite distaste for the whole affair. He had a brassy star pinned to his vest above a dangling Bull Durham tag. He tipped his hat to Mama, and said, "Howdy, ma'am," and then looked at Papa. "You bust into this nigger's cornfield last night, like he says you done?"

"I was plumb out of feed—took a few ears to feed my horses," Papa admitted. "If you hadn't fenced off all the grass in this damned country—"

"Deputy sheriff," the man said. He rested his forearms on the pommel of his saddle, and sighed. "The fence ain't neither here or there, stranger. Thing is, you want to settle with this nigger, or you want to go to court? Tried to talk him out of it, but he swears he'll prosecute."

"I don't want no settlement!" the Negro declared. "White folks think they can steal my cawn jes' because I'm a nigger and got a farm on the road. I want the law on him!"

The deputy motioned across the backs of Papa's team. "Now, wait, boy! Corn ain't worth hardly nothin'. Maybe he took two bits'

[169]

worth of corn. If he paid you five dollars, you'd be ahead, and you'd save the county trouble." He appealed to Papa. "Give him five dollars, and he won't have no case."

"Ain't got five dollars," Papa confessed.

"See?" exclaimed the black man. "Jes' po' white trash, stealin' my cawn!"

This was too much. Papa was still weak from the ague, but he wrapped his reins around the brake handle and bounced down from the wagon seat hot-eyed with temper. "Get off that mule and say that, you black son-of-a-bitch! I'll tear your leg off and beat you over the head with it!"

"You'll get back on the wagon," said the deputy sheriff. "And you, nigger—you keep your mouth shut, or I'll shut it for you! No, I reckon we'll have to go back to town and talk to the judge. There's a warrant swore out, and I ain't got no choice."

Mama's hand was over her mouth. She felt faint, and was sure she was going to scream. The children had crowded up behind the wagon seat, wide eyed and breathless. Little Maude sensed that something was wrong, and began to cry, but Dee and Norah and Jay were waiting to see what Papa would do. They remembered when Papa thrashed a man for kicking a dog . . . they knew he had championed the quail and cut the barbed wire and Roped a House.

Now Papa was about to be arrested. All hell might break loose any minute.

Only it didn't. Apparently Floyd was the only member of the family who had made a correct estimate of the situation. Still regarding Papa with a disdainful air, he chose this moment to regurgitate milk on his dress front. There were no dramatics, at all; there was nothing but an ancient hatred in the eyes of the Negro farmer, and a slump in Papa's shoulders as he turned the team around.

The deputy rode alongside. The man on the mule rode in the dust behind the wagon, accustomed to letting white folks go ahead.

Everybody in the wagon was silent for a little while, and then Jay piped up in a shrill and hopeful tone: "Will Papa have to turn outlaw now? Will he, hey?"

Mama swung around, white-faced. "Jay, you hush your mouth!" she said sharply. Then she began to cry.

There was a considerable Wendish settlement near Bastrop, and a number of Germans. The justice of the peace was of some Teutonic strain—perhaps Prussian, by his close-cropped hair and his uncompromising attitude, which smacked of the military. Papa squared his shoulders to face the court with defiance.

Mama did not go to the courtroom. She stayed on the wagon, sniffling a little, telling the excited children to be quiet, and feeling utter disgrace. *If the farmer had only been a white man . . .*

She remembered that she had goaded Papa into crime. She had nagged him . . . she was really to blame for all that had happened. Her tears came anew.

Meanwhile, Papa admitted that he had taken a sack of corn. His only defense was that his horses were hungry. In other times and other places, in Texas, this would have been enough to win him an acquittal and a collection from the courtroom audience. But the times were changing, and the frontier had moved west.

The judge, dressed in a little brief authority, leaned over the bar and said, "It gifs twenty-five dollars, or twelve days."

Papa came out with the deputy to tell the family good-bye for the period of his incarceration, but not to tell Mama how she would feed either the children or the horses for that time.

"I'm sorry, Bettie," he said abjectly, and turned away before he would be crying, too.

There had been a few spectators in the courtroom. One of them followed Papa outside and remained near the wagon when the deputy led Papa away. He was an elderly man, neat in overalls and wearing spectacles.

"Excuse me, please, lady," the man said a little while after Papa had gone. "You dond't cry no more now. You dond't haff money? You dond't haff some place to go? You are vorried about the children?"

Mama pocketed her pride for once, and admitted that she was in

[171]

desperate circumstances. The old man smiled, and his eyes sparkled, and he chucked Floyd under the chin and took great pleasure in a baby's laugh.

"See that vagon, yonder? You follow that vagon, und ve come to my place, und you meet my Anna. Ve vill take care of you."

To Mama, this kindness was Heaven-sent, and she remembered it all her life. Papa always spoke of her benefactor, later, as "that nice old German," but he wasn't German at all. He was a Wend— the member of a diminishing Slavic people who had come out of Serbia. He and his Anna, now graying and stocky, had reared their children and had married them off. They were lonesome, and loved having Mama's young'uns on their thrifty farm.

Mama made camp just outside the neat white paling fence of the yard, and the three horses were put on good pasture. Every day, the farmer or his wife brought milk and eggs and vegetables to help stretch the staples remaining in the chuckbox. Dee and Norah and Jay tried to help repay all this by performing chores around the barn.

On the day Papa was to be released, Dee caught up the horses and hitched them, and Mama thanked the farmer and drove to Bastrop. Nobody spoke as Papa came out into the sunlight, looking paler, but well nourished. He grunted, and climbed the wagon, and Mama moved over to give him the reins and make him the captain of his fate again.

They rolled westward. Toward the end of a long day, Papa made one general observation, loud enough for everybody to hear: "If I live to be a hundred, I'll never go near that damned town again!"

Fourteen

*T*he cotton-picking season of 1895 ran out from under Papa's wheels and left him low in the pocketbook. Illness in the family had taken its toll, and while Papa languished in jail the cotton was at its ripest; when he came out, the peak was passed. Now the course he was steering for Old Mexico became devious indeed; he was not looking for new country half as much as he was seeking work of any kind.

He turned southward. For some reason of his own, he avoided the bigger towns such as Austin and San Antonio. The children wanted to see the Alamo, but Papa said it would still be there later, and, being older, he had the greater claim to its heritage, so they accepted his ruling. He drifted through Lockhart and Seguin and Floresville, camping in any place where he could help build a house or barn; and by such odd jobs he managed to keep a marginal supply of provisions on hand. For a few weeks, around the New Year, the Studebaker wagon rested on the prairie near a farm worked by a family named Cooper.

Old Man Cooper, so-called, was really no older than Papa, but had ways that marked him as an individual. He seemed to have been engaged, principally, in raising hogs and sons, and he told

Papa, ruefully, that sometimes he found it almighty hard to tell which was which.

"Take them boys of mine," he said, "damned if they ain't just eating me out of house and home! They ain't big enough to make hands around the place, but every one of 'em eats more'n a full-growed man. Plumb full of tapeworms, I reckon."

There were five or six of the Cooper boys, ranging from nine to fifteen years of age—the exact number could not be determined, because all of them were like Indians, and at any moment of muster one or more would be cleverly concealed in the brush as if to escape being counted. They had black hair and black eyes, and were filled with Indian stealth and cunning. Most of the cunning was employed toward getting their bellies filled without having Old Man Cooper lay his rawhide quirt on their collective backsides. He did that every time he caught them in the kitchen between meals.

The day after his visit with Papa, Old Man Cooper went off to town to sell a few pigs, and the younger Coopers moved hungrily upon the Studebaker wagon, like so many Comanches. There was some shaking of lances: they pulled Ivanhoe's pigtails at first meeting, and rolled in dusty, indecisive combat with Dee and Jay. And then they were blood brothers with the Bosworth tribe.

"Ast your Ma for somethin' to eat," urged Tom, the oldest boy. "Ast her if they's maybe some beans she was fixin' to throw out. Or maybe some cornbread 'n' bacon."

It was just past the midday meal at the wagon when Dee relayed the request. Mama wasn't throwing out many beans, those days. If they soured, she either added water and boiled them again to kill the fermentation, or threw them into a skillet of hot grease to make *frijoles refritos*. But the asking troubled her. "I declare!" she said. "You'd think those Cooper young'uns were sure-enough hungry! And there's not a bite around here till I fix supper."

Tom Cooper took the news stoically. "Y'all come over to our house," he suggested, tightening his belt. "Pa's gone to town, and we can ride the calves. Pa ketches us ridin' the calves, he quirts the billy hell out of us."

Riding calves had no appeal for Norah, who was now twelve and quite grown-up, but Dee and Jay were excited at the prospect of a sport later legalized by rodeos. On the way, however, the Cooper boys grew more empty, and changed their plans.

"We'll sneak up behind the barn, so Ma can't see us," Tom decided. "Then we'll make a beeline for the smokehouse, and get ourselves a mess of side meat. Only you got to do it the way I tell you, or we'll all get quirted. Come on, now!"

Dee and Jay marveled at the way the Coopers blended into the brush for protective coloring. They held council at the back wall of the barn, where they stripped cedar bark from a post, rolled it into pieces of catalog paper pilfered from the privy, and smoked it. Then Tom pointed out the smokehouse, distinguished from the privy by being slightly larger and having no vents. One by one, the members of the raiding party dashed across the intervening space and assembled in the smokehouse's pungent gloom.

Old Man Cooper must have been holding back his cured meat in hope of a rising market. More hams and sides of bacon were hanging from the sooty rafters than Dee and Jay had ever seen in a grocery store.

"Listen, now!" Tom whispered. "We got to make it look like the dawgs done it, not us. I'll show you. Watch!"

He mounted a wooden box that was high enough to put his head up into the stalactitic meat, gripped the rafter with both hands, and sank his teeth into a slab of bacon. Then he released his hold on the rafter, lifted his feet, and went swinging toward the farther wall.

Nothing else sounds like the tearing of flesh, even after it has been smoked and cured. The bacon ripped, and Tom landed catlike on the balls of his feet with that Indian grace all the Coopers had.

"See?" he asked, chewing happily. "Looks just like the dawgs jumped up and done it. Joe, you get down from that box, and mind your manners, damn you! Company first."

Dee and Jay tried it, not so much from hunger as for the sheer novelty of putting the blame on the dogs. They had only moderate success. The Cooper boys all had remarkable teeth. They might have grown up to join a circus and go rocketing under the big top, hanging from a pulley strap by their teeth and carrying girl aerialists under each arm.

But they didn't. Not Tom Cooper, anyway. I was to know him, in my teens. He was already a legend then: they told it that he had changed his name and turned outlaw until there was a price on his head. And then he had the audacity to join the Texas Rangers under his real name, and spend several years helping to hunt himself.

I was the second person, at fourteen, to look upon the body of a man Tom Cooper shot and left lying face down in a dusty West Texas road. I saw him arrested, and heard his scornful laughter.

But that story belongs later.

II

The new country of Papa's everlasting search turned out, all too often, to be very much like the country he had left behind, and this was a great disappointment to the children. But now, with the beginning of 1896, Papa proved up his often-repeated promises. He drove down south of Pearsall, in Frio County, into a country like none of the young'uns had ever seen.

It was not a pretty land, unless the traveler viewing it had some measure of Papa's love for limitless space and his need for freedom unfettered by fences. The sky was wide and blue, except on days when clouds came rolling from the Gulf, softer than seagull wings. The land rolled gently, but that was all it knew of gentleness: on both sides of the narrow and dusty wagon road were head-high jungles of mesquite and *huisache,* catclaw and *huajillo,* rat-tail cactus and Spanish dagger and *amargosa.* In February, the *agarito* perfumed it with delicate yellow bloom, and later yielded tiny berries of exquisite flavor. There were thickets of prickly pear high enough to hide a cowboy on a tall horse, cruel enough to drive him mad with the torture of a thousand spines if his horse threw him there. Every shrub, every dwarfed tree, was armed with thorns, and the worst was the plant the Mexicans call *junco*—this, they said, made the crown the Saviour wore when He went to the Cross.

1. *Mama*

2. *Papa*

3. *The Pecos River*

4. *The Pecos River*

5. *A Crockett County ranch scene*

6. *A trail drive through a West Texas town*

7. *Freight wagons on the main street of Ozona*

8. *The Bosworths traveled in wagons like these*

9. Dee

10. Willie and Ivanhoe

12. Mama, circa 1908

11. Dee
at twenty-two

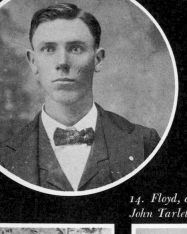

13. Jay

14. Floyd, a student at
John Tarleton College

15. Papa in Mexico

16. *Floyd*   17. *Bert*   18. *Allie*

19. *Floyd (with bottle) and Bert*

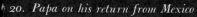

20. *Papa on his return from Mexico*   21. *Allie, Maude, Norah, Bert, Dee and Jay*

22 & 23. *The house on the rocks, before and after the addition*

24. *The first schoolhouse, Ozona*   25. *The new school building*

26. *The fifth and sixth grades, Ozona, 1911. Front row, Allie, fourth from left. Second row, Willie Baker, with mouth open. Third row, "Hop" Hoover, fourth from left; Ora Mae Cox, seventh; Miss Glee Stafford, teacher. Fourth row, Daphne Meinecke, first on left.*

27. *The courthouse in Ozona*

28. *The bank and "Mammy" Kirkpatrick's hotel*

29. *Ozona, looking west from Waterworks Hill*

30. *Main Street of Ozona looking north*

31. Chuck wagon

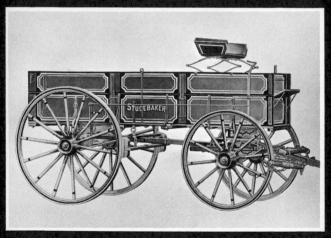

*32. Studebaker
ranch or farm
wagon*

PHOTOGRAPH
COURTESY
STUDEBAKER-PACKARD
CORP.

*33. One of the first cars
in Ozona*

Papa liked this land. The Mexicans had named it *brasada*—the brush country. It had legends old and current; the early Texans had learned the cowboy's trade here from the *vaqueros,* and that was why Texas cowboys roped with a short loop—larger ones would have been snagged by the brush. Papa was late on this ground, as he was always late, but even in his time men did not try to farm the *brasada.* They stalked wily longhorned cattle in the chaparral, or went to infinite pains to capture mustangs at infrequent waterholes. And all the time they fought out their allotted portion of a hundred years of undeclared border warfare with the Mexicans.

Old Mexico was close at hand, now. Papa probably would have made it across the Rio Grande if malarial fever had not continued to plague the entire family, and if it had not turned into something more serious—a typhomalarial sickness.

And if tragedy had not struck. Everybody was ill by turns, but four-year-old Lily May was sickest of all. Her fever hung on, strong and raging. It wore Mama down with sleepless vigils: she was up all night to wring out cold cloths and keep them on the child's forehead. Papa rode to Pearsall and found a doctor who made daily calls in his buggy. Like all doctors of the time and place, he prescribed calomel, which was good for a number of ailments. Every child was presumed to be infested with intestinal worms—and very likely most of them were—and calomel is an anthelmintic.

Lily May was weak, and not well nourished. The calomel salivated her, and her baby teeth fell out from bleeding gums. She swallowed some of them. Her fever did not subside.

The family was living in a small frame house that Papa had rented, and Lily May's illness became so desperate as to turn the house into an isolation ward, with all the other children sleeping outside in the February weather. Mama nursed Floyd, and Norah gave him all the other care he required, and he continued his infantile disapproval of Papa.

Papa was having more luck hunting for meat than he had in looking for paying jobs. The brush country was full of deer, wild *javelina* hogs, and maverick beef. He came back home one evening

[177]

after sundown, with fresh meat on the forks of his saddle, and saw the doctor's buggy still standing near the wagon. This meant, to Papa, that the doctor had been there an uncommonly long time.

He dropped the meat on the gallery, and entered the house. The doctor and Mama were sitting at Lily May's bedside, their heads close together. It did not occur to Papa that the doctor was taking Lily May's rapid pulse, or that Mama was leaning anxiously near to listen to the child's breathing, and to keep the cold wet cloth on her forehead. Papa viewed the tableau in a different light—that of sudden, insanely jealous rage.

"Look here!" he shouted. "What the hell do you think you're doing? Get out of my house, goddamn you, and get out fast!"

There was a .30-.30 Winchester in his hands. The doctor leaped up, overturning his chair.

"Woodie!" Mama exclaimed. "What's the matter with you? Are you crazy?"

"I ain't so crazy that I can't see what the two of you are up to! Thicker than fleas!" He advanced on the physician. "You heard what I said! Get out!"

The doctor snatched up his satchel, and backed out the door. Mama began to cry.

"Oh, Woodie—Woodie! She's awfully sick! Maybe she can't live! We *need* the doctor tonight! Please listen to me . . . please!"

Papa was listening, instead, to the departing sound of hoofs and wheels. He stood the gun in a corner, and said, "Now, you listen to *me!* If I ever catch you that lovey dovey with a man again, I'll by God kill him! And you too, before I'll ever let another man have you!"

He stood in the doorway, the yellow light of the coal-oil lamp showing the fury on his face and striking a wild glitter from his eyes. He swayed there, and came out toward the center of the room, walking strangely. "I reckon," he mumbled, "that I ain't good enough for you! You're too fine-haired. . . . I haven't got money enough for you . . . no education . . . I—"

[178]

Mama caught him as he fell, and half-dragged him to the rocking chair, where he collapsed and babbled things she could not understand. She shouted, "Dee! Dee—your Papa's sick!" and unbuttoned his collar and felt his forehead. He was burning with fever.

Dee saddled and rode to overtake the doctor. It was something of a credit to the breed of old-time horse-and-buggy practitioners that this one returned, readily, to the place where he felt he had run the risk of getting shot. Papa was delirious. They got him to bed and dosed him with powders. He muttered incoherently of Mexico, and of killing somebody—the doctor, no doubt—and raved about being up to the wheel hubs in quicksand. It was long past midnight before his fever broke and he sweated and slept.

By then, Lily May was dead. It was some comfort to Mama when the doctor told her, later, that the child would have died anyway, and that Papa's feverish accusations had nothing to do with it.

Mama was still a pretty woman—an attractive woman, indeed, most of the time. But she had been worn down by sleepless nights at the side of the sickbed, and it happened that she was several months pregnant, and only a man sick in mind and body would have harbored the suspicions that drove Papa into his tantrum. He was tough, and began to mend, but he was not able to attend the funeral. Lily May was buried in a grave Mama never saw again.

As soon as Papa could climb to the seat of his wagon, he began backtracking to Floresville, in Wilson County. He was wild with grief and self-incrimination: one morning, when he thought nobody was looking, Mama saw him beating his forehead on a wagon tire. And his dream of Mexico had been shattered: Mexico would have to wait, now, until the new baby came. Papa once more had been thwarted by love and the processes of fertility.

In Floresville, he suffered relapse in payment for having left his bed too soon. This was just after the birth of my fourth brother, who was named Bert.

"I remember when Bert was born," Norah says. "We were

living in the least little old bitty house you ever saw—there wasn't room to turn around in it. And that was where Papa got real sick, all over again, and didn't have any money."

Papa, or somebody, swallowed pride and wrote to Aunt Docia and Uncle Nick for help. The sheep business Papa had always heartily despised suddenly became a respected and honored institution—Aunt Docia promptly sent a check for twenty dollars. The amount was small, but the fact that she and Uncle Nick had money in the bank and could write a check was an arresting thing. In all his life, Papa never put his signature on a piece of paper that said, "Pay to the order of . . ."

But cashing the check was another matter. Papa was still abed, and the food was running out. Mama made the rounds of the Floresville merchants, willing to convert the entire twenty dollars into provisions and grain for the horses and a gallon of coal oil for the lantern, but the storekeepers were exceedingly wary of out-of-town bank drafts. It was an anxious week before she found a man whose cupidity exceeded his judgment.

Then Dee hitched the horses, and the Studebaker wagon's tongue was pointed westward. Uncle Nick had supplied financial aid in a time of desperate need: what more natural than that the recipients should flee to his bosom in Schleicher County? If a man had money in the bank, then times in Schleicher must be booming. . . .

It was a country not much different from the high and windy Lipan Flats, where the wagon had been before; it was a tableland, a part of the Edwards Plateau, running level and shading abruptly into rocky cedar brakes. There was high grass, but no timber.

"You could see," Dee remembers, "for miles and miles across the divides, and sometimes you could jump whole bands of antelope, and man, how they could run! I was just getting big enough to hire out on some of the ranches, punching cattle or herding sheep, and there was a kind of land boom on around Eldorado—the country was just opening up. Papa could have taken up a section of land free, and then he could have bought adjoining land for a dollar an acre, or even less.

"Well, I told Papa it looked to me like that dollar-an-acre land might be a good thing. But I wasn't but fifteen then, and what I thought didn't count for much. Papa just looked at me and shook his head. He said, 'Why, hell, it won't be worth more than a dollar an acre a hundred years from now.' "

A far-sighted man, my father. He had his eyes on the horizon, on tomorrow, on Mexico and *mañana*. Schleicher County was a place to rest the wagon wheels. It is fortunate that my brother Dee was always blessed with a saving sense of humor. In 1958, after the land had yielded a number of fortunes in livestock, Schleicher County pumped 2,440,985 barrels of oil.

But how was Papa to foresee this, back in 1896? Oil was a chancy thing; if they had found it in Schleicher County, they would not have known what to do with it. Nobody had drilled very deep into the Texas earth; nobody had the equipment. They drilled only to depths a windmill could handle; they had not produced the light metals used much later in windmill rods, and no well went beyond four hundred feet until after the first quarter of the twentieth century.

There were a few men in Schleicher, however, who were drilling holes in the ground and finding water where there had never been water before. They used an unwieldy steam-powered rig, but it was a great advancement from the old drills powered by horses walking in a circle.

And there was a strapping, handsome young driller in the crew named Luke Wilson. He was as black-eyed as the Cooper boys had been; he was straight and strong, and had killed bears in the Santa Rosa Mountains of Mexico. He had killed a man, too, in fair fight.

Luke Wilson saw Norah when she was fourteen, and it was love at first meeting. He came courting. Mama looked back down the years, and found them incredible. . . .

Back in Lavaca County, there was a sudden flare-up of the frontier code. Berry Augustus Bosworth, second son of Uncle Gus, was now rising twenty-four years old. He was reckless with the times of the Skinning War Papa had fled, and hot with the spirit of youth that makes so many men of that age die on the battlefields. Nobody remembers now just how or why it happened, but there was trouble over a girl.

On Decoration Day, 1897, Berry (who was nicknamed Wig) met a man named Will Lewis at Hallettsville's Salem Cemetery. They had words, and by common consent withdrew from the ceremonies then being held.

They walked a hundred yards away, and fought a sort of duel without seconds. It was a fair contest. Each pulled his gun and fired simultaneously.

Will Lewis was killed on the spot. Wig Bosworth lived four hours, his brains oozing from the bullet hole in his head.

Legend wove this incident into the old tales of the Sutton-Taylor feud, for the old stories would not die. And in my childhood it was proudly remembered that the Bosworth *did* live four hours. Without brains.

Fifteen

My family gave the Post Office Department a bad time. Letters sometimes found us months after the stamp had been canceled. They were labeled, "Not At," and "Unclaimed," "Forward To," and "In Care Of."

Such a letter tracked Papa down in Schleicher County, shortly after Norah married Luke Wilson and had gone with him somewhere to camp out and drill a well. It was from Papa's younger brother Bob, whom he hadn't seen in a number of years.

"Well, I'll be damned!" Papa said in an envious tone. "Bob's got farther west than we have. Wonder how he did that? Wonder when he moved, and how many times?"

"Where is he now?" Mama asked. She remembered Bob and Will, that time down in Goliad County, when Papa took her to Grandpa Henry's wagon-encircled house as a bride.

"He's out across the Pecos—by Sheffield," Papa said, and read the letter again. "Doing right well, I reckon. He's running a ferry he built—kind of aerial ferry that hoists wagons across the river. He says the Pecos country is just opening up. Cheap land, and lots of it. That's a big country, out there."

Mama sighed. Papa had the gleam in his eyes again, and the itch in his boots.

"Well, Bob was always smart," Papa conceded as he restored the letter to its much-marked envelope. "He could have been an engineer, if he'd tried. He says he aims to stay in that country and grow up with it. That's the way to get rich—if you find the right place."

Mama took down her looking glass and wrapped it in the quilts; as was usual, she had no vote in the matter of moving. She would have been on the losing side anyway, because at this time Uncle Nick's grazing lease ran out, and he had to find new range for his sheep. He saddled up, and joined Papa in a horseback expedition to reconnoiter the Pecos country.

West of Eldorado, they found the land breaking into wide draws, green with mesquite, and white-brush dry watercourses all winding southward toward the Rio Grande between rimrocked hills that were freckled with scrub cedar and cactus, and the coarse-grassed *sacaguista* Mexicans used for thatched roofs. They rode across several wide divides, high and level as table tops, and the last one broke abruptly into the rugged and crooked canyon of the Pecos.

Papa was charmed. This land was unfenced and wild. He had the feeling that nobody owned it, or ever would; it belonged to the lobo wolf, to the coyote and buzzard, the antelope and rattlesnake and centipede. And the river fascinated him. He had heard of the Pecos, in cowboy song and story, all his life. The river has been tamed, now, by a series of irrigation dams, and the idea of an aerial ferry to lift vehicular traffic across it would not be feasible, even if there were no highway bridges. It had been bridged, even then, by the Southern Pacific—but that bridge, 321 feet high, was part of the Pecos legend, along with "Judge" Roy Bean and his Jersey Lilly Saloon at Langtry.

Papa and Uncle Nick rode into the river some seventy miles north of what Roy Bean called his "bailiwick." The water spilled over their boot tops; they felt the buoyant lurch of the horses as they reached swimming depth. In those days, the Pecos was still a wild bitch wolf of a stream, with quicksands and unpredictable holes in its bottom, and it fell down from New Mexico so precipitously that only its incredibly serpentine windings prevented a lesser Niagara. It changed course at will within the mile-wide confines of the rocky canyon, and ran between rank growths of dwarf salt cedars. The water was so strongly alkaline that cattle bawled thirstily along the banks, mad with the wet smell and liquid murmur and mirror sheen of water they could not drink. Old-timers said that a killdee had only to fly across the Pecos to get a bad case of diarrhea . . .

And Sheffield? The town is still there, and not much bigger: a sun-baked cluster of frame and adobe houses worn by the blowing dust, squatting in a hollow between the limestone rimrocks. The hills look as if goats had been pastured on them for years, and the sun on alkali is like a blow across the eyes. But the air is magnificent, and the sky was never more blue.

Less than a hundred persons lived in Sheffield when Papa first saw the place. He liked this.

Uncle Nick and Aunt Docia moved their sheep across the nearly waterless expanse of divide and draw, and found cheap grazing range near Sheffield. Papa loaded the household goods and the family, and made a little better time. His first job was building a house for a ranchman more than fifty miles south of Sheffield, in a country few white men had ever seen. The family moved some of the furniture into a Mexican *jacal*—a one-room hut made of slender sotol stalks and adobe mud, with a *sacaguista* roof and no windows. *Alacranes*—the Mexican brand of scorpions—fell out of the thatch with alarming frequency. They also came out of the walls with a dry rustling whisper, poisonous stingers curled over their backs in the way proud dogs carry their tails.

Mama scalded and scrubbed and kept close watch over the children. She had never come nearer to real frontier life than she found during the months the family lived fifty miles from any store or post office and almost that far from the nearest neighbor, down near the place where Independence Creek empties its crystal-clear waters into the Pecos. The adobe house was a house in name only: Mama still cooked outside, and the wagon was used for sleeping quarters. The rocky hills closed in on the camp, and on a hot and windless day the high, insistent shrilling in the air could have come from either locusts or rattlesnakes. There was a wild Comanche savagery about the place, and when the sotol burst into full waxen bloom, Mama felt that the hills were covered with sentinel warriors in white-feathered warbonnets, their lances ready. In truth, Comanches had come this way only a few short years before, and the country was dotted with charred rock mounds where the Mescalero Apaches had once roasted the cabbagelike sotol roots, to make a type of mescal and drink it and dream their drunken dreams.

Back toward Sheffield, Uncle Nick Rogers was finding even more hardships. Before the Bosworth family returned from the isolated ranch on Independence, a rustling war flared briefly, and a man or two were "pecosed"—which is to say they were shot and then thrown into the river. Uncle Nick found it expedient to lie concealed in one of the many caves along the river canyon until the affair blew over, he being essentially a peaceful man, as befits the keeper of flocks.

Then he rode out one morning to visit one of several Mexican *pastors* in his employ, to check on provisions and see how that band of sheep was doing.

The sheep were out foraging for themselves in the marvelous manner of their kind, finding sustenance where cows would starve, making their usual bleat and blether. The herder, whose job it was to doctor wormy sheep, protect the flock from lobo wolves, coyotes, and other predators, see that they "nooned" in the middle of the day and got back to water in the evening—as well as serving as midwife and obstetrician in lambing time—the herder sat beside the smoking ashes of his breakfast campfire and whetted a long-bladed knife, a *belduque*.

This, Uncle Nick thought, was strange. He rode up and gave the camp hello. The only answer was the thin, sinister *wheep-wheep* of the blade's being sharpened to an edge suitable for cutting a man's throat.

Uncle Nick came closer. *"Buenos días!"* he called again.

The Mexican put down his knife, and, without rising, reached for a .30-.30 that was leaning against a scrub cedar. He pointed the gun at Uncle Nick.

"Dismount!" he ordered in solemn Spanish. "Do you see the spade there by the tent? Take it, and start digging your grave. I am going to kill you."

Uncle Nick was not armed. He saw the wild light in the man's eyes. He knew that loneliness and poverty and never mind what else had twisted the herder's mind, and it was too late for a doctor; the thing, now, was to try to get away. Uncle Nick whirled his horse and hit spurs to him, and leaned low over the saddlehorn to offer a target as small as was possible.

The bullet burned into his back, right side and low down. He lost consciousness, but kept his seat in the saddle. The horse brought him back to his headquarters tent, and he fell off, properly, in the front yard, where Aunt Docia and their children could see.

Papa heard about the shooting next day, and joined a group of neighboring ranchmen—some of them were men from whom Uncle Nick had hidden in the cave. The party rode out to bring in the herder so that he could be tried for aggravated assault, with intent to kill. But they never got back to Sheffield with their prisoner.

Papa never spoke about this. One of the other men said, laconically, "Saddle-colored son-of-a-bitch tried to get away!" and that was all.

Uncle Nick recovered handsomely and thrived long. Once when I passed through West Texas between Navy assignments, he greeted me in his oldest son's trucking lot. Uncle Nick was then eighty-four, and still clear-eyed and ramrod straight.

"Howdy, son!" he said, shaking hands.

"How are you, Uncle Nick?" I asked.

"Well, tolerable. Been kind of down in the back lately."

"I hope it's not rheumatism or arthritis," I said, and he made a little gesture of dismissal for all such ailments.

"Hell, no," he said mildly. "I've been helpin' Charlie load some of that three-inch windmill casin', and it's mighty heavy. Strained my back, kind of."

They don't make them like Uncle Nick, any more.

II

All at once the drums and bugles of the Spanish-American War began to be heard over the land, but they were not heard very much out west of the Pecos, where Teddy Roosevelt could have recruited some fine Rough Riders. Nobody saw a Hearst newspaper out there when that sensation of American journalism was rattling the saber; nobody came that way waving the flag. Dee was seventeen and spoiling for adventure: he likely would have signed up in a minute, if given the opportunity.

Instead of a recruiting sergeant, along came a hard-bitten man named Hamilton, who had bought a herd of cattle west of the Pecos and was going to make a considerable trail drive all the way back to Hico, in Hamilton County. He offered Dee a job.

Mama had given up Norah in marriage without a murmur. It was different, now, with her first-born; it was always different with her sons. She wept, and called Dee "honey boy," and said she didn't see why he had to go so far away. But she knew he was going.

Papa gave Dee a horse, and shook hands with him, and Dee rode off tall and proud in the saddle. He had already been working a little, around Sheffield; he was remembered there for his testimony concerning a Saturday-night shooting scrape.

"Where were you when the first shot was fired?" asked the justice of the peace.

"I was in the dance hall," Dee said.

"Did you shoot?" the judge wanted to know.

"Yes, sir. When the first shot was fired, I shot right out the door and just kept going."

"Witness excused," said the judge, rubbing his chin.

Dee was headed eastward for three hundred miles or more, with the longhorned cattle. By now, Papa was disillusioned with the Sheffield country, and Uncle Bob had already sold his ferry on the Pecos and had moved on. But Papa lingered awhile, practicing a skill new to him, but older than the Pyramids. From the Mexicans he learned how to make sun-dried adobe brick, and began putting up adobe houses in and around Sheffield. The trans-Pecos country is a land of little rain, and some of the adobes Papa constructed are still standing—the only monuments left to his memory.

Mama's ninth child, a girl she named Ninah, was born in Sheffield on October 11, 1899. Before she was a year old, an itinerant photographer came that way, carrying equipment that looked as if it might have been bought second-hand from Mathew Brady. Ninah was photographed seated on a pillow, wearing a starched white dress so long that it concealed her bare feet.

Floyd and Bert had their picture taken together. Bert was almost four, chubby, freckled, and entirely unconcerned about his lack of shoes. But Floyd, nearly six, remained constant in his grown-up character, and glared at the camera with a fierce, smoldering wrath—which, of course, was really directed at Papa. Papa should have provided shoes. All through his boyhood, Floyd was painfully conscious and ashamed of being poor.

He resented that photograph, and a week or so later he wetted the lead of an indelible pencil and defaced it by drawing a circle on the sole of Bert's foot, so that it looked remarkably like a tattoo. Some years afterward, when Mama had a crayon enlargement made of the picture, the enlarged version came back with the indelible pencil mark faithfully reproduced. This preserved what may have been Floyd's first practical joke upon a younger brother. There were to be a great many more. . . .

Little Ninah died in January of 1901, in Sheffield, and hers was another grave Mama never saw again.

Perhaps Papa grieved much more than anyone knew, when there was a death in the family. He had fled from Pearsall when Lily May died, and now he could no longer bear living in Sheffield. The wagon was swung across the Pecos on the aerial ferry; the horses swam the salty stream. Papa hitched up on the eastern shore, and backtracked to San Angelo.

He didn't go into the town itself, hating towns as he did, but pitched his tent some nine miles west, just off the stage road to Sherwood and squarely between those curiously-formed buttes known on the early topographical maps as the Teats of Venus and the Breasts of Cleopatra.

This was the McGill ranch, and Papa did some work for Mr. McGill, who ran cattle. Dee was still far away, in Hamilton County; Norah was down beyond Eldorado, not far away at all, but too far for Mama to be on hand for the birth of her first grandchild.

Papa stayed at the Twin Mountains about a year. Along toward the end of the following October, a whirlwind almost big enough to be classified as a cyclone came twisting between the two mammiferous peaks, shaking the tent, lifting its dust spiral a mile into the sky, and carrying tin cans and pieces of paper that glinted high in the sunshine. Jay and Ivanhoe watched this out of sight with a vast excitement, and concluded that it was what was left of the notorious Galveston Hurricane, which had killed nearly eight thousand people on the coastal island a year before. Texas was mighty big; it took a long time for a high wind to cross it.

Mama's last child was born in the wake of that high and dusty wind, and if there were other signs and portents in the heavens, they went unrecorded. All Mama wrote in the family Bible, at the end of a long list of names, was "Allie Rucker, born October 29, 1901."

She was finally honoring the memory of her father, the mysterious Thomas Rucker, he of the romantic pride. From that day forward, consciously or not, the dream of a college education for her children began to be concentrated on her youngest son, the namesake of a Greek and Latin scholar and a professor of botany.

There were several things wrong with Mama's dream. Her boys were poor, they were self-willed, and they were also Papa's children.

For no evident reason beyond his eternal restlessness, Papa turned westward to Sheffield and the Pecos again when summer came. It was a hot summer, and dry; Mama, nursing me on the wagon seat, suffered painful sunburn of one breast. Perhaps the place of my birth had made me stubbornly discriminating: I would have nourishment only at the left breast, and completely refused the right one. This amused Papa a great deal. At least I did not lie studying and disliking him, as

Floyd had done. Floyd was still demonstrating that he had never needed Papa. When a ranch house where we were camped one day caught fire from the flue of the cookstove, Floyd manfully carried water from the tank, placed a ladder against the eaves, and put out the blaze while the grownups were hurrying in from a mile away.

"Place would've burned up before *you* got here!" he told Papa scornfully.

There was no work in Sheffield, and Mama did not even have time to visit Ninah's grave. Papa had embarked upon one of his longer journeys. He followed the winding valley of the Pecos northwestward, where the country was wild and the towns were few. The wagon came quite suddenly, one day, to a sign that marked the State line.

Beyond was New Mexico Territory. The country over there looked just the same. Rocks and cactus, mesquite and scrub cedar, and the slanting afternoon sun making a dazzle of limestone and alkali.

The boundary was purely political. A barbed-wire fence would have been a more definite line 'of demarcation. But the country over there wasn't the same, of course. It wasn't Texas, and Mama sat bolt upright on the wagon seat.

"Woodie!" she exclaimed. "You're not fixing to leave Texas, are you?"

Papa cleared his throat in the manner of a man deliberating a grave decision. "Why not?" he asked, finally.

"I just don't think we ought to get clear out of Texas. Dee's back there. And Norah. It's just too far away."

She could find no words for a my-own-my-native-land speech, but the thought of leaving Texas stirred strong emotions in her breast. The people of Mama's generation were Texans first, Southerners next, and citizens of the Union after that. When she said "Texas," she wasn't thinking about the harsh country of the Pecos, or the *brasada* in Frio County, and not about the windy Lipan Flats. She was remembering that all her children were Texas born; she recalled the moss-hung liveoaks and grass-green prairies and the happy childhood of Sweet Home.

Papa saw her nose turning red—and knew she was going to cry.

"Well, we sure as hell can't camp here!" he said testily. "And it's too far back to water. And besides, I haven't seen any jobs growing on the mesquites along this road!" Then, having come this far, he remembered the time when he had felt a bit ridiculous—the time when he drove all the long way to the Red River and didn't wet his wheels. That decided him. "Get up!" he barked at the horses.

III

The summer of 1902 found us camped near Carlsbad. Jay was sixteen, Ivanhoe was nearly fifteen, and Maude was twelve. Floyd was more like a man than ever, at eight, Bert was approaching six, and I was nearing my first birthday. The other children played around the rim of a gash in the sun-baked earth that was called Bat Cave, because at dusk millions of bats poured out of it like a column of smoke, and at daybreak were sucked back into it again as if into a vacuum sweeper.

"It just shows you!" Floyd said caustically, after he had really grown up. "I'll bet you Papa could have bought a couple of sections of that land for two bits an acre. And today you and I would own Carlsbad Caverns. Man alive!"

Then we pushed on to Roswell, and beyond, and looked back on a colorful chapter of the Old West instead of forward to the days of automobiles, motels, and tourists dropping their dollars in "Bat Cave." We were in Lincoln County. Although Billy the Kid had been dead just over twenty years, Sheriff Pat Garrett was still alive, and so were the memories—and some of the hatreds—of the notorious Lincoln County War. Papa steered shy of any argument on the subject. He had been through all of this in another time and another place, with the Sutton-Taylor feud.

The winds blew cold that winter. Snow-clad Carrizo Peak, and the even higher Sierra Blanca lifted proudly on the horizon, dwarfing man and all his works. Papa did moderately well, which is to say he was barely getting by. With summer, he began a variation on a familiar theme. Arizona Territory! They said it was all new country, out there, rich in silver and copper, and maybe gold.

"Just opening up," he told Mama.

Mama's rebellious reaction was unexpected; it was violent and immediate. In her own words, she "just put my foot down." She was not going to have half of Texas and all of New Mexico Territory between her and Dee and Norah. She said bless Patty, she would simply not stand for the family's being separated like that.

This caught Papa between a rock and a hard place. He sulled, and would not talk. He sat on his box in the shade of the wagon and wore his hat brim down over his eyes, and no longer looked for work.

Mama reminded him that the children were still not going to school. Bert was old enough to start, Floyd had missed a year, Maude and Ivanhoe belonged at their books right now, and Jay had never had a full year of study in his life. Besides, the schools in the thinly settled Territory were even fewer and farther apart than they had been in Texas.

No answer. Might as well try talking to a fence post.

"I'll just swanee!" Mama said, exasperated. "Well, you just put this in your pipe and smoke it: I am not going to Arizona!"

Silence.

Something happened at suppertime, in the camp, in the firelight by the wagon, under the star-heavy sky. Nobody remembered what started it, but Papa had a sudden burst of temper, and threw a plate full of thickening gravy into Jay's face.

Jay was nearly six feet tall, and strong as a young mule. He could have taken Papa apart, but he controlled his anger and only sat there, white-faced and trembling. It was Mama who reacted.

"That settles it, Woodie!" she said quietly. "Get out! Go on to Arizona! Look for new country—keep looking for new country until you die! But there'll be no use to come back, because we won't be here. I'm leaving you."

Papa suffered in silence. His head was lower. More of his face was in shadow.

"You don't think I'll leave? You just go, and see!"

Papa grunted his disbelief and got up, loosening his collar as if it were strangling him. He stalked into the darkness and looked after

[193]

the horses. Horses—even when they were beaten on occasion—understood a man.

Jay drew a long breath, and began wiping the gravy from his face and his shirt front. I was too young to know what this was about, or to remember it, but Bert and the girls were crying. Only Floyd was unshaken.

"Are we sure-enough going back to Texas?" he asked eagerly. "Are we, Mama? Man alive!"

With morning, Papa saddled and rode to scout somewhere—perhaps across the Arizona line, maybe not that far. He had been forced into doing this. Mama had called his hand, and if he was going to wear the pants in the family he had to go. Mama would still be here, all right enough, when he came back; she wasn't the kind to kick over the traces. And a man by God had the right to go where he wanted to go, because it was a free country.

Oh, she'd be sorry that she ever argued with him, one day . . . someday, when he found the right country, when he made his pile. . . .

Papa rode out of camp with a ramrod stuck up his spine, and didn't look back. The sun was already an hour high over that land of magnificent distances; the light was deceptively clear. Carrizo Peak looked so near you could walk there and back before breakfast, but it was fifty miles away.

In a cruel light like that, Mama could see Papa for hours, still going away. Nothing else moved along the whole saucer of the world. The sun climbed higher, and Papa was still going.

He went until he and his horse were but a microscopic speck, crawling toward the world's rim, and then the heat waves rose and shimmered and made mirages, and Papa was gone.

Mama opened her trunk, and took out the last letter Dee had sent her, with a postal money order for forty dollars. She began wrapping her looking glass.

Jay and Floyd took down the tent.

Sixteen

*T*he decision Mama made in New Mexico, in that long-ago summer of 1903, took a desperate sort of courage. No man would have understood it. It was a quiet and sorrowful thing, without temper and without heroics. The Rough Riders who had stormed San Juan Hill not long before were reckless and had pride of outfit and country, and courage and the fear of showing fear spread contagiously among groups of fighting men. Mama was alone and desperate, but not reckless; her bravery was purely feminine and feline. She had finally and reluctantly acknowledged that Papa's way of life imperiled her young, and her claws were out.

It had been twenty-four years since Papa lifted her to the seat of the first Studebaker wagon, on the rosy morning of their elopement. She was thirty-nine years old, lean and spare, but not gaunt like so many Western women of her time; she still had that rawhide strength and suppleness in her body, and sunbonnets had preserved her soft, clear complexion. Mama always kept her vanity, and cared how she looked. She dressed simply, but as well as she could, remembered that a lady always wore gloves—even though they were cheap ones, made of cotton—and kept her hair brushed and neatly done up with tortoise-shell back and side combs. There were a few streaks of gray in the once rich auburn of her hair now, and years of reading and sewing by campfire and lantern light and coal oil lamps had taken their toll—she was beginning to need reading glasses.

She had eight children living, with only Norah married, and only Dee gainfully employed. Dee's pay, back in Hamilton County, was average for ranch hands at the time. He earned twenty dollars a month, and grub.

The wagon rolled southward, near the winding valley of the Pecos. During the first few days of the journey, Mama lapsed into occasional sad and thoughtful reveries.

"You don't need to worry, Mama," Jay told her with the confidence of his seventeen years. "I'll get me a job of work."

"Me too," Floyd declared. "We'll take care of you, Mama."

Mama's nose was red, but she smiled, and as the days passed she smiled more, and sat straight on the wagon seat. For the first time, she was wagon boss and camp boss, too. She could pick her own course.

There was nothing she didn't know about handling a team of horses, or picking a place to make camps. But Jay had learned those things too, and Mama—who loved being dependent upon a man—soon yielded the helm.

"Here, Jay boy," she said. "You take the reins for a while. You pick a good spot to make camps."

It was the first time, too, that Mama could ride the wagon in reasonable comfort and enjoy the scenery, neither pregnant nor holding a suckling babe on her lap. I was nearly two years old, and quite able to get about the wagon. I came under the fun-loving eye of Floyd. For some strange reason, he called me "Bit-fit."

"We're comin' to a hill, Bit-fit! Here, grab hold the sideboard like this, and push! You got to help the horses pull this hill, Bit-fit. Push hard. Grunt!"

I pushed and grunted manfully. Floyd rocked with laughter.

"Floyd!" Mama called without looking back. "Stop teasing that child!"

He stopped—for a while. But Floyd had taken an especial interest in my education, and even more in my physical development; he was soon to make this a regular campaign to which he devoted a great deal of time and effort.

On hot days, we pinned up the tarp so that a breeze would blow through the sides. We played games, riding on the upholstery of the featherbeds and quilts, and wondered what tonight's camping place would be like. The wagon made its music, and everyone had his dreams. . . .

"I can get myself a job of work," Jay reiterated.

"Of course you could, honey boy. But I wish you'd go back to school when we get settled. For a little while."

"Oh, Mama, I don't want to do that! I'm too big. I'd have to be in a class with a bunch of little bitty snot-nosed kids!"

"Jay, don't use that awful word!"

All of Mama's children either wanted to go to work or get married. All of them chafed under the loving parental yoke for the same reason. It was time, they said, that they went out and made some money, and took care of Mama, for a change. It was time that she took it easy.

Mama never took it easy in all her long life, beyond enjoying an hour or two in her rocking chair, with a few dips of snuff. Snuff was her only vice, and she never practiced it in public.

Both Jay and Floyd went through periods, in their latter teens, of calling Mama "Old Lady," and pleasing her immensely and scaring her half to death at the same moment. Each would come in, filled with high young animal spirit, seize her suddenly, waltz her around the room a few times to the accompaniment of her shrieks and giggles, then lift her high and toss her on the nearest bed.

"You just stick with me, Old Lady, and you'll be wearing silks and laces!" Jay would say. "Because I'm going to get rich. I'm going to rob the Southern Pacific!"

(Floyd went through the same exuberant period. He was Papa's child: he was going to make his fortune all at once. Floyd, however,

[197]

had made a few slight modifications on Jay's plan. *He* was going to hold up the Santa Fe. As it turned out, *I* was the only one who ever robbed either railroad, and Floyd had a large hand in that.)

But now, rolling down from New Mexico Territory, with Papa gone and maybe gone forever, it was Jay who was the real "honey boy" of Mama's heart. She didn't want him to take a job of any kind, but she was especially anxious that he not punch cattle or herd sheep. Jay had an inborn mechanical ability. At fourteen, in Tom Green County, he had climbed a windmill tower and put the mill in working order after several adults were unable to fix it. At fifteen, he had built a miniature windmill. The tower was about four feet high, and when you stood it over a bucket of water, it actually pumped the bucket dry, because Jay had whittled a tiny wooden pump, too.

"Jay was just born with wheels in his head!" Mama used to say. "I declare, he ought to have been an engineer, or an inventor."

At the moment, the wagon wheels were turning, as the Studebaker came down from New Mexico and made twenty or thirty miles on good days. The signs marking the State line loomed ahead, and this called for ceremony and celebration. This was repatriation, and homecoming, and penitence. Jay stopped the team, and everybody got out of the wagon.

Jay picked up a small sotol stalk, and scratched a mark across the white alkali dust of the road. Mama and the six children toed it— Ivanhoe and Maude in pigtails, Bert and Floyd in short pants. I was wearing the disgracefully long dress that served as rompers for the two-year-old of the time. But I could run.

Jay looked down the line and began to chant:

> *"One for the money,*
> *And two for the show;*
> *Three to get ready,*
> *And four to go!"*

The race was on to see who was first back in Texas. Jay won hands down and laughing, but everybody was laughing. That evening, camped by a waterhole, Jay constructed a whole system of irrigation dams in miniature, and showed the rest of us how to move a little earth and open the gates to let life-giving water run down the rows of plants. Somehow, although he had never been around a real farm, he managed to impart something of the drama of irrigation to the younger children. They would remember it many years later, when the dams came to the Pecos country, and his little show was enacted full scale.

That was a happy evening, with Mama smiling all the time. The horses were fed and hobbled; the shadows stretched, and firelight gleamed on the wagon tarp, and a little wind brought coolness. There was a good supper, and everybody was ready for bed under the stars. And nobody mentioned Papa, at all.

II

Mama could have saved herself quite a few miles if there had been any way to get across the Pecos. She was west of the river, and knew of only one crossing. So she backtracked, and came finally to Sheffield, and to the aerial ferry Uncle Bob Bosworth had designed and operated.

Never argue with me about Fate, Destiny, and what the Orientals call *karma*. Some things are down in the Books, and are going to happen. This ferry had lifted untold numbers of wagons, hacks and buckboards across the Pecos, without mishap. There had been no recent rains to soften the earth. But when the Bosworth wagon came along, not at all overladen with this world's goods, that something happened.

A dead man pulled up. (A dead man is one of those anchor posts you see in the ground, holding guy wires for a telephone or power pole.) This dead man was suddenly uprooted, or exhumed. The cable slackened. Mama's Studebaker wagon fell with a splash into twelve feet or more of alkaline Pecos water.

Several cowboys were on the banks of the stream. It was late afternoon, and their work was done; they were watching the operation in the same mournful, interested way they would have ridden for miles to watch a railroad train come through some small whistle-stop station. Such things made their day: they were a small glimpse of the world.

The cowboys yelled, and shucked off their boots, and those of them who could swim dived into the Pecos with creditable gallantry and had themselves a hell of a time. It was more exciting than getting drunk and shooting up a dance hall. They managed to save some of Mama's things, and Jay was in the river with them, diving to the sunken wagon and bringing up items that were going adrift in the current. They got ropes out, and tied them to the wagon, and used a lot of horsepower to snake the sodden Studebaker to the eastern shore. On high ground again, it shed copious amounts of the Pecos, and Mama wept.

The books that had belonged to Thomas Rucker were ruined. The featherbeds and quilts were a mess. Food supplies suffered: the sack of flour in the chuckbox was soaked, but not all the way through. The outsides of the sack formed a wet, crusting, hardening dough, but there was an inner core of flour Mama could use to make her hot biscuits two or three times a day.

Her looking glass was mottled around the edges, and needed a resilvering job. She never had this done. It would have meant being without the mirror for some time.

Mama camped near the mouth of Liveoak Creek for two weeks, while things dried out. She hung up the featherbeds and quilts. It was still summer, and the family slept for several nights on nothing but dry ground.

This was on the Old Spanish Trail, and hard by Old Fort Lancaster, of Indian days. Uncle Nick and Aunt Docia had a sheep camp there later, and told of marks on a liveoak tree, and of a freshly-dug hole—"big enough to bury a horse in"—and the marks of a rusty iron pot in the bottom of the hole. Somebody had dug up a Spanish treasure. Somebody was always digging them up, before anybody actually found them.

It was Floyd who was dissatisfied, and critical, during that two weeks. He said, well, Uncle Bob was Papa's brother, wasn't he? He said, what can you expect from a ferry built by Uncle Bob?

"Hush!" Mama said out of her sea of troubles. "Don't talk like that, Floyd boy! It just happened."

Nothing dismayed Jay or Floyd for long. They improved the enforced delay by setting trotlines in the Pecos, and catching catfish of considerable size; they explored the old fort, which had been abandoned when Texas seceded from the Union, and was never manned again. And finally the team was hitched and the wagon rolled again, down Howard's Draw and into Val Verde County for a visit with Norah.

But Mama's return would not be complete until she had been reunited with Dee, and we had to drive deep into the heart of Texas to do that. The last, northeastward leg of our homecoming was about three hundred miles, and memories assailed Mama at every turning. Twin Mountains . . . Lipan Flats . . . San Angelo . . . Coleman County . . . Brownwood . . . Comanche . . .

"Yonder's where you were born, Allie. Jay, do you remember when we were first living here, and you asked me where babies came from? I told you we found them in the bushes, and next morning you were out in that mesquite flat, just looking everywhere for babies!"

And then, "It was somewhere along here that your Papa let the other fellers skin that beef for him, then got so mad at the barbed wire." Or, "See that house over yonder? If I'm not mistaken, that was one of the first houses your Papa built, not long after Dee was born. I don't remember the front gallery, though—I reckon that's been added since then."

And, "Maude, this is pretty close to the place where your Aunt Frances and Uncle George lived, and you just scared me half to death that time when you got the grassbur in your throat. And I remember when the older young'uns came running in the house and hollering for your Papa and me to come look—there was a balloon going up at a fair in Dublin, and we could see it just as plain!"

[201]

(He was *your* Papa" now, and would always be that, in the family. To outsiders, he was never "my husband," and not even "my former husband," but simply "Mr. Bosworth." "Mr. Bosworth and I were parted, up in New Mexico," Mama would say, giving no details. For a long time, however, her nose would redden when she spoke of that parting.)

Hico is in the extreme northwestern angle of Hamilton County, almost on the Erath County line. We found Dee near there, and he found a rather large and rambling house for us to live in, on the ranch where he was working. Claudia Ivanhoe, following the pattern of at least three generations, was married before she was sixteen. Her husband was a soft-voiced young school teacher in Stephenville, named Will Jones. He was, in fact, the younger son of Uncle George and Aunt Fanny Jones—and our first cousin. Never mind that: it was a love match, they reared three perfectly formed and rather highly talented children, and were extremely happy . . .

III

I have vague memories of that ranch in Hamilton County, and perfectly sharp ones of small things that occurred there. We had a mother cat with six kittens, and one day Floyd and Bert and I overturned an old abandoned horse trough near the barn, and an equal number of woodrats ran out. The cat tried to catch them all, and only partly succeeded. Jay was talking about getting a job, and I envisioned a job as something tangible, with shape and color, and told Mama that I was going to get a little red job, and then a little blue job. She was amused at this, but not at what she overheard me saying in the back of the wagon as we returned from a trip to Hico. I was pointing to each crooked fencepost and saying, "That's the devil of a post . . . there's another devil of a post!"

"Allie!" Mama exclaimed. "You mustn't say that word, honey boy. It's a bad word!"

To Mama, the devil was always "the Bad Man," and the place we would go if we sinned was "the Bad Place."

We lived on the ranch for the biggest part of a happy year, and

then the ranchman for whom Dee worked had to move his cattle to
—of all places—the Lipan Flats. Dee went along with him, jobs being
what they were—and Mama, torn at this new separation, moved the
rest of us over the line into Erath County, and rented a house in
Stephenville. Ivanhoe was there, and Jay had found a job there as
night engineer in a plant that produced cottonseed oil.

Our house was hard by the Frisco railroad tracks, and Floyd and
Bert and I were determined to be railroad engineers. Floyd and Bert
and Maude were now in school steadily, but Maude would be fifteen
that fall, and was already talking about getting married.

Floyd and Bert brought their schoolbooks home. I learned the
alphabet from a calendar that was on the wall by the oilcloth-covered
table where we ate. It advertised a vegetable oil called Cottolene,
showed a pretty girl, and used all the letters of the alphabet except
"Q" and "Z." Observing that I knew the ABC's, Floyd borrowed
Bert's school reader, and then graduated me to his own. The first
story I remember reading for myself, at the age of three, was about
Dick Whittington's going to London with his cat, and becoming
eminently successful there. With this as a beginning, it was easy to
move on to other success stories, found in the works of Horatio
Alger, Jr.

Life was very exciting that fall when I was three. The world of
letters opened. I learned to identify every train and every engineer on
the Frisco line by the locomotive's whistle. I shocked Mama again,
and mystified my older brothers, by announcing certain rather inti-
mate information pertaining to Rose McAllister—a neighbor girl of
about Jay's age, to whom he was paying court. I do not remember
how I came by this intelligence, but at the supper table, I said:

"Rose McAllister would sure be a good Indian fighter. She's got a
mighty big nabel!"

(It was common knowledge among the boys in our family—and
to most Texans of the period—that all really *good* Indian fighters had
big navels. I feel sure that Bigfoot Wallace had one.)

Mama was horrified. Maude blushed at my indelicacy. Jay choked
on his soup, and Floyd looked at me admiringly, and said, "Well, I'll

just say! Man alive!" But nobody pursued the subject, and all I remember now is that Rose McAllister was a very pretty girl.

That fall, Mama and I went by train to San Angelo, and spent six weeks in the cow camps with Dee, living most of the time in his wagon. There was a bunkhouse at the ranch headquarters, peopled by some of the last old-time cowboys: a man named Sandy, a laughing adventurer known as Missouri, and riders called Curly and Pecos. I earned my first money by manfully struggling to pull off their boots in the bunkhouse after dark, when the work was all done. They gave me nickels and dimes, which I proudly kept in a Bull Durham sack.

We camped out on the Flats when the northers were beginning to shriek around the wagon. There were splendid sunsets, and I looked across the level land to see the clouds touched with pink and gold, and felt certain that London—where Dick Whittington took his fabulous cat—lay somewhere not too far beyond. And I suffered terribly from leg ache. It may have been "growing pains," it may have been rheumatic fever. The *cocinero,* an ancient Mexican with a wrinkled and leathery face and an angelic white-toothed smile, would not allow me to cry. He sat across the campfire, and at my first whimper would smile and begin to shake his gray head slowly.

"No, señor, señor!" he chanted softly. *"No, señor, señor—no, señor, señor!"*

Watching him, listening to the drowsy monotone of his musical voice, I was ashamed to cry and soon fell asleep on Mama's lap.

When we returned to Stephenville, Floyd and Bert had been to see their first circus, and were full of exciting stories. They had been particularly impressed by a tight-wire performer who not only did acrobatics on the wire, but built some sort of fire there, and cooked and ate a chicken while keeping his precarious balance. That impressed me, too, because I had observed a large number of campfires. How could anybody build a fire on a wire?

My Bull Durham sack contained a dollar and ten cents. Mama let me buy a huge "glassy" marble with the dime—it was bigger than a golf ball, and looked as if it had peppermint candy on the inside. She used the dollar to buy Dime Brand condensed milk for me to eat spread on biscuit halves.

That spring, I had a month-long siege of typhoid fever combined with double pneumonia. Uncle George, who lived too far out of town, was not called in. Mama had two other doctors.

No food, they told her. No liquids. My temperature was running 105 degrees and higher; it remained for long periods at 104.

The third week, the doctors consulted, shook their heads gravely, and told Mama I could not live.

It may have been because I remembered the high-wire story Floyd and Bert had told, but I do not think it was all that. I think I have known, since the age of three and a half, what it is like to die. Dying is simply turning loose all holds. Dying is losing your balance and falling.

During that third week of delirium, I was on the high wire, walking it endlessly across a crimson gulf, and I knew that if I fell I would die.

Mama said, bless Patty, if I were going to die she would give me the water I begged for; she would squeeze me orange juice, and let me chew broiled beefsteak so long as I promised faithfully to swallow only the juice. Mama ran her finger around the inside of my mouth to see that I kept that promise. She also gave me quarts of drinking water.

Then I happily confounded two of the leading medical men of Erath County by promptly getting well. In another week I was up, rolling the big glassy marble around the house, and suffering severe headaches from weakness. These went away.

That was sickness enough. I had influenza in 1918, and ate beans. In more than thirty years of a health record in the Navy, I had not a single sick day.

But the Stephenville doctors took my pulse, examined my chest, and still shook their heads. They told Mama I would have to be taken back to West Texas, to a higher altitude and a drier climate.

Everybody knew the old, familiar excitement. We were going to move again as soon as I was well enough to stand a wagon trip. Everybody but Maude, who had other excitement. She was getting married to a young railroad man named Will Lancaster.

Seventeen

Jay, who was still the night engineer at the cottonseed oil plant, slept daytimes in the barn, where my marble-rolling and other childish play would not awaken him. Before we left Stephenville, two incidents occurred concerning Jay and his job, and I still wonder about them.

He left the barn one afternoon rather early, and came to the house.

"You haven't had enough sleep, honey boy," Mama told him. "Why did you get up so early?"

"I had a dream," Jay said. "Dreamed that the boiler busted, and the boss came to get me to help fix it."

"Pshaw!" Mama said. "You should have got your sleep out."

We had no telephone. The cottonseed oil plant was across town. But while Jay was having a cup of coffee, buggy wheels were heard outside, and it was the boss.

"Boiler blowed up!" he told Jay. "Busted. We need everybody to help put the plant back in runnin' shape."

About two weeks later the foreman at the plant discharged a day-time employee for reasons considered good and sufficient. The man, having no recourse to unions, walked off the job muttering threats of vengeance. And Jay dreamed, that afternoon in the barn. . . .

He had just started up the engine, he said, and as soon as it reached full power, the belt suddenly broke, and the flywheel, normally controlled by the two heavy revolving metal balls of the "governor," began to race madly. It was a long belt, and in his dream Jay was at the far end, near the governor. The big flywheel flew apart, and two huge chunks of metal were hurled through the wall of the plant— one on either side of Jay's head.

"Don't you go to work, honey boy!" Mama begged. "Remember that other dream, about the boiler? You just stay home."

Jay laughed. "Shucks, Mama! It was just a dream."

But he promised her one thing. He would look at the belt very carefully, and make sure nothing had been done to it during the period between the day and night shift.

He looked, all right, but he did not look on the under side of the belt, and an examination later showed that it had been cut nearly through on the under side. He started up the engine, and watched it gain speed under a full head of steam.

The belt parted with a great slapping and winding. The engine raced, and the steel balls of the governor slowed and dropped and were still. Before Jay could get to the boiler to shut off the steam, the flywheel disintegrated.

Two heavy sections of it hurtled through the air and tore holes in the wall of the plant. Both went past his head.

I have been meaning, for years, to report this to Duke University, where such incidents are collected and studied. Let us consider this the report.

We hitched up the horses, and the wagon wheels rolled, and I will always be thankful for that one journey made in a time when I could understand and savor and remember its every mile and moment. It gave me a sense of sharing and belonging, a feeling of comradeship with my brothers that was very important to me. We had been reduced, as a family: Mama and Jay on the wagon seat, Floyd and Bert and I in the back. And in that reduction we felt closer to one another.

Floyd said, man alive, that this was just like old times again, and I understood that we had returned, even if briefly, to the full life, joyous and carefree and not fenced in by the walls of a house or the paling fence of a limiting yard. We bought a fifteen-cent watermelon that was so long it could not be placed in the wagon seat, and kept it for suppertime. Floyd and Bert began planning a big fight with chunks of watermelon rind, but Mama put her foot down. She said, "There won't be anything of the kind! It would get your clothes dirty, and I don't intend to wash until we get where Dee boy is!"

Floyd told me this was the way Papa used to travel, only Papa did it just all the time, and hated to make camps. Mama told Floyd to hush.

Jay was driving. It had rained unseasonally, and the roads were bad; we made thirteen miles that first day, and camped at a country schoolhouse near Dublin. It was deserted for the summer holiday, and the doors were unlocked and dirt daubers had built their dried mud nests in all the corners. The bedding was put down between rows of knife-scarred desks. Clouds were making up for a thunderstorm, and we were no sooner under a roof than the rain came heavily.

"It was a good thing you found this camp, Jay boy." Mama said. "That old wagon tarp leaks pretty bad."

She fixed supper under difficulties, and we had the watermelon. Floyd said, "Now, you want to look out, Bit-fit. Don't you wet the bed. You want to remember two things: eating watermelon, or playing with the fire—they'll make you wet the bed every time, if you ain't careful!"

My brother Floyd had begun his dedicated career of educating, indoctrinating, and instructing me, to the end that I might grow up to be a man. I was careful, that night, and Mama and I slept dry. But with morning came difficulties.

The wagon wheels had sunk deep in the schoolyard. Jay hitched the team, and talked to the horses, and applied the lash. The wagon remained immobile.

He finally concluded that the load had to be lightened. We left a number of household possessions in that country schoolhouse, including a chest of tools dear to Jay's heart. We abandoned an "invention" of his—a gallon glass pickle jar to which he had affixed clock wheels and a crank to make a milk churn.

Somebody found it. Rotary milk churns began appearing on the market a year or two later. It was probably a coincidence, but Mama always thought that Jay boy had been robbed of his patent rights.

II

That was an unusually wet year for West Texas. Rain was with us all the way to San Angelo, holding back the horses, stretching the journey to nearly three weeks. And then, when we got down near flood-famous Ben Ficklin Stage Station, history came near to repeating itself. Mama and I awoke before dawn one morning, with the wagon bed awash and pillows and featherbeds going adrift. She got me out of the wagon quickly, and from higher ground we watched flood waters swirl over the Studebaker.

"Well," Mama conceded, "I reckon we made a mistake. Your Papa would never have been caught like that—on low ground."

The flash flood subsided after an hour. Jay caught the horses and got the wagon back on the rain-rutted road. Nobody blamed him, and nobody remembered that Papa would have never been caught like that. As a matter of fact, the same thing could have happened to Papa very easily: Jay had made camps after dark, when he could not see the conformation of the draw. Besides, nobody could ever predict what flash floods might do, in West Texas. Couples used to get caught between draws in the horse-and-buggy days, and couldn't get home until morning, and wonderful things happened . . .

I suffered tragic loss in that flood, but didn't know about it until weeks later, when I demanded to know what had happened to my drum. The drum, a Christmas present, had been slung in the cooney underneath the wagon. Maybe it was covered with genuine calfskin. It busted, and Mama may have been secretly relieved.

The Studebaker wagon halted on the Crawford ranch, five miles

[210]

from the village of Christoval, on the South Fork of the Concho River. We had a five-room house there, and more than half a century later I have not found a place so nearly ideal. The house was under spreading liveoaks, and a trail ran through the liveoaks and hackberry trees to the river, perhaps a half mile away. When Floyd and Bert and I went to the river, armed with a .20-gauge shotgun, and a .22 rifle and fishing poles, we always came back with a hunter's fry for supper: a cottontail rabbit, a squirrel, a brace of quail, and several perch or bass. We had our own reloading outfit for the .20-gauge shotgun, and could put in more or less powder, as we chose.

There was a big argument with redheaded Homer Crawford, who was a year or two older than Floyd, as to ballistics. Homer swore that birdshot, in a .20-gauge, would kill nothing beyond forty yards.

A test was arranged. Floyd and Homer Crawford checked the impact of birdshot at forty yards in a very personal manner: each bent over, carefully shielded his eyes, and allowed the other to fire a blast at the seat of his corduroy britches.

I may be in error about the distance, and I know that nothing was ever settled about the advisability of using choke or scatter, in this case. I remember only that both Homer and Floyd leaped high into the air, clutched their behinds, and could not sit down in comfort for a few days. But they had contributed to their own knowledge, and that of the scientists.

Life at Christoval was a small boy's idyll. We caught seven possums in one trap—a mother, with six babies in her marsupial pouch, and none harmed. We brought them to the house, and they played with a puppy and a family of kittens for a few days, and then went back to the wild.

We caught a large soft-shell turtle on the river bank, and cooked it and had a feast. It was true what they said about turtles: you could taste all the different kinds of meat. Beef, venison, pork, fish, chicken —anything, because the turtle had them all. Besides, there was a cache of soft-shelled eggs, perhaps two or three dozen, in the sand. We scrambled them.

Floyd threw me bodily into the river that day. It was his firm belief that swimming came naturally to horses, cattle, dogs, and cats; he saw no reason why humans should be excluded.

I did not swim. I sank.

"I'll just say, Bit-fit!" Floyd exclaimed. "You've *got* to swim!"

He threw me into the river again . . . and again. . . .

I would have learned, of course. But there was a little too much pressure on the business of learning, and West Texas was too dry. Just when I was about to master the natatory art, we had word from Dee.

It was a brief but very exciting letter, and it made Mama's nose turn red, and she cried.

Dee had bought a house in the town of Ozona. He had paid two hundred dollars for a house and lot.

This would be the first house Mama had ever had, all her own. Never mind what kind of house it was. Never mind if the roof leaked and there were broken window panes, and warped planks where the floor had gotten wet. Nobody asked if the house had water piped into it, or anything like that. It was going to be Mama's very own house, and she had dreamed wistfully about it for many years.

"Don't cry, Mama!" I begged, and repeated what I had heard Jay and Floyd say. "Don't cry—we'll take care of you!"

Floyd got me by the arm and took me out on the gallery, because what I said was making Mama cry all the more. He said, "You hush, Bit-fit! She's crying because she's glad."

"You don't cry if you're glad," I argued. "Just when you get hurt, or you're sorry."

"Girls and women do," Floyd said out of the wisdom of his twelve years. With Floyd, twelve years was a mature age indeed. He said, "Girls and women are mighty funny. You just leave Mama alone—she'll be all right."

III

Jay rode over to Ozona horseback, and scouted the place, because Dee was out on a ranch a long way from town. And because a long trip in the saddle appealed to Jay. He was just turning twenty, and he had two photographs taken around this time which reveal his secret desires. There was not much opportunity for him to exercise or increase his mechanical skill around the Crawford ranch, or around Christoval: the only machines in those parts were windmills, and Jay could put a windmill engine together blindfolded. One of the photographs showed him with a guitar suspended from his shoulder by a wide ribbon, and gave him a sort of troubadour look—but the guitar was a studio prop. The more revealing picture was a full-length shot done in profile: Jay was shown standing by the bank of a stream, which I naturally took to be the South Concho, but later was inclined, reluctantly, to believe was a river painted on a backdrop. He was wearing a .45 Colt's revolver, prominently displayed and was on the *qui vive,* ready to draw and shoot.

Jay gave Mama this picture, and wrote at the bottom, "The u.s. Detective." His Stetson had just the right tilt. He was six feet tall, curly-haired, blue-eyed and handsome, and all of us were very proud of him. For a long time, I thought he really was a u.s. Detective.

He came back from Ozona, and loaded Mama's things into the aging Studebaker wagon. It was an occasion that called for some sort of retirement ceremony, such as awarding the Studebaker a plaque, or a gold watch for meritorious service, because this was to be the last trip the wagon ever made with the family aboard—except for a few forty-mile expeditions to visit Uncle Nick and Aunt Docia, on the Pecos. Mama now owned a house, and would not be going anywhere.

Jay hitched the team. The team had changed, while we were on the Crawford ranch. It now consisted of two small but powerful Spanish mules, one sorrel, the other brown. They could pull twice the load of any two horses in all West Texas; they were fat and glossy and sassy, and loved to go in a spanking trot.

The wagon rolled out on the road to Eldorado. We had about eighty miles to travel. It was early September, and the roads would be good unless the Texas ranchmen got their prayed-for September rain earlier than anybody expected. Eighty miles meant three or four camps under the stars, with mesquite smoke blowing into Mama's face to prove that she was still the prettiest of the company, and the hunger-sharpening smell of meat frying; it meant bedding down under the whole wide sky, and waking to feel good and find your hair damp with dew, and hear the yellow-breasted field larks rejoicing at another sunrise.

The slope-fronted chuckbox was gone from the end gate, because Jay had been using the wagon occasionally, on the Crawford ranch, to haul wood for Mama's cookstove. He bolted the chuckbox on the side of the wagon for this trip, and we all decided this was an improvement. More breeze came through the puckered openings of the wagon tarp, and Floyd and Bert and I could sit in the rear of the wagon and watch the brown-rutted road roll out from under our wheels.

We went southward to Eldorado—Mama said nothing, but Papa's ghost must have been on the wagon seat there—and then turned westward, to roll over the wide divides and down the limestone ledges to mesquite flats and white-brush draws. For some reason, Mama had me wearing a tan linen Buster Brown suit, complete with the sailor-type flathat which that early day funny-paper character wore. I had shoulder-length red curls to complete the resemblance to Buster Brown; I needed only more freckles, and a bulldog named Tige.

Floyd studied me with disapproval. "I'll just say, Mama!" he objected. "Allie looks like a sissy in that get-up. And he ought to have a haircut—he's got hair like a girl!"

"He's got pretty hair," Mama said, reaching back of the seat to give me a hug. "He's my baby, and bless Patty I'll keep him a baby as long as I can. They all grow up too fast."

Floyd grinned at me, and moved back over the cookstove and the sewing machine and the rest of Mama's widely-traveled belongings. "Come here, Bit-fit!" he called. "I want to show you something."

I should have seen the fun devils dancing in his dark eyes. When I joined him at the end gate, he snatched off the Buster Brown hat and threw it into the road.

[214]

"Mama!" I yelled.

She didn't look back. "Floyd, you quit teasing that child!" she ordered over her shoulder.

I struck Floyd with my fist, but he fended the blow, and laughed, and then helped me out of the wagon. The gravel hurt my bare feet as I ran back to retrieve the hat. Just then the mules went into a faster trot on the downgrade, and the gap between me and the wagon widened rapidly.

Floyd stuck his head outside the tarp to cheer me on. "Run, Bit-fit, run!" he called. "Pin back your ears and lay your nabel in the sand!"

I ran, bawling and breathless, for something like a quarter of a mile before the team slowed on level ground. Then when I reached for the end gate, Floyd pretended he was going to bang my fingers with a hammer. But finally he helped me aboard, and—as always—tried to rationalize his teasing with principles of instruction or training.

"Running's good for you, Bit-fit," he said in that smooth, confidential tone that always won me over. "Good for your wind. You ought to run a mile every day and build up your wind, because you'll have a lot of fights when we get to Ozona."

"I ain't mad at anybody in Ozona," I said sulkily.

"Don't make a bit of difference. You'll have fights, just the same." He spat between his teeth, man-style, in a way I greatly admired. "Look," he explained. "We're coming to a new town, and that's the way it is. Bert will have to whip a few boys his age, before they'll leave him alone, and I'll have to whip some my age, and you'll have to whip some your age. Anybody older'n you picks on you, you just tell Bert, or me."

I nodded, but I didn't see why it had to be that way. Floyd looked at me speculatively.

"You wear them curls, and, man alive! you'll have more fights in a week than I've had all year!"

We came, near the end of the day, to the western rim of the last wide divide, and over the ears of the mules was a long curving valley, green as a peach orchard with mesquites, and shouldered by the rim-rocked hills. Jay pulled rein on the team, and pointed with his whip handle.

"Yonder she is, Mama," he said. "See the two windmills shining on the top of that hill? That's Ozona—that's the waterworks and ice and light plant. You've got about eight miles to go."

Mama sat up straight and spare, fussing with her starched blue sunbonnet. It was really something for her to have only eight miles to go to reach permanency. She had been sitting on wagon seats like this, watching other people's houses go by, for nearly twenty-eight years.

"It's mighty pretty country, Jay boy," she said. "I wish the girls could see it. I declare to goodness, it seems strange for them to be married and scattered all over the place. Could you see the house from here, Jay boy?"

Jay said no, you couldn't see any of the houses for the hills, because most of the town of Ozona was behind that one with the windmills on it. He said that maybe we could go on into town that evening, but he wanted Mama to see her house the first time by daylight.

"I ought to be wearing my Sunday-go-to-meeting clothes!" Mama said. "I must look like a sight, and coming to a new house I ought to have my looking glass out and get fixed up."

"Shucks, Mama—you'll probably find yourself a beau here," Jay told her. And then gently, as if to prepare her against disappointment, "Of course, it's not a new house, and not very big—Dee couldn't get much for two hundred dollars. It's not as big as the house Papa roped out of the Brazos, that time."

"I just know it's pretty!" Mama said. "I know I'll love it."

But Bert and I had heard what Jay said. Papa was already something of a myth and a legend to me; Bert didn't remember him too well. We both came up behind the wagon seat.

"Where was I?" Bert asked.

"Where were you when?" Mama countered.

"When Papa did what Jay said—when he roped a house."

[216]

"You weren't born. It was back in Robertson County. It was before Floyd was born."

"Yeah, but I heard about it," Floyd said, and spat between his teeth again. "You didn't get to keep the house Papa roped."

IV

Jay drove some three miles farther. After sundown, he swung the mules off the road to make camps in a mesquite flat near the J. W. Friend & Sons horse ranch. Floyd was studying some red-and-white cattle behind a barbed wire fence. "I reckon I could get me a job on one of these big ranches," he said.

"Job, my foot!" Mama told him. "You'll go back to school next week—you and Bert, and maybe I'll start Allie. You can get a job next summer, but not on a ranch. I don't want to have to worry about a horse rolling on you, or pitching and shaking your insides loose!"

Bert looked at me over the freckles on his nose. "Allie ain't old enough to go to school," he said. "They won't let him start till he's six."

"I can go if I want to!" I said. "Mama, make Bert leave me alone!"

"Well, he can already read and write. I don't see that his age amounts to a hill of beans. I'll take him to school and find out."

"He don't write, he just prints," Bert said.

"Both of you hush," Mama said as she got down from the wagon. "Get out and rustle me some wood for the fire."

We gathered dry mesquite wood from the pasture, and threw rocks at the bullbats that were diving with a whizzing noise for insects they could hear but not see. Then Mama sent me back into the mesquites to get her a supply of "toothbrushes," which she used to dip her Garrett's snuff.

"Now, you be careful, Allie—hear me?" she called as she began mixing biscuit dough. "You watch out for rattlesnakes!"

I used the claw hammer to pull up several mesquite seedlings,

[217]

which had more root underground than stalk above; I peeled the thick part of the sweet-tasting roots, and hammered them on a wagon tire until they were shredded flat, and I watched warily for diamond-back rattlers that might be lying along the winding cow trails. On hot days, the snakes waited for evening's coolness to come out. I saw none. But there was another wagon outfit camped a half mile down the road, that night, and a small boy in it just older than I was not so wary.

We had started to eat supper when two horses galloped up, bringing a man and woman in high panic. The man was holding the barefoot boy in his arms.

"Rattlesnake bite!" he cried shrilly. "You folks got any medicine? You know what to do?"

Mama and Jay both knew what to do. Jay tied a thong of rawhide just above the boy's ankle and used it for a tourniquet. Mama slashed the two needlelike punctures on his ankle with a sharp knife, making the wound bleed freely, and both parents held the child, who was screaming more in fright than in pain. Then Mama poured all the coal oil we had into a tin wash basin, and thrust the lad's foot into it.

The kerosene immediately took on a scum of what appeared to be weeks of accumulated Texas soil. With an expression of disgust, Mama skimmed this off, and in the lantern light we all thought we could see the venom being drawn out, making a green thread in the bloody kerosene. An hour later, the boy was all right, except—as Floyd said—his feet didn't match. One was brown and well-encrusted with dirt; the other had a swollen ankle and had been cleaned and blistered a fiery red. Mama rubbed cold bacon grease on it, and the man and woman got back on their horses, stammering their thanks.

"I declare, I never saw such dirty feet on a young'un in all my born days!" Mama said when they had gone. She looked at Floyd and Bert and me. We were all barefoot. "If I ever see your feet like that, bless Patty, I'll take a mesquite switch to you!"

Eighteen

"Ozona's a millionaire town (said Fat Alford). Everybody there owns a big ranch or oil well or both. Them people have got money to spend, and that's why I can get jobs there . . ." —FRED GIPSON,
Cowhand: the Story of a Working Cowboy

During the summer of 1955 I visited Ozona, approximately ninety miles southwest of San Angelo, Texas. This place was famous for its "silk-stocking row" of ten or twelve millionaire families and its tremendous production of wool and mohair. Children of most ranches in the area customarily became part owners of the land and owned their flocks of sheep by the time they had finished high school. Before their twenty-fifth birthday many young men had annual incomes in five figures. But three or four years of continuous drought had brought unbelievable changes." —W. EUGENE HOLLON,
The Southwest: Old and New

The Studebaker wagon rolled into the town of Ozona from the east, along the dusty unpaved street that even then was known as Silk Stocking Avenue. The year was 1907, and I was nearly six years old. I remember 1907 a great deal more clearly than I can remember 1937, say, because it was an unhurried and unworried time, and every sight and sound and smell and taste was fresh.

Crockett County was sixteen years old, and 2,794 square miles big —twice the size of the State of Rhode Island. Ozona was the county seat and the only town. It was ninety miles north to the Santa Fe Railroad, at San Angelo, and ninety miles south to the Southern Pacific at Comstock.

In 1907, the population of the county was something around 1,500 —counting the inhabitants of "Mexico," as the Latin-American village a half mile south of Ozona was called. And nobody in the county owned an automobile.

Jay came to the town square, where the two-story stone courthouse overlooked a small park of mulberry trees and Bermuda grass, and we could hear the throbbing of the light and ice plant's gasoline engines on Waterworks Hill. On the north side of the square was a two-story frame hotel, a livery stable, and a butcher shop. Another hotel, the bank, a drug store, and two general merchandise stores faced the park from the west. On the south was a third general merchandise store, a saddlery, and the offices of a lawyer and a doctor. Not far from the courthouse, on the east, was a small frame building housing the weekly newspaper, the Ozona *Kicker.*

Saddle horses, wagons, and a few hacks and buggies stood around the square. We had come to town at noon, and now when Jay turned along the east side of the park to pass the Public Windmill—with the highest steel tower we had ever seen—there was a group of children scurrying in the dusty street, engaged in loud, unsupervised, and unorganized play.

"School!" Floyd said bitterly. "Must be the first and second grades, but man alive! Look at the size of some of those kids!"

I looked, and worried all over again about the fights I would have to have. Two or three of the boys were as big as Floyd, and wore boots and spurs; most of the rest were barefoot, and so were many of the girls. One of the larger boys spat tobacco juice and stood back, hands on his hips, plainly admiring the sleek little Spanish mules.

There was no other movement along the sunwashed street. The dust stirred and settled behind us; the schoolchildren stood speculating on who we were, and where we were going, lending importance to the event of arrival. And then the house we could hardly wait to see was before us, standing in the sun's pitiless limelight on the shoulder of a low and rocky hill. . . .

It was new only to us, and still it had none of the mellowed dignity of years. The town itself was new and raw from rubbing the rough edges off a thorny and rocky frontier: now Ozona is lovely with spreading pecans and green lawns, but in 1907 trees had not time to grow. Our house, unsoftened by shade or shrubbery, had a chapped and blistered look. It had no gallery to relieve the bare, weathered front wall; it overlooked the road below with a rectangular, windowless face, blind, and still—somehow—watching. The door was centered, making a grotesque nose; the front steps formed a sullen and chinless mouth line.

It could not compare with the rambling five-room house we had lived in on the Crawford ranch, at Christoval. Everybody knew this at once.

"You like it, Mama?" Jay asked anxiously.

Mama's chin quivered, and her nose turned red. The rest of us could remember very few houses at all, except those we passed in the wagon. Mama could remember the gray house of her childhood, at Sweet Home. But, after all, this place was her very own; this was all her dreams come true.

"Of course I like it, Jay boy!" she said. "It sure is mighty nice."

The mules strained and sweated in their collars, pulling the wagon up the rock-slippery hill. We saw now that the house sat on a gently sloping limestone ledge, almost as smooth as concrete and glaring like snow under the sun. This natural pavement was bigger than a double city lot, and narrowed out in paths running to the north, east, and west to make sidewalks. Somebody had conveniently placed the chicken house at the end of one of these, and the privy at the edge of a small canyon at the end of another.

Floyd and Bert and I piled out and ran all over the place, the rock scorching the soles of our feet. There wasn't more than a cubic yard of dirt on the whole place; the only thing Mama could grow here was cactus.

Jay helped Mama down. She was crying a little now. "Just look at all this pretty, clean rock!" she said. "I—I never lived in a place that had sidewalks." Then she blew her nose and looked at us. "There won't be any excuse for you young'uns tracking mud in the house and messing up my floors."

With that, she got her broom out of the wagon, and while we were unloading and carrying things into the house she swept the entire expanse of limestone as if it had been her parlor floor. Except when it rained, Mama swept most of her yard every day, and a terrace of Italian marble could have been no more beautiful to her.

It didn't take long to set up the woodstove in the kitchen, hang Mama's quilting frames from the ceiling in "the house," as she always called the front room, and put up the beds—two in the front room and one in the kitchen. Fortunately, both rooms were quite large.

"Mama, I'm hungry," I said.

She sent me out to the hydrant, which was in the front yard for the very good reason that digging a pipe trench through that rock would have been Herculean labor. I brought her a bucket of water, and she split a cold biscuit and dampened sugar to put on the halves.

"I declare!" she said. "I reckon we were all so excited about the house we clear forgot about dinner! While I'm scrubbing the floors, you boys go rustle some wood, and then I'll fix supper."

II

Floyd and Bert and I started up the rocky hill behind the house. I picked up the axe, but Floyd said we wouldn't need it.

"Ain't any wood up there big enough to chop," he said. "We can chunk down all the dead wood we'll find."

He was right. The hill had a few scattered thickets of scrub oak, and plenty of springy cedar which gave off a delightful odor in the sun but was too green to burn. Floyd picked up a heavy rock and heaved it against a dead oak sapling as thick as his arm. The sapling broke, and he gave it to me to carry. We walked a half mile to get two armfuls of wood, and it was clear that Jay would have to find some that could be hauled in the wagon.

At the top of the hill a cool breeze was blowing, and we stopped and sat on a flat-topped boulder and looked at the town spread out below, making a sprawling L where two valleys ran together. The courthouse had a black, tin-roofed cupola; some of the stores had false fronts. On all sides the rimrocked hills came down, freckled with cedar and prickly pear. Far down beyond the Mexican part of town a ranch windmill turned lazily, catching glints from the sun, and a sizable herd of cattle moved up past town, headed north and following Johnson's Draw. We saw a three-wagon freight outfit swing down the main road, hauling supplies all the way from San Angelo; the twelve-horse team had bells on their hamestraps, making Santa Claus music in September, in a land where it seldom snows.

Then the school bell rang for four o'clock, and we saw there were three frame school buildings strung out a few hundred yards apart, and that the high school was just around the point of the hill from our house. A number of the boys who came out of the high school looked as big as grown-up men. Several of them got on horses that were tethered in a small liveoak motte, and rode away.

"I sure wish I could get a job on a ranch!" Floyd said. "I hate to go back to school."

"Mama said maybe I can go," I reminded him.

A blue-bellied mountain boomer came out on a rock, its throat pulsing. Floyd shied a pebble at it. "You'll have to fight," he said again. "Any old time you move to a new town, you have to whip a few kids your own age."

The big lizard whirled and ran into a catclaw bush with a rustling of dry leaves. It occurred to me that I had never had a fight worthy of the name, and I wondered if I could whip anybody, and if I might not disgrace the family by getting licked. I looked at Floyd, and thought, *Floyd can whip anybody who ain't older than he is!* Size didn't seem to count for so much: age was what mattered.

And Bert, who was ten and had freckles, and was always skinning his nose whether he had a fight or not—Bert could probably lick his opponents. So could Jay. . . .

It was comforting to know, on the eve of battle, that I wasn't required to fight anybody older than I was. I could say, "My brother can lick you! My brother can lick your brother!"

Things summed up like that, and were very important at the time. I was new in this town, and on the brink of great adventures and terrifying ordeals; I had red curls, and Mama wasn't going to get them cut. But I also had brothers of all sizes up to and including Dee, who was twenty-six and stood six feet two. *Just trot out any old brother you've got—I've got one who can lick him!*

And I didn't think about Papa at all. It had been a long time since I had thought much about Papa.

We lingered a little longer on the hilltop, three small barefoot boys caught up in an infinity of blue sky and rocky, rolling, sunswept land, looking at the town that had been built at Tailholt Crossing, on Johnson's Draw. I wonder why they changed the name when they built the town? Just roll the lilting alliteration of Tailholt, Texas, over your tongue. Say it softly, speak it warm and slow the way people talk down by the Rio Grande, and you will wonder too.

Ozona is not the same now either, for the newness wore off. The shade trees grew to make beauty, and pavement came to bind the streets, and trucks roar where once the freight wagons made music. Stilt-legged towers stride the hills to carry the lightnings; the soft, distance dulled chug-chug of the engine on Waterworks Hill is no longer heard in the hot stillness of noonday, and now they have electricity all night instead of shutting it off at eleven-thirty. Now there are many other things, and who can say that all of them are good?

Now there are oil wells, and many more sheep on the ranches than there are cattle. The last glimmer of the Old West, hanging over the rimrocks like a reluctant sundown in 1907, is gone.

I could swear the hills were higher then. And I know the earth was peopled with giants, all of them capable of tremendous feats of skill and strength and daring, and the biggest of them my brothers.

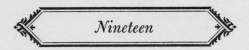

Nineteen

*M*ama forced me to put on the freshly washed and ironed Buster Brown suit. She dipped a comb in water, and dampened my long curls. Then, in all loving pride, she took me to school.

It was on a hot September afternoon when the sun struck a glare from the limestone rocks and the air was shrill with katydid song; it was the season when the green grassburs have turned brown and brittle, and the summer rains have washed them into the Texas roads, and every sharp spine seems charged with venom. I kept finding grassburs with my bare feet; Mama kept urging me on because we were late.

She wore something starched and somber; there was a grayish-blue veil with little dots shimmering before her face like a swarm of gnats, and she almost suffocated behind it. She was clinging to her gentility the way she clung to her looking glass, and for the same reasons: a veil and gloves and a celluloid folding fan, observed in the mirror before she went out, caused her to hold her head high and remember that she had "blue blood" in her veins, and that we were "fine-haired" people. Unfortunately, I remembered that she had worn this same costume to a burying at Christoval, and it lent a funereal aspect to the present enterprise. I wanted to cry—I wanted to run back to the house on the hill, and never go to school. But there were my brothers: each had faced this same ordeal, and all of them would expect me to go through with it.

Mama opened the door on a hot, buzzing classroom, on a sea of curious, staring-eyed faces. The buzzing stopped; the faces swam in a miasma of my own self-consciousness. Miss Minta, a large and bosomy woman with red mottled arms and a kindly countenance, invited Mama to take a chair. I stood at Mama's knee, filled with a nervous desire to go to the closet—there were few bathrooms in town—and looked across the starched lawn of Mama's lap at twenty or more children of the first and second grades—more kids than I had ever seen in all my life. They all appeared either curious or hostile, and I was mortally afraid of disgracing myself and my brothers in their company . . .

"Allie boy," Mama said, "show Miss Minta how you can read."

Miss Minta, dubious of my age, said she would just love to hear me read. I was looking at Willie Baker, who sat at a front desk convenient to Miss Minta's eye and hand, and had emitted an audible snicker when he heard Mama call me "Allie boy." He was a gangling child in corduroy knee pants and black stockings, and I thought of him at once as a type of street ruffian found in *Ragged Dick the Newsboy,* and other Alger books I had read that summer. The indelible pencil he had been eating gave him the fascinating appearance of having been violently poisoned, and I expected to see froth break out on his lips. He was everything, at that moment, that I was not: animal spirits ran rife within him, and his ease amounted to the stage presence of a clown who knows that his face is painted on. That instinct common to dogs and children told me that Willie Baker was my mortal enemy.

Mama patted my curls. "Read for Miss Minta," she said.

Miss Minta handed me an open book, and I saw that it was not by Horatio Alger, Jr.; it was a school reader. My mouth was full of September dust. Willie Baker's eyes were bright with a scheming challenge—he seemed to be daring me to read. I suddenly realized

[227]

he was about seven—an extremely awkward age when you have no brother to match it.

"You hear me, Allie?" Mama asked.

I began in a quavering treble at the page Miss Minta indicated. It was the second reader's watered-milk version of Aesop's already thin account of "The Boy Who Cried Wolf"; it was kid's stuff. I had read it before, and having been around sheep ranches and sheepherders, I suspected the whole story. Nobody I knew used "cry" for "shout"; "cry" meant to weep, or bawl, and therefore the boy was a sissy, and an unsympathetic character from the start. And who had ever heard of a sheepherder's sounding the alarm simply by yelling, "Wolf! Wolf!" and sounding like one of his own dogs? Sheepherders had more poetry in them. They were more likely to come busting through the mesquites hollering, "Turn loose the dawgs, boys, and grab your .30-.30's! There's a goddam loafer after the sheep!"

But I read the fable. Several girls bigger than I was ohed and ahed, but I was at that mysteriously bleak period in which little boys hold little girls in scorn. Willie Baker's sneer was plain. Miss Minta said it was remarkable, and she was not only going to ask the school board to waive the age rule, but she was going to start me in the second grade.

Every kid in the second grade was at least a foot taller than I was.

I watched the door close behind Mama as she went proudly on her way, serenely unaware of the cruelty she had just perpetrated so innocently. It was more than a door closing. This was the end of the preface: the page turned, and the first chapter was filled with unfamiliar words. Miss Minta pointed to a desk and told me to be a guest until she heard from the school board. I went to my seat, feeling all the eyes. Willie Baker purposely dropped a book, and I jumped. Then I sat staring at the second reader, half anesthetized by dread.

Afternoon recess came, and the boys tore outside to start a game of Wolf Over the River—inspired, no doubt, by my reading. I stayed until Miss Minta ordered me to leave the classroom, and then I went apprehensively into the bright sunlight and shrank against the wall.

A large, rosy-cheeked girl descended upon me and called me her "little curly-headed professor," and I was half sick with shame, and wondered if Floyd and Bert were having any fights during recess that day.

The school was a two-story frame structure with all the charm of a scabrous box, and its bilious color matched my mood. Faded green shutters sagged at windows opened for summertime; outside stairs climbed steeply to the higher learning of the third and fourth grades, and Willie Baker was now sliding down the smooth-worn banister in defiance of regulations. The building had been the courthouse when the county was first organized, and horse thieves and rustlers fortunate enough to get any kind of trial at all had been brought to book within its flyspecked portals. Upstairs was a small jury chamber, now used for the more immature deliberations of a study hall, and this had an open manhole to the attic. When a class gathered here for unsupervised study, the boys promptly hoisted one of their number through the ceiling, and he emerged with a pathetic memento of the Calder murder trial—the tiny white lid of a baby's coffin. Waved in the faces of the girls as Exhibit A, this never failed to produce delicious chills and concerted screaming. The latter always brought the teacher on the run, but the coffin lid could be tossed back into the attic before she arrived.

On each floor was a two-gallon zinc bucket, with a tin dipper to nourish and spread the community bacteria. Behind the schoolhouse, on the rocky lower slope of Waterworks Hill, were the other unsanitary arrangements—two three-holers. Boys vied with each other to become drawers of water and hewers of wood: the buckets had to be filled from a yard hydrant, and a day seldom passed without a messenger's being dispatched up the hill to cut a supply of catclaw switches. Nobody considered this a Judas detail at all; the cutter might well feel the cut of his own rods before we sang "I Will Not Loiter on the Way," and heard the four o'clock bell. (For the first few days, I suspected that to "loiter" meant to do something indecent along the road, and then Floyd told me it meant to "fool along.")

[229]

And all of the boys knew that a sharp knife could cut a series of virtually invisible rings around the catclaw switches, making them so brittle they would not survive the first blow.

That same brittleness was upon me now at the first recess. Willie Baker was sliding down the banister, instead of playing Wolf Over the River, because he could watch for me. When Ora Mae called me her "little curly-headed professor," and several other larger girls surrounded me, Willie went into action.

"Allie boy's a little girrul—Allie boy's a little girrul!" he chanted from the top of the stairs. My heart sank. The first fight was coming.

A leggy second-grade girl faced Willie angrily. She had hair much redder than mine, and more freckles than Bert; she was inelegantly known at that time as "Turkey Egg." And she grew up to be a beauty.

"He is *not* a girl!" she shouted. "You leave him alone—you hush your dirty mouth, Willie Baker!"

(The situation, militarily, was fast deteriorating. If Floyd ever heard that I had been defended by girls, I would never know the last of it.)

"Allie boy plays with girruls! Look at Allie boy's ha-ir!"

"Don't pay any attention to him!" crooned Ora Mae. She put her arm around me. "You've got pretty hair."

"Leave me alone!" I begged miserably.

Willie rocketed down the banister, yanked one of my curls, and ran away laughing when my Amazonian protectors grabbed at him. He climbed the stairs again, hitching up his corduroy pants.

"Allie boy's a sissy! Allie boy's a sissy!" he yelled, and launched into another slide. A spectacular crackling sound followed, and a trail of sulphurous smoke burst in his wake. The friction had ignited a handful of kitchen matches in Willie's pocket.

He landed groveling at our feet, rolling and slapping at his smoking behind, kicking up a shower of dirt from which the girls fled. They huddled against the wall, shrieking with mirth, and I was pitifully alone. I wasn't laughing, but when Willie scrambled to his feet he whirled on me, his purple mouth twisted with pain, and his fist struck out savagely. It slammed hard against my nose. The blood spurted, and tears blinded me; I clutched desperately at him, and pulled him down, but he was on top, pulling my curls and pounding my head in the dirt, and I knew I had disgraced the family. I was losing this fight.

Miss Minta finally came, and the hour of white-faced humiliation that followed in the classroom was worse than the fight. I found no solace in seeing Miss Minta build another fire on Willie's seat with a catclaw switch. That was Bosworth blood on the Buster Brown suit, and it had been muddied by the dust of defeat. . . .

I Loitered on the Way, at the foot of the hill, dreading to go home. Mama came out and called me. She threw up her hands and said bless Patty you'd think a teacher could keep things like that from happening, and now what was I going to wear to Sunday school? Floyd chortled with laughter when he saw me, and then demanded to know what the other kid looked like.

I had to confess that Willie was virtually unmarked. "He's two years older'n me!" I wailed.

It wasn't the size. It was the disparity of age, the weight of years, that had been overwhelming.

"Willie Baker," Bert repeated thoughtfully. "I wonder if he's got any older brothers?"

"He better not have!" Floyd said darkly, and spat between his teeth. "Bit-fit, there's one thing you've got to learn. Don't start a fight—I mean, don't pick one. But if you figure there's goin' to be a fight, don't wait for the other kid to begin. Just up and hit him so hard he won't ever get over it!"

He studied me for a minute, and said, "I'll just say!" and then he went out to the chicken house. A little later, while Mama was in the kitchen fixing supper, Floyd appeared at an open window and called to me.

"Stick your head out here, Bit-fit!" he whispered. "And keep quiet."

I obeyed. Floyd produced a pair of rusty sheep shears, and laid the cold blades against my prickling scalp.

There was a snicking sound. The first red curl dropped to the limestone rock, and I was scared all over again.

"Mama'll whip me!" I said. "She'll whip us both!"

"Hold still!" Floyd ordered. "If these curls ain't cut, you'll have to fight every kid in town!"

The job was quick and rough. The sheep shears nicked my scalp in a few places; they left short curls and cowlicks in others. Mama called us to supper, and burst into tears when she saw me. She sobbed that she had wanted to keep me her baby for a little while longer, and then she just picked at her food. She groped her way outside and picked up most of the shorn ringlets to press in the family Bible, and cry over on occasion.

But she didn't whip either of us, and perhaps the haircut had a reverse Samson-et-Delilah effect on me. Because a week or so later, on a Saturday when I had to pass Willie Baker's house on my way to the store, he came out and began throwing rocks at me. He threw small rocks at first, and small taunts. Then he came outside the gate in his paling fence, and threw bigger ones—and a rock hit me.

I was suddenly crying mad. I turned on Willie Baker. He ran, laughing, but I overtook him just outside the gate, and bore him to the ground, and—as Floyd said—beat the whey out of him.

After that, Willie and I were good friends.

II

Oil had not been heard from, but cattle and sheep were bringing money into Ozona, and the town stirred and dreamed of progress. It was planning to hew a temple of learning from the rugged native stone; drills were already testing the depth of ledge rock on the far side of the hill behind our house. At the moment it was only a dream, mainly in the mind of a far-seeing country judge who also was superintendent of schools. He wanted to spend a hundred thousand dollars for a new all-inclusive school building, and a lot of people mumbled that he was crazy. The dream had to wait a little while.

Meanwhile, spring kindled her fires and awoke the restless blood, and Mama had difficulty keeping Floyd in school. It was almost a tradition, in West Texas, for any boy big enough to fork a saddle to leave school when the spring roundups were on.

Dee was punching cattle on a ranch eighty miles from town, and we saw him perhaps three times in a year. Jay was working on a ranch forty miles away; he came to town more frequently. And Floyd argued that he ought to go to work. No reason, he said, that Dee and Jay should support him.

"You might as well just put it out of your mind!" Mama declared. "I won't have it! I'm bound and determined that you three young'uns are going to finish school, so that you can make something out of yourselves. And I won't have you punching cattle!"

Floyd stewed and fretted all that spring, when the roundups were on. The sons of ranch owners—his classmates—were leaving, rejoicing. They would start back to school in September in the same grade. But what did algebra and Latin have to do with raising cows?

Then Jay came to town with a whole week off, early in the summer. He was twenty-one, and his spurs made music the way Papa's spurs had made it at that age, and there seemed to be dash and deviltry in all that he did.

"Old Lady," he said with a twinkle in his eye, "I've decided not to go back to this thirty-dollar-a-month job. Why should I work for thirty dollars a month when I can make a quick clean-up, and get rich? I've got it all figured out. I'm going to hold up the Angelo stage."

I looked at him with admiration. The San Angelo stage was a three-seated hack pulled by four fast horses. They changed teams every twenty miles, and made the ninety miles from Ozona to San Angelo in about twelve hours.

"Jay!" Mama said. "Hush talking like that! I declare, I don't know what's got into you. You just won't do any such thing!"

Jay laughed, and danced Mama around the room, and threw her on a bed so hard two slats were knocked loose. She lay there laughing in spite of herself, and Floyd took a more adult view, although he was still in knee pants.

"Shucks," he said. "The Angelo stage never carries anything—

maybe a couple of drummers' trunks. What you want to do is go down to the Pecos High Bridge, and hold up the Southern Pacific. Or go on up to Angelo and rob the Santa Fe."

"Figured on the Southern Pacific job later, after I got my hand in," Jay said easily. "You could run over into Old Mexico with the dough, and hide out until things quieted down. I thought I'd start on the Angelo stage just for practice."

They worked out the finer details of this conspiracy, while I listened open-mouthed, and Mama became actually alarmed. "I'll just swanee!" she exclaimed. "You ought to be ashamed of yourselves—both of you!" And then, in a sudden burst, she mentioned Papa. "I don't like that outlaw talk," she said, "and I'll tell you why. Your Papa's first name was Woodson. Jesse James's middle name was Woodson, and there was some talk about them being cousins—maybe second or third cousins. And maybe being an outlaw runs in the blood. I want you to hush talking about it!"

Bert and Floyd and I went out of the house and looked at each other, and at the world.

Floyd spat between his teeth. "Man alive!" he said in an awed tone. "Who'd ever have thought that Papa was kin to Jesse James?"

Next day, the letter came from Ivanhoe, in Stephenville. Maude had left her railroading husband. This was followed by a letter the day after that. The railroader, Will Lancaster, had gotten drunk and had tracked Maude down. He had beaten her on the head with a stick of stovewood, so that she had to have an incredible number of stitches.

Jay came up the hill from town an hour after the mail stage had brought the second letter. He had been down at the livery stable, seeing that his horse was all right, and now he found Mama crying over what had happened to her baby girl. The minute Jay read the letter, Mama had a new worry to silver her hair.

He reached for his hat, and his eyes were no longer laughing. He said, "Pack your valise, Mama. We'll catch the Angelo stage in the morning. Take Allie with us, and Floyd and Bert can batch it."

"Where—where are you going?" Mama faltered.

Jay was at the door, not looking back. He said, "To the hardware store, before they close. To buy myself a gun. Because I'll kill that son-of-a-bitch!"

Floyd and Bert and I waited on the rocky hill point for him to come back. Nobody talked much. Floyd spat through his teeth, and said Will Lancaster had it coming to him, and Bert shied a rock at a bullbat that was skittering through the darkening sky with its lonesome call. The bird swooped blindly toward the hurtling stone, and then turned aside at the last instant.

"I guess Will ain't got any brothers my age," Bert said.

There was a hush over everything, the rocky hills softening under the twilight, and a warm, sweet scent of wood smoke drifting up from the town. The bigger engine that made electric light started up with a phut-phut-phut on Waterworks Hill, signaling day's end.

Mama came out of the house, an apron twisted in her hands. We couldn't see her face, but we knew she had been crying again.

"Is Jay boy back yet?" she called.

We told her no, and she went back inside the house. We could hear her moving around, doing the things she had to do. Mama cried now and then, but in a crisis she could work dry-eyed, with tireless, patient hands.

Then we saw Jay coming. He walked in the middle of the dusty road, as if danger lurked in shadowy ambush on both sides; he was tall and strong and hot with youth. As he drew nearer, we saw that he wore two cartridge belts crossed over his lean middle, and a six-shooter holstered on his right hip. He was carrying a Winchester .30-30 loose and easy in his right hand.

III

It is not much of a journey now, from Ozona to Erath County. The pavement runs level across the wide divides; it unrolls a ribbon of progress through the mesquite flats and the red and yellow clay hills of the postoak country, and the tires sing sweetly from the Pecos to Fort Worth or Dallas. But in those days, before the first automobile came to West Texas, even the ninety-mile trip to the railroad was an adventure to be dreamed upon. I lay long that night, feeling the delicious languor of the freshly bathed and the very young, knowing the good, tired feeling that makes children wriggle and smile when they are tucked in their beds.

Still, I could not sleep. There was yellow lamplight in the room, and shadows on the wall: my brother Jay's, ten feet tall as he walked past the lamp with the guns he had just oiled, Mama's, gaunt and grotesque as she bent over the two shoeboxes she was packing with fried chicken and biscuits. The shadows gestured and moved, and a hundred exciting images moved with them. Jay was going to kill Will Lancaster, and I saw Will lying on his side in the dust, kicking like a rabbit. And there was an exciting sequel to this. Once he had shot Will Lancaster, my brother Jay would certainly have to turn outlaw, and then he would really hold up the Southern Pacific.

Mama pleaded with Jay to leave the guns behind. She either had been crying again, or was about to cry afresh. It didn't do any good.

"I'll kill him!" Jay said.

"I don't see how you got the guns, in the first place," Mama said. "They must have cost a sight."

"Sold my horse," said Jay.

"You sold your horse?" Floyd asked incredulously.

"Still got my saddle," Jay said.

That was a saving thing. A man with a saddle could always go to work, because the ranches had plenty of horses to ride. But, as I watched Jay's tall shadow move restlessly across the wall and then shrink before it vanished in a dark corner, I knew he wouldn't be working. He'd be on the dodge west of the Pecos, and in Old Mexico; he'd be hiding out in cedar brakes and rocky canyons. And Mama would take her rocking chair out on the limestone rock, and listen for the sound of a horse coming out of the night. . . .

Then it was dawn, and gray light making mystery of everything that was familiar. The stage came to the bottom of the hill to pick us up. It was a light three-seated hack with a tarpaulin top, with one of the Patrick boys driving the four horses. The horses waited, rolling their bits; the morning was cool enough to make their breaths smoke a little. Patrick was a wiry man, so thin-faced a chew of tobacco threw him all out of proportion. He looked back at Jay's guns.

"Looks kind of like you're loaded for bear," he said, and that was all; his tone acknowledged that it was none of his business.

Jay said, "Yep," and Mama sniffed. She was wearing that polka-dot veil again, as if she intended to go to Will Lancaster's funeral. "He ought to leave the guns here," she said, addressing Patrick. "He'll get pulled, sure as the world!"

I understood vaguely what Mama meant. The sheriff "pulled" people into court, where they paid eleven dollars and seventy cents for fighting.

"I'm traveling," Jay said, helping Mama into the hack. "Anybody traveling's got a right to carry a gun. Get up here, Allie."

Mama and I took the middle seat; Jay was up front with the driver, and the horses were making their harness jingle. Floyd and Bert came down the hill to see us off. Floyd spat between his teeth, and looked slyly at Jay.

"I reckon you'll see Rose McAllister," he said, and grinned at me. "You know—best Indian fighter in the country."

"Won't have time for that," Jay grunted but he turned red. Floyd nudged Bert and laughed.

Mama lifted her veil and looked at the house on the hill. "Don't forget to mind the chickens, you boys," she said, and then Patrick shook reins over the team, and we rolled around the hill point into the main road, and the sky was fresh with morning.

Far down the demeaning years, when the days and weeks and months run faster, when distances dwindle and stature shrinks, it helps to remember the freshness of mornings like that one, when the sky turned yellow over Waterworks Hill. Every sensory perception was sharp; every new scene and sound and smell waited to be examined and classified, because the world was not yet in so much of a hurry. The horses moved into a fast trot, jingling their traces and relieving themselves of the early-morning flatulence; the steel tires whispered through gravel and sand. I remember the green mesquites flashing by, and the broomweed growing strong and rank in the low places, and sometimes a soft honey-sweet fragrance of cat-claw in belated bloom.

Half-wild cattle headed up and broke into lumbering runs away from the road; I grew tired of trying to count the jackrabbits, or the chaparral cocks streaking long-tailed up the road for a half mile before they had sense enough to head for open pasture. There wasn't a town for fifty miles, but in mid-morning we halted at a stage stand to change teams, and by then the sun was strong and high and distilling the homely smells of the corral into one clean and heady scent. The road ran wherever the way was easiest, and an occasional milestone marked our progress. There was time to read it, rolling past.

Jay jumped down now and then to open a pasture gate. "This here's the O-Nine ranch," Patrick would say. Or, spitting tobacco juice and pointing with his whip handle, "Black Jack Ketchum hid out in a cave, over yonder in that canyon." Or, "See that liveoak motte? That's Dove Creek. Had a big Indian fight there. . . ."

I counted back. Twenty years—thirty years—forty years ago, and the Indians had roamed here with the vanishing buffalo. And so had Papa later. Somehow, I began to wonder where Papa was, and what he would say if he knew Jay was heading east with two guns, intending to kill a man.

And somehow, too, I had the idea that killing Will Lancaster was really Papa's job.

It was dark when the stage rolled into San Angelo. There were more lights than I had ever seen, and the Landon Hotel's lobby was a place of vast splendor. When we went through it, Jay let me carry the valise, and he strode ahead on clicking bootheels, walking tall in his blue serge suit and Stetson, the sixshooter on his hip and the cartridge belts bristling, and the .30-.30 in his hand. I saw the eyes following him, and heard the whispers.

"Look at *him!*" they said. "Must be a Ranger!"

"Yeah—I'll bet he gets his man! Hate for him to be on *my* trail!"

Jay looked straight ahead, but maybe he swaggered a little. He wore the sixshooter into the dining room when we ate supper, and the service was excellent. Mama was proud, even when she tried to talk Jay boy out of shooting Will.

Mama said it wasn't enough that she had to worry about Maude's being parted from her husband, or being hurt goodness knew how bad. No, she had to grieve about one of her boys who was bound and determined to kill a man, and get himself sent to the pen. (When she talked about the pen, I could see it very plainly: it was a small barbed-wire corral, with men standing inside like cattle.)

But Jay ate his steak with a good appetite, and laughed. "You stop worrying, Old Lady!" he said. "Eat your supper. This is a man's job, and you leave it to me."

We stayed at the hotel that night, and caught a Santa Fe train early the next afternoon. The same excited admiration followed Jay from the hotel to the depot; it boarded the train with us. He leaned the .30-.30 against the seat and relaxed, and it occurred to me that he could hold up the Santa Fe now, and save himself a trip. The way he bought something every time the news butcher came through reminded me of a verse from the song about Sam Bass:

> Sam always coined the money,
> And spent it mighty free;
> A kinder-hearted fellow
> You scarcely ever see. . . .

Jay bought a whole stack of dime novels: *Adventures of Buffalo Bill, The Daring Exploits of Jesse James,* and *The Younger Brothers.* He got Mama a copy of *Cruel as the Grave,* and then, when the news butcher came through the coach again, he bought *Life in the Mines; or A Crime Avenged,* and a fascinating volume in hard covers called *Wild Life in the Far West.*

The train was rolling through new country; I had been along here in the wagon, but that seemed years ago. Somewhere there was a line between East and West: you crossed it, and suddenly saw ploughed fields, and houses only two or three miles apart, and fences everywhere. The other passengers studied Jay curiously, especially those newly boarding the train, and a warm feeling of superiority and pride swelled my breast. Jay was come out of the West, Young Lochinvar and Wild Bill Hickok rolled into one. I felt sorry for any Easterner who crossed his trail.

IV

There was a four-hour wait in Brownwood, and a transfer to the Frisco depot attended by more of the limelight's glare. We ate the last of the fried chicken and biscuit and preserves; we took another train at last, and it roared through the night smelling of varnish and dusty plush, hot engine oil and spittoons. I woke in a hack that was rattling into the yard of Uncle George Jones, on the southern edge of Stephenville. Dawn was up again, and the white-headed woman I saw at a window was not Aunt Fanny but my sister Maude, her hair cut and her head swathed in bandages. Ivanhoe was there too.

The women enjoyed a little cry, but Aunt Fanny was a practical woman in spite of the fact that she was Papa's older sister. She sent me into the back yard to get some stovewood, and a minute later she was out there with me. She had gray hair and her face was lined and sallow, but her eyes were shrewd and bright behind steel-rimmed spectacles.

"What's Jay aiming to do with those guns, Allie?" she asked.

"He's fixing to kill Will Lancaster," I said.

Aunt Fanny nodded, and pursed her lips. "He's a hotheaded fool, like all the Bosworth men. Either that, or—" and she didn't finish what she started to say. She took my arm and led me past the corner of the house. "I reckon you don't remember much about living around here," she said. "See that place over yonder?"

"You mean the white house?"

"No, that's where Will Lancaster's folks live. I mean the one with the chinaberry trees. I want you to go over there and tell Rose McAllister that Jay is here. Tell her I want her to come right off. I'll carry in the wood."

I went hesitantly down the path by the barn, watching the Lan-

[240]

caster place warily, and remembering—or trying to remember—how I had classified Rose McAllister as a good Indian fighter. Rose must have been about sixteen when I did that. She was more like nineteen now, and her name suited her perfectly. She said, "Oh—you're Allie! My, how you've grown!" and gave me a quick hug. When I gave her Aunt Fanny's message, her cheeks flamed, and she came back across the field so fast I had to trot to keep up with her.

But she was changed, in some strange way understood only by women, when she entered Aunt Fanny's living room. Aunt Fanny and Mama and my sister Ivanhoe were in the kitchen getting breakfast; Maude sat in a rocker, crying, and apparently had just been telling Jay how Will had beaten her. Jay was walking the floor, getting mad all over again.

He looked up and said, "Well . . . howdy, Rose!" and his eyes didn't want to leave her face. Color was high in her cheeks, but she only nodded to him and somehow seemed cool and aloof. Then she looked at the .30-.30 leaning against a chair, and at the sixshooter he wore, and the two cartridge belts around him. She looked at his boots and spurs, and then back at the pistol. She began to laugh.

Jay stood it for almost a minute, then turned red.

"What's so damned funny?" he asked.

"You!" Rose said, laughing again. "You haven't grown up a bit, Jay—you're still riding stickhorses, and playing cowboy and Indians."

He didn't say anything. I said, "Well, he *is* a cowboy! I'll bet you he can ride any old bronc you ever saw!"

"I'm sure he can," Rose said, wiping her eyes. "But he didn't come here on a horse, and folks don't carry guns around here. What are you going to do with them, Jay?"

"That's my business!" he growled.

Rose nodded. "It sure is. But it doesn't take much of a man to pack a gun. Even a coward can pull a trigger. And you look funny!"

She began laughing again, and Jay took a couple of quick steps toward her. I thought he was going to shake her, and I hoped he would. Maybe he intended to do just that, because he said, "No woman's going to laugh at me like that!" and caught her shoulders

[241]

in both his hands, a little roughly. She looked up at him as if surprised, and then he kissed her hard on the mouth.

My sister Maude said, "Well, I'll just declare!" and began laughing, too. Jay glanced at her, and turned away without a word. He picked up the .30-.30 and went out the door, and we heard him stamp down the steps with his spurs jingling.

Maude came out of the rocking chair so suddenly it made pain shoot through her head. "Stop him, Rose!" she begged. "Don't let him kill Will!"

"I don't think he'll do that," Rose said, smiling strangely. She touched her lips with the tips of her fingers. "I don't think he's going to shoot anybody, now. . . ."

I didn't wait to hear anything else, or to see Mama bawl when she found Jay was gone. I hurried out the door and was just in time to see him turn the corner of the barn, the Winchester held loose and easy in his right hand. Then he was out of sight behind the barn, and I ran down through the dew-wet broomweeds, wanting to get close enough to see what happened, and not so near he could send me back. I edged around the barn, and there was Jay going through a patch of sumac and scrub postoak, toward the Lancaster place. I could only see his head and shoulders, and he was walking fast.

I ran, dodging from one clump of bushes to another. There was a woodpile behind the white house, and I sneaked up behind it and heard Jay calling Will Lancaster's name at the kitchen door. I thought, *Now it's coming!* and my heart slammed against its rib cage.

The screen door opened, and there was Will. I wouldn't have known him, but he had on blue overalls and the high-crowned blue cap worn by railroad men everywhere. About Jay's size. But older—maybe two years older, and that was a difference.

I held my breath, waiting for the shattering roar of gunfire, expecting to see Will lurch across the little unroofed back gallery and crumple down the steps and claw at the dirt the way men did when they got shot in the dime novels.

[242]

And then I saw that Jay had left both his guns and both his cartridge belts somewhere.

Will said, "Howdy, Jay."

Jay said, "Come out here, you son-of-a-bitch! Come out here and let's see if you can stand up to a man!"

"I was drunk," Will said. "She left me . . . and then I got drunk."

"Come out!" Jay said.

Will took a deep breath against something inevitable, and came out; he descended the steps with his eyes narrowing, and his head scrunching down into his right shoulder, and then he rushed. There was a shock of collision, a flurry of dust, and a confused blur of swinging fists. Jay tripped on his spurs and sat down.

Will jumped on him, fighting dirty, aiming a kick at his jaw. His ankle struck Jay's shoulder, and Jay grabbed his foot and twisted it. Will Lancaster went down too, and the next thing I knew they were rolling in the dirt, clawing and pounding each other. I remember that I was crying, and that when I saw Will on top and grabbing for Jay's throat I groped for a stick of stovewood, intending to run out from behind the woodpile and hit him on the head. But I didn't have to do that, because both of them were suddenly on their feet again, and fighting around the side of the woodpile, so that I had to get out of their way. I heard Jay grunt as he put his whole weight behind a swing, and his fist cracked against Will's jaw.

Will staggered back and bumped his head on a washtub that hung from the kitchen's outside wall, and then he hinged at the knees and slumped just as grotesquely as any of the villains in the dime novels. There was blood at the corner of his mouth, and I thought maybe he was dead.

Jay dusted the dirt off his blue serge suit, and spat out some blood, and we went back across the pasture without saying a word. When we came to the barn, Jay stepped inside and got the guns he had left there. He was washing his face in the horse trough when Rose McAllister came out, and I don't know what she said, because I had to run to the house and tell everybody about the fight.

But I know that when we started back to Ozona a few days later the cartridge belts and the pistol were in the valise, and Jay had wrapped the .30-.30 so that you could hardly tell what it was. I was the one who looked like a cowboy, because the last thing he did in Stephenville was to buy me a cowboy suit.

I liked this a lot better than that sissy Buster Brown outfit.

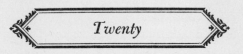

Twenty

*T*he house with so solid a founda-
tion was to be Mama's home for many years, and they were the
happiest years of her life. She left it only to spend an occasional
summer on the ranches where Dee worked, or to visit Norah and
Ivanhoe and Maude and she was always glad to get back. She had
all five of her boys with her, or not far away, and was keeping the
three younger ones in school.

Moreover, the house had been enlarged and improved. Dee and
Jay somehow managed to take two weeks from their jobs at the
same time; each had learned considerable of Papa's carpentering
skill by working as his helper. They added a large bedroom on the
west of the house, ran a wide gallery across the entire front, and built
a shed-roofed kitchen. Then they painted the house gray, with a
green trim. All of us carried stones to build a low retaining wall at
the edge of the front yard, and topsoil began collecting there when
it rained. Mama soon had Bermuda grass and a few shrubs growing
beyond the edge of the limestone rock—and it became my job
to chase Mexican burros and stray cattle out of her "garden."

But we loaded nearly everything into the wagon, that second
summer in Ozona, and went five miles east of town, where Dee had

[245]

been put in charge of the J. W. Friend & Sons' horse ranch. Jay was then punching cattle for another outfit, fifty miles away; he could come to the Friend horse ranch to see us as easily as he could ride to town.

Mama locked the house for three months. The wagon wheels rolled briefly, and it was like old times again. Floyd and Bert and I were disappointed when we found that there were no cattle on the ranch, except a milk cow and her small calf, and one surly Durham bull who always came up from pasture at twilight to drink at the windmill tank and rumble his discontent at the absence of coy young heifers on his range. Neither were there horses bearing the Friends' Spanish Gourd brand. (In later years, the brand became known as the Fiddleback, which perhaps sounds more romantic.) The horse ranch had been grazed off; the livestock had been moved to another of the family's large holdings.

But there was plenty for Dee to do in adjacent pastures, and to his great delight Floyd often rode with him. Mama cooked, and milked the cow morning and evening; Bert and I played around the windmill, or hunted cottontails with our .22 rifles. I had been given a single-shot .22 when I was six, and Floyd, pursuing his avowed policy of making a man of me, had taught me how to shoot. This training had actually begun even earlier, with a Daisy air rifle as the weapon. I could not voluntarily shut my left eye.

"Well, you'll have to shoot left-handed, Bit-fit," Floyd said. "It won't make any difference, in the long run. Now, remember this: don't ever point a gun at a man unless you are going to shoot him. Don't ever point an unloaded gun at anything. And, here—let me show you how to go through a barbed-wire fence with a gun . . . and how to carry it when you're huntin' with somebody else . . . and how to clean the barrel."

So I shot left-handed. Years later, in the Navy, I was to run up such a creditable score at the rifle butts that the drill instructor came my way to see who was getting the bull's-eyes. He was shocked into profanity when he witnessed the 1907 Springfield throwing empty shells into my face, and insisted that I comply with regulations and shift the rifle to my right shoulder. Shortly after that, I became a Hospital Apprentice Second Class.

A thousand cattle came bellowing up from the southern hills, and bedded down in the pasture a few hundred yards from the house, and hard by the half-section horse trap where our milk cow grazed. The herd did not belong to J. W. Friend & Sons, but had been granted the right of passage on a drive to the railroad shipping pens at San Angelo. I stayed up late that night, watching from the gallery, seeing campfire glow on the tarp of the chuck wagon, listening to the complaint of the cattle bedding down, and hearing even the soft unmelodic singing of the first night guard: it was as if I knew, instinctively, that these things already belonged to the past, and would not be seen or heard again. And I think Mama understood.

Dee knew that it was important and exciting and special. When I finally went to bed, on a pallet spread on the floor, he was there with a silver dollar held between thumb and forefinger and looking as big as the front wheel of a wagon.

"Give you this dollar, Allie, if you go to sleep in two minutes!" he promised, smiling.

It seemed like what Floyd called a "lead pipe cinch." It was so certain that I began thinking what could be done with a whole big silver dollar. Five plates of vanilla ice cream at Soapy Smith's drug store, and fifty jawbreakers at Bunger's . . . or twenty packs of nickel firecrackers for next Fourth of July . . . or six whole boxes of .22 shorts, and a dime left over for ice cream. Gosh, with that much ammunition, you could hunt for years!

Dee had his watch out. "One minute!" he warned, and I knew then that I could never win, because the visions of so much money danced through my head more entrancingly than visions of sugar plums. I closed my eyelids tightly and tried to breathe as if I were asleep, but Dee saw the involuntary twitch of an eyelash.

"You're playing possum!" he laughed. "You're not asleep."

"No," I sighed. "Nearly, though. . . ."

He put the dollar back in his pocket. Life has always been like that for me. The big money—the important money like a whole silver dollar—dangles before me now and then, and vanishes in the flicker of an eyelash.

II

That was the night they ran. A crashing, blinding thunderstorm broke over the hills after midnight, and there was a brief dry rattling of hailstones on the roof. I awoke and ran to the window, and Floyd was there, not scared, but laughing with excitement. Another dazzling bolt made the room as bright as day, and the thunderclap jarred Mama's dishes in the kitchen.

"That one may have hit the windmill," Floyd said. It began raining; we could hear the rain coming across the horse trap, moving fast with the wind in the cloud. It ran over the gallery, over the roof; the water streamed down the window panes and blurred the next flash of lightning, but we could see what we called "nigger babies" jumping in a puddle already formed in the yard, when the oversized drops struck.

"Raining like a cow peeing on a flat rock!" Floyd rejoiced.

"Floyd!" Mama said, behind us.

"A *tall* cow, Mama," Floyd chuckled. "Shucks, it's stopping!"

We thought we heard wind, but the sound grew into a roar, and then was a thunder that did not come from the sky. Chain lightning was still playing around the hills, and the intermittent flashes showed a dark wave rolling through the mesquites, with white-faced splashes of foam on its crest. And Dee stamped in from the gallery.

"Stampede!" he yelled.

A thousand terrified bawling, running cattle came up through the half-section horse trap and took the barbed-wire fence with them. They splashed through a little draw, and some of them slipped in the mud, and the others went over them with cutting hoofs. The leaders saw another fence in the lightning flashes, but the hot press of surging, back-humping bodies behind them forced them on. The fringe of the running herd passed so near the house that mud was spattered on the gallery, and I was clinging to Mama's nightgown more in awe than in fright. This was a spectacle; this was something

I would never see again. A cowboy went by like an actor in an early movie film that has jumped the sprockets on the projector: flashes of light, pitch darkness, flashes of light, and the rider in a different place and different posture each time. He was waving his slicker and risking his neck, and on the far side of the turbulent sea of tossing horns one of his comrades was firing a sixshooter.

It was all over in a few minutes. Dee shook his head, and said he hoped the boys got them milling up on the divide. He said there would probably be an awful lot of fence work to do tomorrow.

"Reckon you'll have to help me, Floyd," he said.

"Shucks," Floyd sighed. All the romance had gone out of the stampede. From time immemorial, cowboys have hated building fence.

"I hope nobody's horse stepped in a prairie dog hole," Mama said. "I sure am glad that you weren't out there tonight, Dee boy—I'm thankful none of my boys had to be out there riding."

"Man alive, Mama!" Floyd said. "I wish I had been. You don't see a stampede like that every day!"

And Bert pulled me aside. "You want to go partners with me?" he asked.

"Doing what?" I asked suspiciously.

"There'll be some dead cows out there in the morning. We could skin 'em. Cowhides are worth about four bits apiece."

"You think I can—I mean, you think we could skin a cow?"

"You've got a knife, haven't you?" Bert said.

Next morning, after Dee and Floyd had already ridden forth with wire cutters, claw hammers and staples, and when the trail drive cowboys were five or six miles away, combing canyons and draws for the lost ones, Bert and I stood on the gallery.

We surveyed the sun-bright flat. The mesquite is a desert plant; it responds to a shower, or folds its leaves to hoard moisture in the blazing sun. This morning, the mesquites were beautifully green.

Bert counted, stabbing the air with a forefinger. The first carcasses lay where the horse trap fence had been, and just beyond. Some of the cattle had dropped when the wire sagged and parted and the stubborn cedar fence staves thrust up into their bellies like spears; some had lurched onward, crippled and doomed, until the frantic following tide overtook them and rolled them under . . .

"Twelve—fourteen—fifteen!" Bert said. "Maybe more, in the chaparral. We'll never get 'em all, and we've got to work fast. You get the canteen, and fill it. Let me have your knife."

He sharpened the skinning blades of the IXL Barlow knives that were our indispensable delight, and Mama's despair. They were so heavy they wore holes in our pants pockets. We moved out across the trampled mesquite flat, under the vast blue-hot bowl of the morning.

"This is like when Papa got caught in the Skinning War," Bert said. "I reckon he had a lot of trouble. It was before we were born."

I looked around apprehensively. There didn't seem to be anybody else within miles, except Mama, back at the house. But you couldn't tell about Skinning Wars, and we had to get the hides before the other side moved in to get them. And the buzzards—dozens of them —were already circling in the sky.

"We've got to work fast!" Bert said, looking at the buzzards.

So we did. It was easy enough to slit a hide up a belly not yet distended, or to cut along the inside of the legs still flexible, and strip the hide away from the inert flesh. It was not so easy for two small boys to turn the carcasses over to get at the other side, or the back. Some of the steers weighed eight or nine hundred pounds.

But at sundown we had drunk the canteen dry and had skinned three cows. A dollar and a half. Six bits apiece. We went home with the wet hides weighing a ton—two for Bert and one for me—and ate everything Mama had on the table.

Next day, it being summer, the smell of death and corruption moved with us across the sun-washed prairie, and the buzzards were becoming more aggressive. But we had gained some skill in hide removal: we skinned four cows, and were getting rich.

The third day was bad. Green blowflies swarmed over the first carcass, and maggots were boiling in a wound made by a cedar fence stave. Bert tried to hold his breath while he ran his knife blade up the distended belly, because the smell was strong; the blade went too deep by the merest fraction of an inch, the drum-tight skin ripped and erupted, spewing its fetid gases with an obscene sound of crepitation, and Bert staggered away, blinded and sick. He bent over to retch and vomit. I retreated from the scene and then came back with the canteen of tepid water. Bert was fighting off a buzzard that wanted to duel him for the spoiling spoils. He didn't want water; he wanted only fresh air.

We went out into the mesquites and lay down until he felt better. While we were there, buzzards blackened the carcass.

"Wish I'd brought the .22!" Bert said. "I'd show 'em!" He was getting mad, at the stench, at the buzzards, at the job we had tackled. He said, "Come on—let's finish it! We've got to get three more hides!"

"You think Papa ever had it this bad, in the Skinning War?" I asked. We were plying our knives with one hand, and fighting off a swarm of predatory, smelling, flapping buzzards with the other. The legs of the dead cattle had become as stiff as fence posts, and this helped, in a small way—it afforded better leverage when we had to roll the cows over.

But the buzzards came in increasing numbers, and grew more daring. They brushed us with the tips of rusty, foul-smelling wings, and one vomited on the grass within a few feet of where we were working, and we saw others sick in the air. I have always wondered about buzzards. If they have such queasy stomachs, why don't they pursue some other line of work?

We were both being stubborn. We fought out that day, and the stench; we battled the blowflies and the maggots; we slapped at the buzzards, and skinned the tenth cow. We had made five dollars apiece.

"Well, Papa never had it as tough as that, in the Skinning War!" I said when we headed home at last, with the green hides on our shoulders.

Papa wasn't there to say, oh, yes—it was a lot tougher when you skinned a cow and might be shot for skinning it.

[251]

When we stopped to think about it, we didn't know where Papa was, or what he was doing. But Floyd was quick to point out that things were equal. He figured Papa wasn't worried about us, either.

III

Floyd lured me to the horse ranch corral in the early evening, when the old Durham bull came rumbling up to drink, when the bullbats whizzed overhead and the earth cooled and stretched after a hot day.

"Bit-fit," he said in that smooth and confidential tone I was to know so well, "Bit-fit, you see this little old bull calf? Now, you are just cut out to be a great bronco rider, like Booger Red, but of course you've got to learn. Now, you just climb on this little old bull calf, and ride him to a fare-thee-well!"

He talked sweet. But doubts and misgivings assailed me. Maybe the little old bull calf did not want to be ridden. The little old bull calf was seven months old, and outweighed me by many pounds, and had stubby horns.

Floyd could have been a very successful salesman. He said, "Now, don't you worry, Bit-fit. Why, man alive, you're just built for a bronco-buster. You just climb on this little old bull calf, and bust him so he will know he has been busted!"

The little old bull calf looked as big as a full-grown Hereford to me, but I was susceptible to flattery—I was eager to be the next Booger Red. Floyd helped me on. The little old bull calf tore loose, raised a flurry of corral dust, and speedily disjointed to the accompaniment of shouts like, "Stay with him, Bit-fit! Ride him, cowboy!"

On the third jump, I went over the calf's head and knocked out two front teeth on one of the stubby horns. I rose uncertainly from the dirt, bathed in blood and tears, and bawled for Mama. She came running.

"Floyd!" she exclaimed. "How many times do I have to tell you to stop teasing this child?"

"Why, shucks, Mama," Floyd said. "I wasn't teasing him—I was showing him how to ride. He's *got* to learn how to ride!" Then he turned to me. "Now, let that be a lesson to you, Bit-fit! Keep your head up. Always keep your head up when you ride, so you don't get knocked out on the saddle horn."

I can give you no portrait of Floyd: he would not sit still long enough. He was restless and reckless, grown-up and virile, precocious and entirely capable. He took a job a little later, not yet fifteen, during the summer vacation from school. He was in an isolated sheep camp, forty miles from town, and his only companion was a Yaqui Indian herder. On the third evening, Floyd came back to camp to find this middle-aged man squatting by the campfire, spooning beans into his mouth from the communal Dutch oven.

The herder spoke no English, and Floyd had to express his displeasure in sign language. He picked up the heavy iron cover of the pot, and lowered it forcefully on the man's skull, knocking him unconscious for a spell.

"Let that be a lesson to you!" he said sternly, when the herder had recovered.

The rest of the night, each sat wakefully. The Mexican had his back against a tree and was sharpening his knife. Fortunately, the owner of the sheep rode that way early the next morning.

He fired Floyd on the spot, for his own protection. "Don't blame you a'tall, son," he said. "But I can't run the chanct of you gettin' all whittled up. And that greaser knows sheep, and you don't. Maybe you can work for me some other time."

We went back to Ozona, to the house on the hill, early in September. Mama was the first to unlock her front door and find a five-foot rattlesnake that had moved in sometime during the summer. We were unloading her things, and she did not call for help. We heard her say, "Well, I'll just swanee!" and then there were vigorous thumpings of a broom, and by the time we got in the house Mama had whipped the snake to death on her kitchen linoleum. She let me cut off the thirteen rattlers and a button.

I climbed the stairs to Higher Learning, to the third grade, and the fourth. The textbooks were more interesting. We took up Texas history, and cheered the Alamo and Sam Houston's rout of the Mexicans at San Jacinto . . . and never mind what Washington suffered at Valley Forge. American history could come later.

There was one book which had all to do with crocuses, and the first buds on the horse chestnut, and the miracle of an apple tree from first flowering to fruition; it told of violets and alders and birch bark, and said nothing of mesquite or *huisache* or catclaw or prickly pear. It didn't mention the bluebonnets that run their azure carpets over the Texas hills in the spring. This was a book purely out of Boston, gone far astray. No Thoreau had ever camped at German Waterhole—but a German had, long before, and thus named the place. There were a few wild plum thickets in the hills beyond German Waterhole; the yellow-fruited wild currant called *agarita* (Ozona people pronounced it "algereeder") made wonderful jelly, and in summer you could pick a delicious strawberry-flavored cactus fruit named *pitaya*. But there wasn't a violet, a birch, an alder, or even an apple tree in many miles.

I complained about this at home, and Floyd supported my theory. "It don't do you much good to study things like that," he said. "You take Hop—in your class. His old man must have about a hundred sections down on the Pecos, and a big part of it will be Hop's, some day. Now what good will it do him to know about horse chestnuts? He ought to be on the ranch learning more about horses, and never mind the chestnuts!"

Mama looked up from reading one of her favorite books, *Ishmael; or Self-Raised.* She said, "You just hush, now—hear? You're going to stay in school."

"It's not right for Dee and Jay to have to support us when we get big enough to work," Floyd argued. "I'm big enough. It's time I got a job."

"You're just talking to hear your head rattle," Mama told him. "All three of you are going to stay in school till you finish."

To back up her determination in this regard, Mama applied for and got the job of janitor to the Ozona school system. This involved only sweeping out the three buildings. There were no furnaces; the first boys to reach school on cold winter days built a fire in the pot-bellied stove, opened the damper, and warmed their hands on the stovepipe until the stovepipe got too hot to hold. I helped do this one morning, in the fourth grade. There was a little too much horseplay around the stove before the arrival of Old Miz Snell, the teacher, and somebody knocked the stovepipe down. Flames roared up and licked the varnished ceiling, and several girls who also had arrived early began to cry as they loaded their book satchels and went down the outside stairs toward home. But I was one of a dozen little savages who fell into lockstep and marched around what we hoped would soon be a flaming pyre, chanting: "The schoolhouse is burning, hooray, hooray!" to the tune of "The Campbells Are Coming." Old Miz Snell arrived unconscionably early, and spoiled our fun; seeing her, Boots McKinney picked up the zinc water bucket and set it on the stove to block the flames, then threw a few dipperfuls of water on the charred ceiling.

Floyd and Bert and I helped Mama sweep out the three buildings after school—Floyd handled the high school by himself. I was not big enough to be much good with a broom, but I could pick up papers. I wrote on the blackboards of the other two buildings, "Please do not throw paper on the floor," and signed it "The Janitor."

"Miz Snell," Ora Mae asked the teacher next morning, "what's a janitor?"

"Somebody who cleans up," Old Miz Snell said, and I hated her, because Ora Mae said, "Oh," and looked at me, and so did everybody else. "Sweeps out," or "takes care of," would have been kinder words. (Building maintenance had not been heard of.)

Ozona . . . millionaire's town. You couldn't tell the millionaires from the cowhands by the way they dressed, and nobody in town was snobbish or stuck up, and everybody thought Mama was doing a fine thing for her children. But Mama's children suffered a little, not because *we* were sweeping out, but because she was.

All of us thought that Mama was too soft and too pretty to be sweeping out schoolhouses for forty dollars a month.

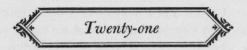

Twenty-one

I do not love thee, Mrs. Snell,
The reason why I cannot tell;
But this I know, and know full well:
I do not love thee, Mrs. Snell.

*I*n the fourth grade, I was well
enough advanced in my reading to be able to handle Tom Brown.
I put that verse on the blackboard one evening after Mama and I
had cleaned the schoolroom, and I took care to print it. Nevertheless, Old Miz Snell, who taught the third and fourth grades, knew
who did it. When school took up, next morning, she called me up to
erase the offending jingle, and then she broke a few well-notched
catclaw switches on my bare legs.

I went back to my seat and surreptitiously carved another notch
on my desk.

The pattern had not changed. My classmates still ran a foot taller,
and although it was no longer necessary to fight anybody but newcomers, I had developed an inferiority complex from the good-natured
shoving around I got in games at recess. But, being light, I was

usually the one who was hoisted to the attic to bring down the baby's coffin lid during study periods in the former jury room. That gave me a sense of belonging.

Floyd had thirteen notches cut on his desk by the first of the spring term. One of the Perner boys had fourteen, and was tied with Ernest Dunlap. The contest was intramural, and there was some talk of handicapping "Hop" Hoover—his real name was Armond—in my class, because Hop had at least twice as many notches as anybody else. Hop got a whipping every day that he attended school. He usually left for the spring roundup, and didn't come back until next year; at times he played hookey even in the fall, and walked the forty miles to his father's ranch on the Pecos—sleeping out on the divide one night, without bedding. But his father always brought him back to school, until he was needed on the roundup.

Floyd depended upon me to keep him informed about Hop, whom he admired a great deal. "Hop get a lickin' today?" he would ask every evening.

"Man, he sure did!" I would say. "Look—this race ain't fair to Hop. He gets so many lickin's he hasn't got time to cut notches for 'em. He sits in front of me, and I know. Every time he gets out his knife to cut another notch, Old Miz Snell calls him up and whips him again, and he loses count."

"How many you got, Bit-fit?" Floyd asked, but he lowered his voice so Mama wouldn't hear.

"Just five," I said sadly. "She can't see me for Hop, he's so big."

At twelve, Hop was nearly six feet tall, had a bull-calf rumble in his voice, and was already shaving. Nobody around Ozona had heard of I.Q. tests in those days; Hop would very likely have come out with a genius rating, because he was very intelligent indeed. He simply wasn't interested in school, in books, in formal education: he only wanted to get back in the saddle again, astride a horse from which he had gotten his nickname—a horse known as Hop-and-Go-Fetch-It. He coasted easily in that second time around in the fourth grade, and spent many hours reading dime novels that were camouflaged by a cover torn from a physiology text. Old Miz Snell noted this strange interest in physiology, and stood by Hop's seat one day to suggest that he trace the circulation of the blood.

Hop was unabashed. He looked at the page before him, and picked the proper paragraph:

" 'A thin trickle of crimson crept down Wild Bill's cheek from the bullet wound,' " he began, and then Old Miz Snell had him by the ear and was dragging him to punishment. While being flogged, Hop whooshed and snorted like a bull calf at branding time. No whipping ever hurt him. He stood there rolling his eyes and making his whooshing sounds until the room was convulsed with laughter, and inspired with rebel spirit. Whipping Hop was bad for whatever discipline Old Miz Snell had ever instilled in her pupils.

II

We called her *Old* Miz Snell, which needed not have been a term of disrespect at all, but was. The word was used indiscriminately, both in affection and in opprobrium. Old Coots Curry had done this or that today, and Old Miz Snell had licked him for it: the difference here, accented by a soft southwestern Texas drawl, was that everybody loved Old Coots—who was perhaps thirteen.

Actually, that year's teacher of the third and fourth grades was somewhere around forty. I wish I had a photograph of her; I know that she was paid little, and endured and suffered much; I should like to be sure unpleasant associations have not distorted her image in my memory—at least not violently. For now she seems to have been the very model for the umbrella-carrying Female Reformer cartoons I saw in later years—a thin, angular caricature of a woman, with spectacles and a long, severe face, and mousy hair worn in a drab and straggling knot at the back of her head, the very antithesis of Mama and of soft femininity. Her husband was the high school principal, and in that capacity had laid the rod upon Floyd and Ernest Dunlap, and the Perner boys, and others too numerous to mention, all of whom fully deserved it. In my recollection, he in

[258]

turn has looked at me from many an editorial page, the Prohibitionist and Blue Law advocate in the flesh.

I still do not love thee, Mrs. Snell. It still seems to me that two more sour-faced individuals, expressly created for each other on a day when God felt unwell, never met. I do not think that such people should ever have been entrusted with the education of the young; I doubt that there was any tenderness in their lives. I imagine the Snells spent their evenings poring over accounts of the Spanish Inquisition, and yellowed treatises on medieval tortures, cackling shrilly at the discovery of some particularly exquisite practice.

Whippings were one thing, simple and necessary, but Old Miz Snell's other punishments were something else, and could get her brought to book if she decreed them today. She lined up four of us at a time—not to face the blackboard, but to look on our classmates so that they could witness our weakness—and made us extend both arms at right angles, with two books balanced on the palm of each hand. Two minutes of this posture become painful, three are excruciating, and five impossible.

Our arms sagged. A book or two dropped to the floor. Old Miz Snell then leaped to the lineup with a pin extracted from her starched white shirtwaist. She jabbed each of us in each arm, deep enough to draw blood and spread diseases of the blood.

This stung the weakening flesh to superhuman effort, and brought forth grunts and yelps—and, from me, hot tears of anger. Nobody in the classroom laughed. Nobody was on the side of Old Miz Snell.

Howard Westfall was a splendid physical specimen. He held the books a long time before weakening. When Old Miz Snell came with her pin, he put the books down, lifted her gently aside, and went home.

His mother brought him back.

Neither Mama, nor any other parent, could believe things were quite so bad as what we reported at home. And there was a common reluctance to tell such tales: relating them brought up the question of what were you doing to arouse the teacher's wrath?

The climax came abruptly on a day late in March, when the catclaw and *agarita* breathed their soft scents from a thousand rocky hills, when the third and fourth grades were mixed and then divided for a spelling match, with lines drawn on opposite sides of the room. Coots Curry threw a fragment of chalk, and was whipped for it. The match resumed.

Hop Hoover, towering at my side, was looking wistfully out the open window at the street.

A Mexican woman went about her lawful occasions there, in the lazy spring sunshine—a brown and buxom Mexican woman pulling a small red wagon filled with laundry. The March wind flirted with her calico dress, dallied with it, lifted and molded it against voluptuous legs and backside. Hop was only twelve, but he had been reared in the cow camps; he had to shave once or twice a week. The frontier was at work on Hop, speeding his manhood. He nudged me, and snorted; he made bull calf whooshings. He pawed the floor like a rutting bull with his spurred boots.

"Warehouse!" called Old Miz Snell.

Nobody answered. It was Hop's turn in the spelling match, but he was lost out the window. He looked out where spring ran at the flood, where Life breathed and stirred and walked with a seductive swirl of calico skirts.

"Armond!" rasped Old Miz Snell. "Warehouse!"

Hop turned his head in his shy, startled manner, and grinned his bashful grin.

"Warehouse," he rumbled. "W-h-o-r-e-h-o-u-s-e, warehouse."

The schoolroom fell apart. Coots Curry and Howard Westfall and Ben Gilbert greeted this Freudian slip with howls of laughter, and so did most of the smaller boys, including me. Boots McKinney let out a particularly loud shriek of mirth. He was twelve, barefoot and leggy, and had all the gifts of the Irish. And he was most handy to Old Miz Snell.

She seized him by an ear and tugged him to the wall. He had been standing near the open door, and now she ordered him to pick up the round rock that was used as a door stop, and hold it at arm's length.

The stone weighed at least three pounds more than a geography book.

Boots's arm sagged quickly, but Old Miz Snell was there to yank the pin from her shirtwaist and sting his flagging biceps. He tilted his hand, dropped the rock squarely and very deliberately on her toes, and then ran chortling from the classroom.

Pandemonium broke. All hell tore loose. Rebellion was instantaneous and unanimous—now that the tyrant was crippled, even the girls struck a blow for liberty. Whizzing chalk and hurtling heavy board-backed erasers filled the air. Somebody overturned the desk of authority. Ben Gilbert—my especial chum—found himself strategically near the water bucket; he seized the tin dipper and began sloshing water into every face in range.

"Stop it!" screamed Old Miz Snell. "Stop it! Class come to order —do you hear?"

Nobody heard. Juvenile delinquency joyously inundated the entire second floor. Old Miz Snell tore her hair, and it came down in strings; she wept in impotent rage, and was most unlovely. The noise brought Miss Minta up from the floor below, and she bulked large in the doorway, stout-armed, kindly, and well remembered. She restored a semblance of order.

It didn't last long. The McKinneys lived just across the rocky hill point, only a hundred yards from the school. By the time the desk had been righted and the students had returned to their seats, Boots McKinney's mother suddenly charged through the doorway and seized Old Miz Snell by her mousy hair. She dragged the teacher out of the classroom, and pulled her all the way down the outside stairs where they could fight in the yard. It was not an even match: Old Miz Snell was never able to lay a hand on her assailant.

I will always suspect that it was from the McKinney family that *McCall's* magazine later stole the concept of "togetherness." That afternoon in Ozona, the McKinneys put on a display of togetherness that has seldom been matched. At the very moment Boots's mother was yanking Old Miz Snell down the stairs, his father—Ralph McKinney—was at the high school with hot Irish anger in his eyes, and a skinning blade in his hand. Only the concerted effort of several larger boys, including his own eldest son and my brother Floyd, prevented McKinney *père* from disemboweling Professor Snell on the spot.

School kept no more that day, and in the evening Floyd and other members of a high school committee called on the Snells at Mammy Kirkpatrick's hotel.

"You'd better be long gone by April Fool's Day!" they warned.

On the first of April, a number of things happened. The high school privy was overturned, of course, but that was standard order of procedure, and required neither imagination nor skill. The buggy on the high school's two-story roof, on the other hand, testified to some mute, inglorious engineering talent and considerable exercise of the steeplejack and rigger arts. There was a dead skunk tied to the bell rope at that very moment when a polecat—like a pear—is at its most flavorful. The entire male segment of the student body, which is to say perhaps fifteen boys, solemnly lined up to march into the building, but each executed a smart right-face at the door and went whooping off over the hills to explore Dudley's Cave, seven miles distant. And, when the teachers opened the classroom doors, they were nearly swept off their feet by an escaping zoo. The lower floor was thronged with cows, burros, excited chickens, and even one white male duck that quacked lonesomely as he waddled to the exit.

The second in command at the high school watched the duck, and even followed him for several hundred yards. Practically nobody kept ducks in that arid country.

The drake went up the San Angelo road and turned off toward a horse trough at the Dunlap house. The teacher wrote down the name of Ernest Dunlap, who was one of Floyd's fun-loving pals.

But Professor and Old Miz Snell were not there to view the menagerie. They rose before daylight, that morning, and at five o'clock they boarded the horse-drawn stage for Comstock, and the Southern Pacific Railroad. At Comstock they could catch the Sunset Limited. Whether they went west or east I do not know, but I rather imagine they had had enough of the west. They never came back to Ozona.

III

It rained a lot that spring. The lily-white blooms of wild onions sprinkled the rocky hills like stars after every shower; pink sweet william and fragile yellow and white buttercups and hollyhocks gladdened the flats, and bluebonnets ran wild. I woke in the cool and freshened night to hear the quiet, steady music of rain on the shingled roof, and the fluted accompaniment of rills liquid on the limestone ledges of the yard. No sleep was ever half so sweet as the drowsy surrender to that melody. . . .

"Allie boy?"

"Yes, ma'am?"

"Did you put the washtub under the corner of the kitchen, like I asked you?"

"Yes, ma'am, I put it there."

The town water was wonderful for drinking, but it left lime deposits in Mama's kettle, and she always tried to catch soft rain water for her washdays. Nobody ever did washing or ironing to suit her, and when there was a laundry in later years she would have none of it: she complained that the bedclothes smelled of soap and bleaching compounds and a scorching iron. Mama's bedclothes always smelled of cleanliness and sunshine. She boiled her wash in two fire-blackened five-gallon kerosene oil cans, on an outdoor fire, and stirred the soapsuds with a bleached broom handle. It was my job to rustle wood for washday, and to carry water from the hydrant. She used two rinse waters and half a cup of bluing, and dried the wash in the sun and the high windy air.

Then she dipped the soapsuds from her tub and scrubbed the white limestone rock of the yard, until it was a clean as the floors in the house.

Rain in West Texas was high grass, and money in the pocket and credit at the bank. It meant bigger calf and lamb crops, and more jobs for ranch hands like Dee and Jay. The broomweeds and Johnson grass would grow rank at the side of the road; there would be more

blue-bottle flies and more screw worms to plague the livestock . . .
more quail whistling on the hills, more cottontail rabbits and woodrats, more rattlesnakes and prairie dogs . . . more of everything that
drew sustenance from the thirsty earth.

When it rained in the night Floyd and Bert and I sat up and
listened and hoped. If the rain was heavy enough, Johnson's Draw
would come down, and there would be swimming for two weeks or
more.

When Ben Gilbert and I were small boys and planning to become
rich ranchmen, we swore that we would drill two wells and erect
two windmills near the head of the draw, so that there would be an
unfailing supply of water to fill the swimming hole north of town.
The thought of perpetuating our memory by constructing a swimming pool did not occur to us: we had never seen a swimming pool,
and we wanted running water.

Johnson's Draw took its twisting course through the mesquite flat.
Scrubby wild walnut bushes lined the banks along the shallow reaches
where the bottom was covered with smooth, skeletal white stones;
hackberries and big liveoaks shaded the deeper pools. This was a high
plateau country, a tableland tilted southward; the rocky hills and
slanted flats made a swift watershed and produced flash floods both
spectacular and dangerous. After a heavy rain, water remained in
the swimming hole until it became "too thick to swallow, and too thin
to chew," and shrank into puddles rimmed by sun-cracked mud, and
the waterbugs danced prodigiously across its surface. The mud was
churned into a loblolly by the hoofs of cattle come to drink; many
a "ganted" cow got down in the mud to bawl piteously and finally
die lacking human aid. The next hard rain would hang a pathetically
shriveled bag of hide and bones in a high tree crotch farther down
the draw. Old Shanghai Pierce had made jest of this, in Papa's youth
and down on the coastal prairies: when a visitor wondered how it
came about that hides and horns were so high in the trees, Shanghai
trumpeted that those cattle of his were great browsers. Said they
climbed and foraged for the tender buds, and sometimes slipped and
"hung theirselves in the tree forks."

The spotty rains of West Texas fall not alike on the just and un-just, but on the just lucky. Many a cattleman has watched dry shod and filled with envy while a wet black cloud breaks over his neigh-bor's pasture. Heavy rain up around Four Mile Hill used to bring the draw down while the main street of Ozona was still dusty.

Someone usually got the word and yelled that the draw was com-ing down. Running water has always had a terrible fascination for West Texans, who see so little of it, and half the town hastened to the draw to watch the rise. A shout, "Here she comes!" and the crowd would fall back from the banks as an angry wall of water swept around a bend in the channel, rolling rocks with it and folding the rank green walnuts under and lapping out to lift the blades of the mesquite grass and drive cottontails from their covert. The water slowed to fill the deep places; it roared down the rocky shallows faster than a man could run, bearing dry cowchips and assorted driftwood on its foaming crest. When it had settled to smooth, swollen flow, hundreds of toads came out of hibernation and floated downstream, riding tandem and croaking happily. They made love all the way to Devil's River, and perhaps to the Rio Grande, and we wondered if the lower Rio Grande wouldn't be knee deep in toads.

Floyd couldn't even remember when he had learned to swim, and Bert certainly had been swimming before we lived in Christoval. Here was I—six, seven, and eight years old in successive summers, and unable to swim a stroke. This was like fighting: it was some-thing I had to learn to do. Floyd said again that ducks, puppies, bullfrogs, and small boys should swim naturally.

We were mother naked beside the brown waters. Floyd took hold of my wrists; Bert grasped my ankles. They began swinging me like a sagging hammock.

> *"One for the money,*
> *Two for the show;*
> *Three to get ready*
> *And four to go!"*

[265]

I soared over Johnson's Draw and splashed flat on my back, in water ten feet deep. I went under, came up strangling, and heard Floyd's voice faintly through the water in my ears. "Swim, Bit-fit— swim!" he shouted.

I threshed the water wildly, and sank again.

It was well known that a drowning man sinks three times and only comes up twice. Also, on the third submersion—according to what I had read—his whole past life flashes in review.

When I went down the third time, I remembered that. Sure enough, the tapestry of past works ran through my mind, displaying a shockingly evil pattern. There was the window I had broken one summer at the schoolhouse, right beside a placard that warned that defacing the building was punishable by a fifty-dollar fine or thirty days in jail, and I wept because Dee wouldn't have the fifty dollars and would have to go to jail for me. There was the time when I was first given a Daisy air rifle, and in my eagerness killed a mockingbird by mistake. The most scarlet thread of all marked the day Mama caught me under an overturned wagon bed with Annie Rooney. We were both six. . . .

Floyd let me go down three times, then dived in and brought me ashore. "I'll just say!" he exclaimed. "What's eatin' you, Bit-fit? You swim like a rock, and dive like a feather! Well, let's try again."

Bert also looked upon me with reproach. "Time I was your age," he began, "I—"

"Well, you had a river!" I told him. "You had a whole slew of rivers. If I had a river, instead of this old muddy draw—"

"Water's water," Floyd said. "One for the money . . ."

The third time out, I rebelled and fled into the mesquites. Floyd confiscated my clothes. I was afraid that he was going to tie knots in them so tightly that I would have to use my teeth to loosen them. I knew what was generally conceded to be the dirtiest of all dirty Irish tricks: tie the knots tightly, and then pee on them.

Floyd didn't do that. He just laughed and asked me how I was going to go home naked. And just then three teen-aged girls strolled curiously along the road, surreptitiously seeing what they could see through the revealingly scanty mesquites.

I fled back to the swimming hole, and was thrown in again and again, and each time Floyd saved me from drowning. We wore each other out, that wet summer. I was filled with a great appreciation of what he was trying to do. But it just didn't work.

"Could Papa swim?" I asked, hoping to put the blame on heredity.

Floyd was beginning to use grown-up man talk—when Mama was not in hearing. "Why, hell, yes!" he said, spitting between his teeth. "Everybody can swim but you!"

The summer when I was nine brought little rain, but all the boys in town ran barefoot through the cow trails of the mesquite flat to a new windmill on one of the Henderson ranches. There was a big dirt tank, and swimming water well over my head. We peeled off our clothes on the run, a half mile away, and shouted: "Last one in's a rotten egg!" and "The one that made it up has to eat it!"

Enlivening this sport were thousands of wasps and yellow jackets that had built their nests in the mesquite trees. The leaders in our dusty race knocked down the wasp nests, and fled the consequences; the smaller boys could not leave the trails because of cactus and grassburs and mesquite thorns. We ran naked through the buzzing swarms of angry insects, and sometimes had to put blue mud on the stings when we reached the tank.

Floyd tied string to the handles of two one-gallon cans that had once contained windmill oil, and made me a pair of crude water wings. Buoyed up by these and his always smooth sales talk, I paddled all over the big tank.

Then one day when I was in the middle of the tank and terribly alone, the string broke under my chest. Both cans leaped like corks released under water, and were far beyond my reach.

Floyd and Bert and all the others had climbed high on the windmill tower, the better to observe a pair of belligerent bulls that pawed the ground and were intent upon locking horns and settling a dispute arisen over some particularly attractive heifer. It was a loud and spectacular war of movement; it surged to the very foot of the windmill, and trapped the noncombatants on the tower.

So it would have done no good to cry for help. When the string broke, I could only remember the title of an Oliver Optic book I owned: *Sink or Swim*. I splashed the tank water desperately, and all at once found myself staying afloat.

"Look!" Bert yelled from the windmill. "Allie's swimming!"

Floyd looked and admired. "I'll just say!" he declared. "Probably could have done it two, three years ago, if he had tried."

It was the summer after that when Ben Gilbert and I and the Holmsley boys—Peery and George and Larry—made an important discovery that virtually brought swimming into the home. Of the two stone reservoirs on Waterworks Hill, one served the householders and the business part of town; the other fed water to the courthouse, the jail, and the schools. This one had a conical roof and a small observation tower, with a trapdoor and ladder leading down to the shaded water.

The discovery we made one summer day was that the trapdoor padlock could be picked with a bent piece of baling wire.

"Just look at that water!" Peery said in awe. "It's been here all the time."

Ben and Peery were the leaders; they were three years older than George and I. "Last one in's a rotten egg!" Ben announced.

He began shucking his clothes right there in the observation tower. I was scared.

"What if they catch us?" I asked.

"Ain't going to catch us," Ben said. "We'll hide our clothes, and pull the trapdoor shut. And maybe we'd better hide the lock, too—just in case."

Peery was getting undressed, too. I looked down into the gloom, and suffered claustrophobia. This would be a strange kind of swimming, in a covered tank. I had visions of being unable to reach the ladder, of swimming in slow and agonizing circles and trying to hold on to the perpendicular, moss-slick wall, until there was only a weak flutter of the last hand going under.

But I didn't dare admit that I was frightened. The thing had to be reasoned out.

"Say," I said. "This is the water for the courthouse and jail!"

"Don't make any difference," Ben said. "There ain't anybody in jail except that Meskin that busted into the hardware store. And maybe Albert-the-Dutchman-the-Bootmaker—they throw him in jail every Saturday night, when he gets drunk."

"Allie's scared!" Peery Holmsley jeered.

"I ain't either!" I denied. "But this is school water too. We'll have to drink it, next month."

Ben pointed to a thin trickle of water that poured into the tank as long as wind turned the windmill. "Remember what it said in the physiology?" he asked. "It said in the physiology that running water purifies itself every forty feet. That water has run a sight more than forty feet, because the windmill's a hundred yards away."

"Yeah, and it runs more'n a quarter of a mile before it gets to school!" Peery added. He went on down the ladder, and made a cool and inviting splash.

I remembered reading the same thing in the physiology text, so I couldn't argue any more. We swam. We swam every day for a month, and nobody ever found out that we could pick the trapdoor lock.

And when school reopened that September, there wasn't any difference in the taste of the water at all.

Twenty-two

We heard, quite unexpectedly, from Papa. I remember it well, because the intelligence gave him much greater stature in my eyes. He was in Old Mexico, where he had recently gone through a revolution, or some sanguinary phase of one.

Papa did not write to us, but to his sister, Aunt Docia. Uncle Nick and Aunt Docia Rogers were still sheep ranching on the Pecos, but they now had a house in Ozona.

Aunt Docia brought us the letter. It was a curious missive, scribbled with indelible pencil on ruled tablet paper decorated with a gaudy rose. Papa was working in the mines. Of the revolution he had too little to say: he had been forced to occupy a trench for several days while bullets whistled overhead, but whether he was an active participant or enjoyed noncombatant status was not clear. He liked Mexico and its people, and indicated that he might look for some new country down there. He did not care for the local Mexican priest, who, counting his beads in the plaza, muttered *"El Diablo! El Diablo!"* every time he passed Papa. Papa demanded to know if he was being called a devil; the priest said no, he was castigating Satan. Papa had never been a very religious man; he suspected the *padre* was really trying to form an unholy alliance with the devil.

By this time, Papa had become a misty legend to me. I could not really recall his image. When I asked questions about him, Mama was sometimes inclined to be vague, and Floyd was quick with his filial scorn. But other boys had fathers in residence, and spoke of them—not always with affection or respect. There was the Run Under the House, Here Comes Papa! school, and there was a more enviable class, in which Papa was a solid citizen and a respected member of the household; and there was the man who smeared himself with engine grease after evenings in the pool hall.

These various classes of the father image confused me a little as I grew up, but in family pride I tried to keep the Papa Legend shining. Papa had Turned Loose the Quail, he had Roped a House, he had been Mixed Up in the Skinning War.

Now there was something new. He was a military man. He had been in a war, just in time to round out a completely satisfying picture to my boyish imagination. A great deal of the literature available to me dealt with one armed conflict or another; along with G. A. Henty I had been with Lee in Virginia, and in company of lesser literary lights with Ethan Allen at Ticonderoga, and—many times— with Davy Crockett at the Alamo.

I basked in the afterglow of Papa's martial experience, but Floyd scoffed at it. I wondered, aloud, if Papa had done any shooting in the battle. Floyd said, "Sure—just like Dee said he did at Sheffield that time. When the first gun went off, Papa probably shot right out the door and kept going."

Mama told him to hush. "After all," she said, "your Papa could have got killed."

Not long after that conservation, Mama and Bert and I nearly jumped out of our hides when we heard a shot in the living room. We dashed in there from the kitchen, and found Floyd sitting in Mama's rocking chair, doubled up with laughter. He had the .22 repeating rifle across his lap.

"Floyd!" Mama exclaimed. "What on earth? I thought maybe you had shot yourself!"

"Ha ha!" Floyd roared. "It wasn't me. Ha ha! It was Papa!"

He pointed. Hanging on the wall was an enlarged crayon reproduction of the tintypes Papa and Mama had made just after their marriage; the artist had made it appear that Papa was standing just behind Mama's shoulder. Now there was a neat little round hole in the glass, and an even neater one squarely between Papa's eyes.

"Why, Floyd!" Mama said reproachfully. "I declare, I just know you did that on purpose!"

"No, I didn't," he said solemnly. "I was cleaning the gun when it went off. Just happened to be pointed that way. Let that be a lesson to you, Bit-fit—always keep a gun pointed high like that when you're cleaning it." Then he started laughing again. "Well, we can always say Papa got shot while he was down in Mexico."

There were a few more letters and postcards from Papa, all to Aunt Docia. He did not ask about his children, or about Mama, who had divorced him at Stephenville. Papa was now near his middle fifties, and perhaps he could see that he had rolled his wagon wheels over a lot of beautiful new country, and past a great deal of happiness. . . .

II

Mama was fighting a losing battle of her own, trying to keep her boys in school. She really had lost it the day she took the job as janitor: Floyd and Bert and I were determined that she should not work as a cleaning woman to give us an education. Mama's argument prevailed for a year, but she could not win.

Spring was the season when the processes and the confinements of education seemed unbearable. In March the hills turned soft with bluebonnet blue, and the air was honey sweet with *agarita* scent. There were March days when northers whistled past the high school and dust banners rode the sky; there were nights heady with spring and starglow, and always the restlessness that burns the blood. Spring was the beginning of epic movement in the ranch country: the tides ran full through roundup and branding, tally and sale and shipping drive. All of us could sit at our desks and hear the herds swinging up through the mesquite flat with a music as primitive as the beat of Indian drums.

It was the time of year when anybody big enough to straddle a horse could get a job, and many a graduating class was made up entirely of girls.

I had an argument with my new teacher, in the fifth grade. It was in the spelling class. She asked me what a cobbler was, and I told her it was a peach pie.

Her name was Miss Glee Stafford, and she was from somewhere in the North. She was small and dainty and blonde, and when I was turning eleven I was madly in love with her.

"No," she said. "A cobbler is a shoemaker."

"It's a peach pie!" I insisted, even though I adored her and was dreaming about her every night.

She whipped Ben, and Hop, and Shotgun Bunger so soundly with a strap that blood showed on their shirts. But Miss Glee had no trouble with me. I was a model pupil that year.

"Mama," Floyd said firmly, "I'm big enough to work. I'm not going to have Dee and Jay feeding me any longer."

He pushed his chair back from the table, reached for his hat, and said he was going out to look for a job. Floyd was seventeen, and in the ninth grade.

"If Floyd's big enough to work, I am too!" Bert said. "I can get a job driving the meat wagon for Bob Cooke. He said he'd pay me fifteen dollars a month."

I turned green with envy. *Four bits a day, every day of your life!* The most money I had ever had, except for that five dollars from the cowhides, was two bits on the Fourth of July.

"You'll both just stay in school!" Mama said. "Bless Patty, I'll keep you in school even if I have to take in washing!"

That scared us—for a while. The threat to take in washing was unfair; it was a feminine weapon very akin to the tyranny of tears. Every time I carried wash water for Mama, after that, I was afraid she would go out and solicit laundry while she had the hot soapsuds.

Mama said it was no disgrace to be poor. She said to look at some of the people in town who put everything they had on their backs, but didn't educate their young'uns. This, she said, was false pride. What she was trying to pass on to us, she said, was the real pride of being fine-haired and blue-blooded.

We could see it made a difference, all right, but we turned the argument against her. Taking in washing would be a definite step down the ladder; it was even worse than sweeping out the schools. And we told her she should know, very well, that Dee and Jay would never let her become a washerwoman.

Things were happening fast. Jay, being Papa's child, succumbed to the lure of far places. He could find nothing around Ozona to satisfy his bent for machinery; he wound up in Wichita, Kansas, working for the railroad—and getting married.

And Floyd, as if knowing that time was short, intensified his campaign to Make a Man of me. . . .

He left school in the ninth grade, despite Mama's pleading. He went to Stephenville to live for a while with Ivanhoe, and to enroll at John Tarleton College. But his finances ran out, and he did not finish the term.

He came back to Ozona when Mama and Bert and I were living temporarily on one of the Friend ranches with Dee, forty miles from town. We had not been to Ozona in two months, and I had a formidable growth of curly hair, something like a denizen of the Australian bush.

"Floyd," Mama said, "you worked around the barbershop one summer. Before we go to town, I wish you'd cut Allie's hair a little —just fix it so he won't be a disgrace when he goes to the barber."

Floyd chuckled deep down in his chest, and anybody should have known that he was up to mischief. "Why, sure!" he said cheerfully. "You come out here, Bit-fit!"

He put a chair in the yard behind the house, hard by an old abandoned concrete cistern that was twelve feet deep, and had once been used to store rainwater from the roof before a well was drilled. He had a pair of hand clippers. When I sat in his chair, he tied a bed sheet around me for a barber's towel—and tied it so tightly I was helpless.

Then he ran the clippers from my forehead to the nape of my neck, cutting a single swath close to the scalp. Having done that, he tossed the clippers down the old cistern, and yelled: "Next!"

I came out of the chair struggling with the sheet, and yelling for Mama, and I was fighting mad. But Floyd had soft and smooth words.

"Why, Bit-fit," he said, "that's the latest style. They call it the Denver Curl. All the girls are just crazy about it!"

He fended my attack, and laughed again. He said, "Now, you let that be a lesson to you, Bit-fit! You want to be careful about going into just any old barbershop. You want to pick a barber carefully, so you don't get barber's itch."

Mama cropped the rest of my hair the best she could with her scissors, and when we made the long wagon trip to Ozona I had my head shaved and started all over again.

The let-that-be-a-lesson-to-you theme was recurrent. On a Sunday afternoon, Floyd took me to the vacant lot behind the store of Chris Meinecke & Son, where he had just gone to work. "Want to show you something, Bit-fit," he said, and led the way to a cluster of empty gasoline drums. The first two automobiles had come to Ozona; there were no garages or filling stations, but just Tom Smith's blacksmith shop and drums of gasoline at places like Chris Meinecke's. The drums had been emptied by the siphon method—which left an inch or two of fuel in the bottom of each. They stood under the hot summer sun, expanding their gases.

Floyd unscrewed the cap of a gasoline drum while we stood close. He struck a match on the seat of his pants, and dropped it inside.

"Run, Bit-fit, run!" he yelled.

There was no time to run. The drum went six feet in the air. Floyd and I were both blown flat. He got to his feet dusting off his clothes, and laughing.

"See?" he said. "Let that be a lesson to you. Never fool around gasoline with matches."

[275]

Mama had finally been prevailed upon to give up her janitor's job—the new stone schoolhouse was near completion, and would be much too big for her to handle. Prior experience in sweeping out got me my first salaried job: I took care of the Baptist church, ringing the bell on Sundays and for Wednesday-night prayer meetings, and building fires in the potbellied stove in the winter. This paid me two dollars and a half a month, and I bought a second-hand bicycle from Boots McKinney.

Riding north on the San Angelo road, toward the Dunlap place, I remembered that this was where Floyd and Russell Dyer had sheeted themselves to lie in wait for Ernest Dunlap on a Halloween. They had Ernest worried for a moment, but did not frighten him noticeably, because he remembered what day it was. Then they went over into "Mexico," and haunted a ditch and moaned until the householder came out.

This man happened to be the last surviving veteran of the Battle of San Jacinto, which was fought in 1836. He was reputed to be 110 years old, and for some time had diplomatically asserted that he fought on the side of Sam Houston, as a scout.

He came out into the road, saw the shrouded specters rising from the ditch, keeled over with a heart attack, and died.

Floyd and Russell Dyer were chastened and sobered—to an extent. No charges were brought against them.

"A hundred and ten years!" Floyd said later. "Man alive! What could you expect? And besides, we didn't even know he lived there."

He went to San Angelo to work in a wholesale liquor store—a busy place in a town of ninety or a hundred saloons. I went there that fall, to attend the West Texas State Fair. I was nearly thirteen, and had saved five dollars for this trip. Two schoolmates, Harvey and Bud, accompanied me on this high adventure, and we were lucky enough to get a ride with A. C. Kincaid, a rancher who owned a brand-new Packard car. He had a Colt .45 and a belt of ammunition lying in the rear seat; there was an increasing amount of border trouble.

Harvey and Bud took a room at the Landon Hotel. I moved in with Floyd at his boardinghouse, but saw very little of him. He was always shaving and putting on a clean white shirt, and going out in the evenings.

Hamburgers were a nickel, and milkshakes a dime. I lived high on the hog for three days, secure in the knowledge that a big, strong, generous brother would see that I got back home. The schoolteachers in Ozona had encouraged this trip: the fair, they told everybody, would be very educational.

It was. I witnessed baseball games and quarter horse races—both dear to a Texan's heart. I saw death-defying motorcycle rides on the perpendicular walls of the Motordome, and watched my first airplane—a two-winged craft piloted by Karl Kuhl, the Fool Flyer from Florida and the star attraction of the whole show. There was a marvelously designed working model of the Panama Canal, which had been opened only recently. And I somehow managed to get on the viewing platform of a show called "Pussy in the Well," but just as a nude woman began fleeing a nude man below—she was greased, and extremely elusive—I was thrown out as being under age.

After three days, it was time to leave the carnival-tented reaches of Chadbourne Street, and head homeward. I told Floyd that I was down to two bits. I said I would like to borrow two dollars and a half for the rail fare to Barnhart, where the Kansas City, Mexico & Orient Railroad had recently built its westering tracks, coming within some thirty miles of Ozona. From Barnhart, I told him, I could ride the mail stage on credit.

Floyd was shaving and putting on a clean white shirt, and thinking about a girl. I felt a sadness, knowing instinctively that he was soon going to be lost to me, that he would have no time for me, and that I would have to make the rest of my way toward manhood without his help. He looked at me from the mirror, darkly handsome and scented with bay rum. "Got two bits, you say?" he asked, struggling with a collar button. "And all you have to do is to get to Barnhart?"

"The ticket to Barnhart is two-fifty," I said.

Floyd became confidential. "Look, Bit-fit," he said, "you haven't been around. You don't know the ropes. No Big Corporation—like the railroad—ever pays its employees enough. The conductors have to knock down on the company when they can, and I don't figure it's a crime to rob a Big Corporation. See what I mean?"

"Well . . . not exactly. I need—"

"Now, you've got two bits. I'll tell you just what to do. Don't buy a ticket. Get on the train. When the conductor comes around and asks for tickets, just slip him the two bits, and say, 'Here, brother—drop this down in your pocket and don't tell the company anything about it.' You got that? That's all there is to it."

"You sure?" I wavered.

His voice was honey sweet. Of course he was sure. He reminded me that I had only ridden a railroad the time Jay went to Stephenville to kill Will Lancaster. Floyd, on the other hand, had gone to Fort Worth with cattle, and once even to Denver. He had Been Around.

Besides, he said, he didn't have two-fifty just then.

I looked up Harvey and Bud a little later. They were resigned to a dull evening, because they had just enough money left to pay their hotel bill and buy their railroad tickets.

I broke the glad news that they didn't really need more than two bits for their railroad fare. Something of Floyd's bland plausibility had rubbed off on me, and they believed. They paid their hotel bill and put aside two bits apiece, and then we went out on the town with the rest of their money. We saw Spidora, the Girl Who Lives in a Web—Floyd told me later it was a trick done with mirrors—and we chunked the cats, and we got thrown out of another outer sanctum of a show for men only.

Next morning we met at the depot, our confidence slightly wan, and boarded the train. It had one passenger coach, one mail and express car, and more than thirty cattle cars which would be loaded at intervals, down the line. I moved nervously into a window seat at the front of the coach; the other boys went farther back.

The train moved, and I began rehearsing the lines Floyd had given me. Just across the aisle was a big man wearing some kind of star on his vest and that didn't help. I felt much the same as I had felt the time Floyd coaxed me into diving from a thirty-foot windmill tower into a tin water tank that looked like a teacup. But I was committed.

After an eternity, and thirty miles out on the prairie, the conductor appeared. He had a broad and honest face; I knew at once that he was not the kind of man who would knock down on a Big Corporation. I realized that Floyd had played another of his jokes upon me, and I clutched my two bits in a sweating palm, and waited miserably for a tap on the shoulder.

It never came. Somehow, the conductor passed me by. He went on down the aisle. There was a sudden stir, back there, and a voice rising above the rattle of the train, which was pulling onto a siding by some loading pens filled with close-packed, bawling cattle.

"Trying to beat your way, eh?" the conductor asked in a loud and virtuous tone. "Well, we know how to handle that on *this* railroad! Now . . . you see them cows out there? You just drag your butts out there and help punch 'em on board!"

Harvey and Bud went by the window where I sat in cushioned comfort, trying to stifle my laughter and still feeling like a Judas. They gave me some black looks before and after their labor in the choking dust of the corrals and the loading chute, and for some weeks I had the feeling that they might be laying for me after school.

Floyd came down to Ozona a few days later, and was sitting on the front gallery when I came from school. He watched me walk up the rocky hill, and burst into loud, thigh-slapping laughter.

"Got thrown off the train, didn't you?" he asked. "Had to walk forty or fifty miles—had to sleep out on the prairie. Well, *that'll* make a man out of you, Bit-fit! And it'll teach you a lesson. *Always* pay your way—never try to beat your way anywhere!"

I smiled a superior smile, and he was puzzled. "You *did* get thrown off the train, didn't you?" he demanded.

"Why, hell, no!" I said, borrowing some of his own grown-up

talk. "See this? This is the same two-bit piece. I've got a better system."

"I'll just say!" Floyd marveled.

It must have taken them nearly two years to build the new schoolhouse; they had started it before Floyd left high school. The rock was quarried from the far side of our hill, and dynamite blasts rattled Mama's dishes, and Dee left his ranch job to drive a wagon hauling the rock and be at home for a while.

Jay came back home and worked on another ranch for a few months, his romance temporarily on the rocks. He found solace in a Curtis Cyclone motorcycle, and came roaring into town wearing goggles and gloves instead of Stetson and spurs.

The Automobile Age was coming to West Texas. Twelve-horse or sixteen-burro outfits still brought freight into town, but they were doomed. A half-dozen automobiles were already roaring around the square.

The feeling that the Old Frontier was passing . . . that people were getting soft, was inescapable. Besides, there was another feeling that we hadn't known before. Troubles were kicking up along the Rio Grande, as they had for ninety years, but all at once they were United States troubles, whereas before they had belonged only to Texas. And, about the same time, things just flew off the handle in Europe.

Ben and Peery and I and the Joslin boys sat under the Big Tree, a liveoak under the hill from Mama's house, and discussed the international situation as we saw it. All of us were on the side of Germany, because so many countries had ganged up on her.

It was August, 1914, and I was nearly thirteen. . . .

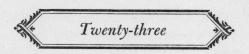

Twenty-three

*S*eptember began the string of months with R's in them. In West Texas this had nothing to do with oysters; September was when furs began getting good, and by November they were prime. For a prime polecat—the fur catalog called them skunks—you could get maybe two dollars. There was a legend, unsubstantlated locally, that a pure white polecat's hide was worth more than a hundred, and that pure black was just as valuable.

Nobody had ever seen an unstriped polecat, so far as we knew, but there was always hope that such an animal existed. Ben Gilbert and I consulted Mr. Nick Wigzell about the matter. Mr. Wigzell, a small bowlegged man with fierce blue eyes, had gone up the Texas Trail with cattle in his youth, and had been a professional trapper for many years. When we found him he was sitting in the doorway of a shed back of his house, holding a battered stewpan and narrowly watching a hound dog in a wire pen. Outside the wire, half the dogs in Ozona were hopefully assembled.

"Ol' Queen's in heat," Mr. Wigzell informed us in his gentle drawl. "I been tryin' to get her to make some water. When it comes to makin' wolf bait, there ain't anything can beat water from a bitch in heat."

We asked him about pure white polecats, and he bit off a chew of tobacco and said he had never seen one. But it was true, he said, that a pure white polecat fur was worth a lot of money.

"You boys figgerin' on trappin'?" he asked, keeping one eye on Old Queen.

"We've got seven traps," Ben said. "Three Number Ones and two Number Twos, single-spring, and two double-spring Number Fours for lobo wolves."

"Now that's where the money is," Mr. Wigzell said, nodding approval. "State pays a bounty, and most times the rancher does too. Last year I ketched thirty-odd lobos, but they're thinnin' out. I got about seventy-five coyote skelps." He rose to his feet, but Old Queen was just fooling and coquetting with the dogs beyond the wire. "Driest dawg I ever seen!" he complained. "Where you goin' to trap?"

"Close to town," Ben said. "So we can run the trapline in the mornings, before school."

"Well, that's good for polecats and wildcats and coons, and of course the lobos and coyotes ain't necessarily forty miles away either. Know how to make wolf bait?"

Ben said that we did. He said the way he heard it, you could tie a bottle under a stud horse or a dog, didn't make any difference. Then you chopped up the liver and lights, or any other bloody parts of a beef, and added garlic, and you corked the bottle tightly and buried it for three weeks. Then it was ready.

"Left out one thing," said Mr. Wigzell. "Assafidity. You put a few little bitty pieces of assafidity in that bottle, and there ain't anything like it to make it work. Be shore you tie the cork down before you bury it."

It looked to us like Mr. Nick Wigzell had a pretty soft life, just sitting there in the warm September sunshine, watching Old Queen and waiting for her to cooperate. But we knew better. He spent months at a time out on first one ranch and another camping out with a wagon, and running his traps on foot. On most ranches, his job also called for him to put out poison for prairie dogs, and he was out in freezing northers and scorching suns. His right index finger was off

[282]

at the middle joint, and I could remember the time when it happened.

"Tell us about when you got rattlesnake bit, Mr. Wigzell," I urged.

"Well, wasn't much to it. I was out about fifty miles east of here, and was settin' my traps one evenin' about sundown. Spread a Number Four with both feet, and put her in the hole I'd dug, and put a sheet of paper over the trap like I always do. Reached behind me to get a handful of dirt and leaves to sprinkle over the paper, and wham! Felt that snake hit my hand and knock it clear out of the way, and it was like havin' a couple of hot needles stuck into you. Well, it made me so durned mad I turned around and lit out after that snake. Chased him through four or five clumps of catclaw and cedar, and he run under some rocks, but I finally cornered him and stomped him to death. After that, I got to thinkin' I'd better do somethin' about the bite, but I cut off his rattles first—still got 'em—fourteen rattles and a button. I tied up my finger, and had to go out and ketch my team. Hitched up and started for town, and by then it was plumb dark. Had a bottle of whiskey along for jist such thing as snakebite, or I shore wouldn't have made it. As it was, I come in here about noon next day, and couldn't hardly get off the wagon. Wasn't the snakebite itself that caused me to lose this here half of my finger —it was blood poison settin' in when the durned thing was nearly well."

We hung around a little while longer, and Mr. Wigzell told us to wash our traps with coal oil every few days, to keep the human scent off them, and said he always tried to wear gloves when he was setting traps for lobos or coyotes. Wasn't wearing gloves that time he got snakebit; wouldn't have done any good, anyway. Coyotes, he said, were smarter than lots of people. Lots smarter than Old Queen, yonder.

"Well, I shore hope you ketch a white polecat," he said as we thanked him and rose to go. And when we were around the corner and starting up the dusty street, we heard his patience snap.

"Durn you, Queen!" he shouted. "You think I ain't got anything to do but set around here all day?"

We were ready for the enterprise that made the Astors rich and built St. Louis. Ben had a dog, a brown-and-white shepherd named Ring. Both of us had .22's, but money for ammunition was hard to come by. First, we would have to sell at least one hide, and to do that we had to ship it to Funsten Brothers—in St. Louis.

Meanwhile we could kill anything we caught with our nigger-shooters. Ben owned an ancient .32-caliber bullet mold, and we melted scrap lead and turned out pellets that went hard and true and could have cracked a man's skull. We slung the traps over our shoulders on an evening after school, and went jingling over the hills, where we killed two woodrats for our first bait.

Next morning, up with the frosty dawn, we met our first disappointment. Nothing had happened. We went back after school and killed a cottontail for fresh bait, and on the following morning a patch of white in the gloom of the postoaks made us catch our breaths in excitement. But it wasn't an albino polecat worth a hundred dollars; it was an ordinary, back-fence variety of tomcat, not at all injured by the jaws of the Number One trap, but spitting and yowling mad.

He scratched both of us severely, and we had to find some wire and rope him around the neck before we could set him free. That made us late for school, and for days thereafter I remembered the look in his blazing yellow eyes.

Dee came home for a few days at this time, and laughed when he learned what Ben and I were doing. He said he doubted that anybody in the Bosworth family would ever be a good trapper.

"Probably take after Papa too much," he said and winked at Mama. "Like when he turned the quail loose. Couldn't stand to see anything penned up."

"Couldn't stand to make any money!" Floyd said.

"Now Floyd, you hush," Mama said. "I guess your Papa was kind of funny that way. Seemed like he never had much use for money."

"Well, it sure never had any use for him," Floyd declared.

When we went out over the hills at daybreak, the air was fresh and chill and spiced with cedar scent, and sometimes after a rain and a "silver" freeze, the cedars were all Christmas trees with a million crystal pendants that hurt the eyes when the sun came up and made them sparkle. Our breath made steam, and we stopped on the rimrock after a hard climb and saw woodsmoke lying blue in the little canyons, and heard the engine on Waterworks Hill start its thrumming as if it were many miles away. Sunup brought a breeze, and the cedars moved as if waking to dance music; the icicles tinkled and fell in a shining shower. I remembered the way Papa felt about trapped things, and understood; I remembered the tomcat's yellow eyes, mingling pain and defiance and a momentary hatred for man that was new, and yet ages old. We went on, and I was half glad and half sorry when we found the next trap unsprung.

But the savage was only latent in my breast. One morning we came expectantly and eagerly to a Number Two trap carefully set in a postoak thicket, with Ben leading the way. He peered cautiously around a cedar bush, and let out a yell.

"We got one!" he cried, and drew back the sling of his niggershooter. "We got one!"

When it came to using a niggershooter, Ben had just about the fastest draw in the West. But the polecat beat him to it. There was a *whish,* and Ben gasped and stumbled blindly into the cedar, making a choking sound.

I leaped forward to fill the breach in our rampart, and the polecat beat me to the draw, too. I rolled on the ground, suffocated and blind.

It was several minutes before either of us could see well enough to dispatch our quarry, which had run out of ammunition. We buried the carcass where it lay. Ben said that was the only thing to do; the earth would absorb most of the scent, and we could return that afternoon and take care of the skinning job. We intended to "case" the hide, slitting it up the legs and then pulling it over the head the way you do a sweater, after which we could stretch it, inside out, over a fork cut from a cedar, until it dried.

"What do you suppose it's worth?" I asked.

"Pretty nice hide. Maybe two-fifty."

We were in the money at last. I began to notice a curious thing. I couldn't smell myself any longer, and neither could I smell Ben.

It was time to get to school. We buried the trap too, so it would be ready for resetting, and took our triumphant way back over the hills. The take-up bell was just ringing as we ran into the school yard and fell in at the tail of the marching line. Our seats were near the stove, and it glowed plump and cherry red with morning's first stoking. All the windows were down.

Ora Mae turned her pretty head. "Pee-uw!" she said, wrinkling her nose and looking across the aisle at me. Peery Holmsley yelled, "Miss Glee—Miss Glee! There's a polecat in the room!"

Miss Glee rose to her feet and held a scented hankerchief to her nose. "All right, children!" she said with a slight adenoidal twang. "Who is it?"

Ben pointed at Peery. Peery pointed at me. I pointed at Hop, and he whooshed like a bull calf:

"You might as well tell me!" Miss Glee said. "I'll find out."

Ben and I exchanged glances, and I saw the gleam in his eye. He held up his hand. "It's me," he said. "Me and Allie."

"Well, you and Allie get out of this room this very minute, do you hear? Go home and take a bath and change clothes, and—get out right now, before it gets worse. Peery, will you please open a few windows?"

We went rejoicing, knowing that with luck we could escape a whole day of school. It was funny that we couldn't smell ourselves, but it wasn't at all funny to Mama, who said bless Patty, it was hard enough to keep me in clothes so I could go to school, without having everything ruined. She made me undress in the chickenhouse and drop everything in a tub half filled with coal oil. I had to take a sponge bath in the cold, with coal oil in the water. Then I pointed out to Mama that I couldn't go back to school smelling like kerosene, either, and besides, it would be dangerous to sit near that stove all soaked up like a lamp wick.

Mama said she just declared, she ought to take a switch to me. But she hadn't done that since I was nine or ten, since a day when she whipped me and I laughed. She said then that it wouldn't do any good to whip me any more.

The polecat hide brought two dollars from Funsten Brothers, and proved what Ben and I had contended all along—that there was money in trapping. But Mama put her foot down. She said if I wanted to trap, I'd have to wait until school was out for the summer. She hadn't heard that rule about months with R's in them.

II

Mama was never an actively religious woman—she neither taught Sunday school nor served on committees—but she knelt in prayer every night, and always derived a quiet comfort from her membership in the Baptist Church. When evangelists came to town for revival meetings, she attended faithfully. and required her younger boys to do the same.

Sometimes these revivals were not too far removed from the old-time camp meetings, for in the summer they were held in the little park of mulberry trees. Much of the congregation sat on the Bermuda grass, which was filled with tobacco-spitting grasshoppers, and at night great swarms of moths were attracted by the unshielded electric light bulbs.

Even in the Baptist church itself some of the revivals could be so spectacular that as a small boy I was watching the show rather than receiving the message. I remember when a backslider first began to "Amen!" and then to groan horribly; he progressed from that to shouting, and finally he came up the aisle to prostrate himself on the rug. He groveled there, grinding his brow into the dust, and loudly implored God to "look right down here between them joists in the ceiling, and have mercy on this here pore, miserable, black-hearted sinner!"

And I remember the time when little Mrs. Brown reached for a hymn book on the piano, and fell into the baptismal pool wearing her best frock.

I was still sweeping out this church, and the revival put an extra load on my labors. But Mama helped me. I asked her about the back-slid brother. Anyone so repentant, I thought, must have committed a murder or two, and maybe even had stolen a horse.

"Of course not!" Mama said in the starched-Sunday-dress tone she used for church matters. Mama at least believed in dignity in the house of worship; she did not approve of such spectacles.

"What did he do then?"

"He danced out of the church," Mama said. "He's done it before, and he'll do it again."

There was a dance at the courthouse about once a month, with music from a Mexican guitar and two fiddles. Cowboys rode in to take their turns in barbershop chair and bathtub; they had their boots shined by a colored man who never had any other name but "Shine," and they wore silk shirts; each held a handkerchief in his left hand to protect his partner's dainty shirtwaist when he waltzed out on the talc-powdered floor, smelling of bay rum.

At Mama's house on the hill, we could hear the courthouse dance music quite plainly on summer nights, and even at eleven and twelve I wondered why the two-step and the turkey-trot were sinful.

There was talk I only partly understood, about Being Converted. Mama felt about church as she did about school; she wanted all her boys to be Converted, and I had the idea that this was something like graduation. But it wasn't that simple. How did anybody know when he was Converted? Was there a burst of light? What happened?

Floyd had been persuaded into the Baptist faith the previous summer. I asked him about it. He said he didn't feel any different. He was vague on the whole subject.

Bert took me aside and enlightened me. "Don't you know why Floyd joined the church?" he asked. "He's stuck on a couple of girls who go there—you know. Frances and Ruby. He had to join the church to see them."

"You mean he's a hypocrite?" I asked aghast. "You mean he ain't really Converted?"

"I ain't saying he wasn't converted," Bert said impatiently. "I'm just telling you *why* he was converted."

[288]

Mama had been in the Baptist Church since she was a girl, and was baptized in Little Brushy Creek at Sweet Home. Being baptized in a river sounded like fun. But in Ozona—which was forty miles from a live stream—the church performed the rite in a concrete pit under the rostrum. It was a deep and narrow affair, unpleasantly like a tomb.

"Did Papa belong to the church?" I asked Mama.

She admitted that Papa was not a very religious man, and told me stories about the old camp meetings, and wound up with the account of Berry Bosworth and Will Lewis shooting each other to death in the church cemetery.

Norah had learned to read out of a big Bible full of colored pictures, Mama said. That was when they lived near Eldorado, and the Bible belonged to a sheepherder who taught Norah to sing "On Jordan's Stormy Banks I Stand." She was very young when she was Converted. But she was developing, and the shepherd's mind was not in green pastures, nor beside the still waters. Papa ran him off the place with a gun.

One way or another, it appeared to me that the religious aspects of Papa's life has been strangely mixed with violence. I decided I would not be in a hurry about being Converted. Heaven could wait.

Bert was converted not many months after that discussion about Floyd and religion. I examined the circumstances closely, and could find no girl connected with them, and for a month or two he led a life so saintly that I got the idea he was miserable. All this gave me pause, and so did the things John McDonald told me.

John was about three years older than I, and the McDonald house was not far from our place. I wasn't long in learning that he believed the Spradlin house—just across a little canyon from us, and vacant since its owner's death—was haunted.

"There ain't any such thing as a ghost," I told him.

John eyed me solemnly. "Maybe you don't think there's any such thing as a vision," he said.

"A vision? You mean like the one Sir Launfal had? That's just in a book—it's a fairy story."

"My father had a vision," John said. "One day in the spring he was driving along, and he had a vision right there on the wagon seat. He said the trees turned brown and the grass turned yellow, and it was cold, and somehow he knew it was the thirtieth of November. He told us all about it when he got home. He said it meant he was going to die on the thirtieth of November."

"Well, shucks!" I said. "It must have been a dream. You can ride along on a wagon, and doze easy enough."

"My father," John went on in his solemn voice, "died on November thirtieth, just like the vision had told him he would."

March brought a revival meeting, not long after Ben and I had been forced to give up trapping. It brought a red-faced, shouting evangelist who called hell by its proper name, and flung the word hot and smoking into the teeth of the devil, and the faces of all backsliders and sinners. It was a two weeks' campaign. My old friend, the backslider and first-nighter, had danced out of the church again; he promptly banged his brow on the rug and begged God to look down between them there joists in the ceiling, and then he startled everybody by saying that he had heard the Call and had answered it in the affirmative—he was going to be a preacher.

The temper of the tabernacle was such that they made him a deacon on the spot. By the end of the first week, the aisle matting was frayed by wayward feet hitting the glory trail. By Sunday, the evangelist's voice was worn to a husky pleading, and he was reduced to a shoddy trick. Sunday school had always been dismissed, and the bell for the sermon came a few minutes later. This time there was no break. They drew back the curtains that separated Sunday-school classes, and the evangelist hoarsely announced that his text would be "Suffer little children to come unto me."

We were trapped. There were nine boys in my Sunday-school class, all of us squarely in front of the pulpit. We had entertained hopes of playing baseball a little later. The evangelist began his sermon. His voice came back strong as he painted a lurid picture of hell fire and damnation; he lost it again, and spoke in a hoarse pleading whisper as he begged us to come and be saved forevermore.

I looked down the row of knickerbockered knees, and saw that Harvey was on the aisle. And Harvey's legs were trembling. I knew that if he weakened the rest of us would follow like sheep. Mama was watching from a seat across the aisle, and I saw her urging me with her eyes.

Bud was next to Harvey, and I counted him a strong point. John McDonald sat next to Bud. The congregation sang "When the Roll Is Called Up Yonder." The preacher dropped on one knee and held out his hands to Harvey, begging him to come.

Harvey suddenly went. Bud held out for another stanza, but John McDonald was pushing him.

The whole line suddenly gave way, in exactly the same fashion a forward unit can do in battle; we were all on our feet, and moving. I looked across the aisle and saw Mama crying happily, and I was glad.

III

John McDonald and I filled the next week with serious theological discussions. We were to be baptized, with about forty others, on the following Sunday. The evangelical drive had moved over into the Latin-American quarter.

I had tried to back out. I told Mama that I wasn't really sure I had been Converted. I didn't know the words, but I tried to make her see that maybe I had been the victim of mass hypnotism and herd psychology.

But she said she could tell. I had been Converted, all right. Now all of her boys had been Converted, and she was very happy.

John McDonald became high priest and spiritual advisor during that indecisive week. "John," I asked him, "what would happen to us if we died right now?"

"We'd go straight to Heaven," he said. "It just takes three days to get there. That's what it says in the Bible."

"But we haven't been baptized, yet," I pointed out. "The Bible says you have to be baptized."

"Gosh—that's right!" John said. "I don't know what would happen in a case like that. We better be mighty careful between now and next Sunday."

"But why do they take such a chance?" I asked. "Why don't they baptize people right off? Brother Williams is over in Mexico, and he has converted about twenty Mexicans. He has to baptize them, too."

"Where?" John asked.

"In the church. There ain't any other place, unless it rains and the draw comes down."

"I don't like that," John said. "Some of them Mexicans have got lice."

On Saturday, a cold blue norther whistled down over Four Mile Hill, making me wish I had gone over to the Methodist church, where they just sprinkled a little water on you and let it go at that. The norther was still blowing Sunday morning, when the kids in my Sunday-school class gathered at the back of the church, dressed in their best. I had on a suit that had been tailored for Floyd, and then passed successively to Bert and to me.

There was no way to heat the water. After the baptism, both John and I would have to walk nearly a half mile in our wet clothes, against that icy wind.

"What if we get pneumonia going home?" I asked my spiritual advisor.

"Oh, we'd go straight to Heaven, that way. We would have been baptized."

"Well, gosh!" said Harvey. "I wish they'd let us *dive* into that cold water. It wouldn't be so bad if we could just dive into it!"

The congregation began singing "Washed in the Blood of the Lamb." The members of the congregation would sing one stanza, then pause, and the convert would take one more step down into the icy water, feeling it rise in a chill circle around his legs. Another verse, and then the local pastor, standing in the pool with water well above his middle, blue-lipped and shivering, would stutter the baptismal rite and plunge his charge backward.

It took forever, and the waiting was the worst. I remembered a hundred burlesques of this in the old swimming hole. We seized somebody, and bent him over backward, and rocked him a few times, and chanted:

> *"In the name of the Father and the Son,*
> *And in the hole he goes!"*

But the water was warm there. It was summer, and all the promises of Resurrection were bearing fruit; the whole scheme of things was much more believable.

A loud splash. Bud had pretended to slip on one of the steps. He got wet all over at once, and that was what he wanted. It was my turn next, and I went down into the icy water still wondering if I had been really Converted.

And I wondered too why the evangelist didn't pitch in and do some of the cold-water work, instead of leaving it all to the local pastor.

Then I went over backward, and was cold all over, and would have to walk home against the icy north wind.

The Mexicans, I noticed, went in last.

That afternoon, once again dry and reasonably warm, John McDonald and I wandered over the hill back of Mama's house, and tried to adjust ourselves to this new spiritual alliance under which we were safe. We felt good—the bath in cold water had set all our nerves tingling. We ran down the farther slope near the new rock quarry, and jumped from a limestone ledge to land on our heels.

John lost his balance in the jump, and sat down, laughing. His hand touched something.

"I'll be G—, I mean, gee-whillikers!" he exclaimed. "Look at this! Dynamite!"

Just behind him, neatly bundled, was a stack of a dozen sticks of high explosive which someone apparently had stolen from the quarry. Each stick was capped, and John said that it took only a forty-pound jar to set them off. He pointed out that each of us weighed more than forty pounds. God, he said, was directing our footsteps, or we could have been blown to pieces.

We looked at each other, and drew deep breaths. We were in.

Twenty-four

*B*etween our house and the Spradlin place was a small rocky canyon, its slopes well covered by scrub cedar. Unlike John McDonald, whose father had seen visions, I did not believe the Spradlin house was really haunted; still, I didn't like its looks. It sat on a knoll, with a low, frowning gallery across the front, and had been vacant for a long time.

Then, when I was eleven, the Spradlin place became sanctuary for a man personally haunted by old and secret fears. It was he who brought the first music and the first romance into my life. He was known as Albert-the-Dutchman-the-Bootmaker.

"Mein poots," Albert would boast through a mouthful of tacks, "fit like the baper on the vall!"

Cowboys east and west of the Pecos, cowboys in Arizona, *vaqueros* in Mexico and even *gauchos* in the Argentine agreed. Albert's boots were sculptured to fit every bunion; he fashioned them from minutely exact measurements and penciled outlines of his clients' feet, and orders poured in. The only trouble with Albert was that he had snakes in his boots, and he had a whole shopful of boots to have snakes in.

✤
Albert was not really a Dutchman, but a Czech, a small, bald, shy man with pale eyes and a pale, wispy mustache. His shop was in the center of one of Ozana's three business blocks, made of lumber and sporting a false two-story front like most of the mercantile establishments of the era. On two or three evenings each week, Albert worked late, and when the electric light plant shut down at eleven-thirty, he was just sober enough to light several coal-oil lamps and resume his labors. There was a bottle at his side, and at intervals he ceased hammering and strained a swig through the dozens of tacks he kept in his mouth. So far as anybody knew, Albert never swallowed a single tack, but it appeared that whiskey strained through such a spiked filter was particularly productive of delirium tremens.

"I see Albert-the-Dutchman-the-Bootmaker is working tonight," one of the town's more responsible citizens would tell Ben and me if we happened to be abroad at a late hour. "Here's a dime apiece. Watch him till he closes up, and see that he don't set the town on fire."

This became a genteel and lucrative racket. We could earn a dime while watching what to us was a screamingly funny show. Albert worked industriously and with a craftsman's skill up to a certain point, when his eyes bulged like pale blue grapes, and the sweat popped out on his bald head. Then he would drop the boot on his last, and stare at it in horror, and the show was on.

"Mein Gott—schnakes!" he yelled, leaping to the top of his work bench and dexterously grabbing the bottle to take along. Then he laughed and wagged his finger playfully at the boot on the floor. "But I fool you, you Gott-tamn schnake! I fool you! You can't get me now!"

Another drink in celebration of his escape, and a careful survey of his elevated position. The bench was always half covered by boots in every stage of construction and repair. Albert's eyes bulged anew, and he clapped a hand to his brow.

"Mein Gott—more schnakes!"

He leaped nimbly to another table. The oil lamps jarred and flickered. Albert shouted with mirth at his nimbleness, only to find that every boot had its reptile. Sometimes he fled the shop; sometimes, when he grew exceptionally agile and a fire or a fracture seemed imminent, Ben would keep watch while I ran through the park of mulberry trees, and summoned Sheriff Jim Moore from the jail. Albert spent many a night in protective custody.

Sundays at the Spradlin place, where he had moved for reasons known only to himself, and where he lived alone, he lay on a cot on the gallery, and played his gramophone. It had an ornate morning-glory horn, and had to be wound for every third record. If it gave out needle scratch or any other sounds of low fidelity, they were lost in the little cedar-green canyon: the lilting strains of Strauss waltzes and light opera floated to my ears undefiled, and I listened with growing enchantment. We had a gramophone too, a machine that Dee or Jay had acquired in some ambiguous swap, but the records that came with it were mostly nasal narratives of "Uncle Josh at the Telephone," "Uncle Josh and the Elevator," and other monologues of a Yankee hayseed recited with an alien twang. I envied Albert-the-Dutchman-the-Bootmaker.

But he drank as he played his music. There always came a time when the gramophone ground to a groaning halt while Albert lay on his cot feeling that the world and all that was in it were his to command.

He rose on an elbow and glared at the offending machine. "Blay!" he ordered imperiously.

Silence. Albert had been born forty years too soon for automatic phonographs, for long-play records, for remote control. He took another drink.

"Blay!" he thundered.

The concert was over. Albert sought strength in the bottle, and came up from the cot menacingly.

"Gott-tamn you, haf I not told you vun thousand times to blay?" he shouted, seizing the gramophone and heaving it from the gallery.

Then he started on his collection of records. He became a discus thrower, swearing and grunting as he sent the records sailing out over the canyon. Many of them were Victor Red Seal records, and cost as much as two dollars apiece. Some of them caught in the swaying foliage of the scrub cedars, and were not broken.

On Monday mornings, Albert tenderly retrieved the machine, straightened the dented morning-glory horn, and had needed repairs made to the tone arm. Once a week a music store drummer from San Angelo came to town, and Albert always ordered new records. Finally he acquired the new-style hornless Victrola—he smashed one of the table models, and then bought the larger cabinet that was to stand in parlors all over the land. It was a little too heavy for him to throw out. But he still had to wind the motor, and he still sent records spinning over the canyon when the machine ran down.

I searched the canyon every Monday. I found "The Beautiful Blue Danube," "My Hero," "Beautiful Lady," "The Glow-worm," and the "Barcarole" from *The Tales of Hoffman*. Before the time came when I could afford to buy "Dardanella" for myself, I had built up a fairly extensive collection.

"Now, Allie boy," Mama said, "you ought to take those records back to Albert-the-Dutchman. It's almost like stealing!"

"No, it's kind of like they are mavericks," I told her. "Besides, I can't go over there and tell Albert-the-Dutchman that I've got some records he threw away when he was drunk."

There came a day when Albert-the-Dutchman-the-Bootmaker called at the post office for his mail, and received more than the usual bills and catalogs from leather supply houses, and more than orders for boots. He opened the letter with a shaking hand. He read it hastily, and began to laugh.

Half the town of Ozona was always around the post office when the mail stage came in. The assemblage saw Albert run into the street and do a dance there, waving the letter above his head.

"Py Gott!" he shouted. "I feel vun thousand years younger!"

Everybody thought that this was a new onslaught of the DT's, but Albert wasn't drinking that day. In fact, he took a pint bottle from his pocket and smashed it on a rock. He said he was through with drinking, forever.

"My vife!" he said, waving the letter. "My family—in the old country. Now I can send for them. The boliceman—he iss not dead! Ha ha! The boliceman—Gott-tamn him, he iss still alive!"

It took a while to get the story out of Albert, in that emotional state. Eleven years before, in the Czechoslovakian town of Klatovy, he had gotten as drunk as he ever did in Texas, and had beaten up a policeman so thoroughly he thought the man was dead. Albert didn't even say good-bye to his family. He fled to Trieste, changed his name, and took ship for America. For eleven years he had not dared write home, but at last he sent a cautious letter to his wife.

That evening he was drunk on headier brew than comes in bottles. He lay on the gallery at the Spradlin house, and laughed a lot, and cried a little, and played Viennese music without throwing a single record into the canyon.

Albert's reformation, of course, was somewhat disappointing to me. He was no longer a one-man vaudeville show I could be paid to see; the music he bought no longer grew on cedar bushes. For the next two months he was busy fixing up the house, painting it, planting flowers, moving furniture into rooms that had not been occupied by anything more solid than Mr. Spradlin's ghost. He whistled at his work bench, hired two helpers, and paid more attention to his personal appearance.

Finally the automobile stage from Comstock rolled up to the Spradlin gate, and Albert's family disembarked.

Every kid in the neighborhood was watching. Until now, Albert had been the only "foreigner" we had ever seen. Suddenly, here were five new ones: Mrs. Albert, two boys nearly grown, and two girls. Ben's sisters reported that the younger girl—Anita—could say, "Thank you," almost as plainly as any twelve-year-old Texas kid. She had been less than a year old when Albert fled. I looked at her with new interest. She was exotic. She was small and pretty, and my age. Within two weeks I was mooning around the hills with a hammer and chisel, cutting hearts and initials into the ageless rock. Very probably they are still there.

"Allie plays with gurruls! Allie plays with gurruls!"

"Don't either!" I told Ben and Peery. "Nishka—that's how her folks say her name—Nishka comes over to our house because she likes Mama. Mama makes a fuss over her. Gives her things, like fried peach pies. And all I'm doing is, I'm kind of trying to help her learn English."

She showed me Klatovy on a map of Europe, and I told her about Graustark, which was somewhere down that way even if it didn't show—I had been reading a lot about Graustark.

And she was surprised and pleased to find that I had the same tastes in music as her father—even to identical Red Seal records.

II

At thirteen, every day was a generous slice of eternity, unhurried by the clock, unspoiled by yesterday's regrets or tomorrow's fears. I remember a world bound around with that day's horizons, and nothing beyond them mattered, or could touch me. The hills were higher, the miles were longer, and Time was a road running straight into Forever, climbing as it went. Ahead on that road were my brothers, looking back at me to laugh, and urge me onward, each taking successively longer strides so that I despaired of ever catching up with them. And somewhere on the far heights, biggest of all and misty with legend, was Papa.

But a legend lives only so long as it is needed and used for precept and inspiration. Somewhere down the quickening, shortening years, when my own strides grew longer, Papa ceased to be a giant and became merely a tall and mortal man, perhaps even owning some of the shortcomings Floyd so often ascribed to him. It was no longer necessary, by way of apology for his absence, to build him into a Bunyanesque figure too large to fit the local screen. My brothers had supplanted him: Dee was foreman on a big ranch, Jay had his own wife to support, Floyd was twenty and getting married, Bert was working as night operator for the telephone office. I had to think about making some money for myself.

Papa was as much to blame as was my own expanding, maturing

consciousness, and the small triumphs that built my self-sufficiency. He had stayed away too long; he was not at hand when we needed him. From a very tender age I had nurtured a fond dream that Papa would turn up someday, the way people did in books, to tell us that he had made a fortune and was ready at last to settle down and share it with all of us. This didn't happen, and it didn't happen, and the years went by until I knew that Horatio Alger was right. A man had to make his own way.

The war was several months old in Europe, and nobody in Ozona was selling newspapers. I wrote to the Fort Worth *Star Telegram,* and one of Amon Carter's minions hired me so quickly that Mama and everybody else was amazed. Twenty-five papers came by return mail. They were only one day old, and that was a small matter in a town thirty-odd miles from a railroad, in a day when radio had not been invented.

Floyd came down from San Angelo, and applauded the venture. "I'll just say!" he exclaimed. "How much are you making?"

I told him the papers were billed to me at four-fifths of a cent each, and that I sold them for a nickel. Twenty-five copies made me a dollar and five cents a day. Plenty of grown men were working for forty of fifty dollars a month.

"What are you going to do with your money?" Floyd asked.

I told him, proudly, that I was paying part of the grocery bill, and then showed him a magazine advertisement for a popcorn machine. I had written to the company asking for its literature.

"Probably costs too much," Floyd said. "When I was working for Chris Meinecke, there was a popcorn-and-peanut wagon in the warehouse. Ask them what became of it."

I did. Mr. Meinecke took me into the warehouse behind his store, and showed me a red and gilt and glass machine, covered with dust and cobwebs. I could own it for fifty dollars, and about three weeks later a cash deal was made.

I rolled the wagon through town and up the hill, and Bert helped me clean it up and wash all the windows and oil the spring mechanism.

I bought a hundred-pound sack of popping corn and a fifty-pound sack of peanuts through Mr. W. L. Watters, of Watters' store, who was so amused at the venture that he allowed me wholesale prices.

We fired up the machine in the front yard. The popcorn began to make its miniature snowstorm within the glass, the peanuts gave off their appetizing roasting smell. I wheeled the wagon down the hill in proud excitement, and parked it before the post office in time to make a dollar and five cents selling newspapers.

It was that easy. One day I thought of myself as an Algerian Ragged Dick, the Newsboy; the next day and I was a tycoon, surrounded by half the kids in town, and beset by prosperity and problems. There was no place to store the wagon overnight. Movies had come to Ozona on a three-nights-a-week basis. There were always hangers-on eager to push the wagon over to the movie palace, or to the courthouse dances, for a bag of peanuts.

I needed a costs accounting service. How much the handouts ate into the profits I never knew. But when the first supplies had been paid for I discovered that I was making three or four dollars a day and the weekly newspaper wrote me up in an item that concluded:

"Allie is a humdinger, and will be one of Ozona's most prominent business men someday."

Papa wasn't needed after that. I reflected that I just might be doing better than Papa was doing himself. I paid a larger share of Mama's grocery bill and even banked money. The business grew, and I became insufferably rich, and paid some other kid two bits to sell the twenty-five newspapers; I paid another one a dime to mind the store while I went to the drugstore for a soda that cost me another dime. Winter came, and business fell off because there was no place to garage the popcorn wagon.

I finally made a deal with the proprietor of the pool hall, which was the only social club of the town. In return for keeping the machine there, I would sweep out the pool hall every morning before school.

The barbershop was in a railed-off space in the pool hall at that time, and there was an altercation one morning at daybreak with Shine, the barbershop porter, over who swept out the hair clippings.

Shine pulled a razor on me, and I hit him with the broom. After this joint burst of temper we reached an amicable settlement—Shine swept his part and I swept mine.

I did not mention this for more than thirty years; I was well past forty when I recalled the incident on a visit to Texas. Dee and Floyd and Bert were sitting on the gallery with me; Mama was inside, where she couldn't hear.

My older brothers had not lost their protective instincts. "Why, I remember that shine boy," Dee said. "He was about my age. Good thing you didn't say anything at the time!"

Floyd and Bert looked at each other, and Floyd spoke for them both. "Do you remember his real name?" he asked. "Do you know where he is now?"

Twenty-five

Mama's fiftieth birthday had come in 1914, just nine days after the war started in Europe. She sat long before her beloved looking glass that day, examining the new gray in her hair and saying, "I just declare, I'm getting so old!" She used some Creole Hair Tonic, which was supposed to darken gray hair, and powdered her nose with prepared chalk, and fussed with her dress. I could see that the half-century mark was a milestone that really worried her, and I made her happy by saying, "Shucks, Mama—you're not old! And after this you are always going to be just fifty. No more."

She gave me a hug, and went about her household work with a song. She said, "All I want to do is to live long enough to see my boys grow up and amount to something."

If Mama could have had her way, however, her boys would never have grown up. Hers was a Peter Pan world. It was a shame, she said, that puppies and kittens and frisky little calves had to pass from the playful stage to the dull usefulness of maturity. She had looked upon all her children the same way—keeping me in curls as long as she could, still greeting Dee with baby talk when he came in from the ranch, even after he had passed thirty and was sporting a fine sorrel mustache. After she acquired the house on the rock, Mama saw no valid reason—not even marriage—why any of her boys should ever leave it. And she was fortunate, during the next two years after she turned fifty, because Jay was back and working not too far away, Floyd was clerking in the L. B. Cox store, and Bert and I were still in school. There were occasions when all of us were at home.

Mama had filled a box with earth at the end of the front gallery, and planted morning-glory and madeira vines in it to provide shade. This was one time she saw her planting come to fruition. All of us sat on the gallery in the summer evening, feeling the earth grow cool after a hot day, watching colors change in the sky and along the land in that lovely way they can do only in a desert country. This was something new and vaguely satisfying: an hour of family communion, for the most part silent. Sounds drifted up from the flat where the purple shadows flowed and deepened, from the scattered town, where in those days every light was a friendly beacon and not a garish advertisement. Locusts fiddled in the mesquites, a cowbell tinkled, cool and mellow, a freight wagon outfit went by. Coyotes sometimes howled from the rimrocks, and if there was a dance at the courthouse the music might come to us with a faint sound and the charm of a tune only half remembered. Over everything and behind it was the steady deep thrumming of the light plant on Waterworks Hill.

When Dee and Jay were there, they would sit through the hour of dusk and quiet, and then rise, stretching, to be drawn to the lights of the town for a little while. It all changed when Floyd married, and when Bert took the job of night telephone operator, and when I was either lost in a book or out in the moon-drenched night, about the mischief common to boys.

Then Mama sat there alone, listening to the sounds of the night, enjoying her dip of snuff, rocking on the gallery where a moss-green cedar bucket hung in the coolness with its tin dipper, waiting until one or more of her boys came home to take a shower under the tall hydrant in the front yard, and maybe to sleep in a bedroll on the clean rock.

So long as she knew where we were, and that we were coming

back, Mama was happy. The house on the rock suited her; the roots she had put down so tardily were strong, and she was content.

II

Not all the violence or the murderous gunfire of 1915 was confined to the fields of Flanders, or any other part of war-torn Europe. Pancho Villa was in the saddle in Mexico, singing "La Cucaracha" for his marching song. We heard the song in Texas—it was only in later years that I learned there were verses fit for singing in mixed company—and many a Texan, including Papa, heard the hoofbeats of the Villista horses.

The trouble may have seemed a new thing to the citizens of New York and Boston, but it was eighty or ninety years old to those living along the Rio Grande. It was an expected and accepted thing: border ranchmen buckled on their gun belts, and lived with it, and sometimes died with it. Historians trace a number of reasons why the trouble was intensified in the middle teens of this century. The Madero Revolution against President Diaz—the one in which Papa had some small part; Madero's assassination by followers of General Huerta; the revolt and rise of a provincial governor named Carranza; the later rise of a man whose real name was Doroteo Arango, but who admired an earlier *bandido* called Francisco Villa, and changed his name to that.

Bullets began to whine in greater numbers across the border river. Carranza and Villa fell out in their common fight against President Huerta. Americans had well over a billion dollars invested in Mexican mines and oil wells; the United States Navy had a coaling station under lease on Magdalena Bay, in Baja California, and there was dispute over renewal of the lease. Unarmed U.S. sailors were arrested at Tampico when buying supplies. The United States demanded a salute to the American flag, and it wasn't given.

German agents were busy in Mexico, promising the Mexicans their old territory of Texas and Arizona if Mexico would make war on the side of the Central Powers. A German ship was on its way to Veracruz with munitions. President Wilson acted, Veracruz was seized by the Navy—and now both Carranza and Pancho Villa were against us.

The ranchmen of Texas had to read about all this much later. They were too busy dodging bullets from lesser Villas, and trying to keep their cattle from being rustled over the Rio Grande. All at once, no Mexican could be trusted.

Mama worried herself into new gray hairs. Dee was out on a ranch, toward the border, working with Mexicans every day, and Jay was on another one. Dee laughed, and said he understood Mexicans. If a man had one for a friend, the Mexican would die for him. If he had one for an enemy, he would get stabbed in the back. By and large, the Mexicans of that part of Texas were almost pure Indians. And Dee had no enemies.

Crockett County ranchmen began wearing their guns openly, and no law enforcement officer cared. In the summer of 1915, there was a newcomer from the East, running sheep on a leased range down below the Harrell ranch. He sported a .32-caliber pistol.

"You know, mister," one of the lean and salty old-timers told him one day, "if you ever shot me with that thing—and if I ever found it out—I would be Godalmighty mad!"

The man from the East stiffened. "Why, this gun's big enough!" he said. "It'll kill a man."

"Might kill him," admitted the old-timer. "But it won't knock him down, like a .45 would."

And it didn't. A week or so later, two Mexican herders with a grudge jumped the ranchman with their knives. He shot one in the forehead, and the .32 slug glanced on the bone and ploughed a furrow to part the Mexican's hair. The other closed in from behind, and stabbed him.

When he was down, the Mexicans stomped his face with their bootheels until his eyesockets were caved in, his jaw broken, and his teeth knocked out. They also castrated him, after stomping in most of his ribs.

The body lay in the ripening Texas sun for two days before it was found. It was brought to Ozona and put on public display on the lower floor of the courthouse. I filed by the corpse along with score of ranchmen. It was the first lifeless body I had ever seen, and it was beginning to smell, horribly.

The cattle and sheep men looked, and went outside, and got on their horses. They rode southwestward, and trailed the killers for two or three days. But the trail was already cold, and the Mexicans were safely across the Rio Grande.

Ozona suddenly remembered that it had a very rich bank, and was only fifty or sixty miles from the Rio Grande. The county judge sent a telegram to Austin, requesting Texas Rangers.

Austin complied in that same frugal fashion with which it always assigned the members of its famed state police force, or the "one riot, one Ranger" method. Austin sent a Ranger named Tom Cooper.

Dee laughed heartily when he read about this in the Ozona *Stockman,* which had succeeded the Ozona *Kicker.*

"Tom Cooper!" he said. "Why, I know him. He's about my age. He was the one who jumped up and caught the meat in his teeth so that it would look like the dogs had been after it."

Tom Cooper was a black-eyed, black-mustached man, still filled with a Comanche cunning. His arrival in Ozona coincided with the advent of a cheap .22 pistol supposedly designed to fire nothing but blank cartridges. But it was made of cast iron, and any kid could see that a rat-tail file used to ream out the muzzle would make it possible to shoot live ammunition. The thing began in the category of a cap pistol, and then became a weapon. And every boy in high school was carrying one.

Sheriff Jim Moore took alarm, and ordered all the guns turned in at the jail, but nobody paid any attention. At least ten of us were gathered one evening in front of the new school building. We had not yet fired a shot, but were preparing to do so. Somebody warned, "Psst!" and here came Tom Cooper, riding out of a dark street, and some of the boys quickly threw their illicit guns over the schoolyard fence and into the high Bermuda grass.

I have always been proud that I kept mine in hand, because it is something to have been disarmed by a Texas Ranger. Tom Cooper rode up, and got down out of his saddle. He said, very quietly, "All right, boys—give me your guns." And he said, after collecting those in hand, "Now, the rest of you shinny over that fence and get the guns you threw in the grass."

That was uncanny, and we talked about it for days. Tom Cooper could not possibly have seen anybody throwing the guns into the grass. He had simply figured out that if he were in our place that would have been the thing to do.

One town, one Ranger.

I had just finished sweeping off the wooden sidewalk in front of the pool hall on a summer morning, before sunrise, when a Model T Ford sputtered up, and a rancher said he wanted to use the telephone. He called Sheriff Jim Moore at the jail, and told him there was a Mexican lying dead in the road about half a mile out toward the Friend horse ranch.

"Shot," he said. "Shot twice—in the back."

I rode back out on the Sonora road with the ranchman, and we got to the scene before the sheriff arrived. The Mexican was a thick-set man, lying face down in the summer dust, his lips curled to show his white teeth. There were horse tracks in the road.

Jim Moore and a deputy followed the horse tracks. They led back through a ranch pasture. They went straight to the jail, where Ranger Tom Cooper was still sleeping. His job was that of night guard.

By ten o'clock, the whole town knew about the shooting. But Tom Cooper was still sleeping the sleep of the just, and nobody dared awaken him. At noon he arose, and came out to get some breakfast. The sheriff and the deputy fell in with him in the little park of mulberry trees, one on one side and one on the other, because the man was already a legend. Half the town was watching. I saw them grab Tom Cooper's arms, and take away his gun, and tell him he was under arrest.

And I heard him laugh. He said, "Why, sure, I shot the saddle-colored son-of-a-bitch! He was a stranger in town, and he couldn't explain what he was doing here. He's one of Pancho Villa's spies."

The latter charge remained unproved, but Tom Cooper had

emerged as a hero, and no charge was ever proved against him either. Meanwhile the Mexican troubles grew worse, until we lived in a zone of undeclared guerrilla warfare.

III

Partly because of my earnings in the popcorn-and-peanut venture, Mama had a new cookstove. It burned coal oil, which was a considerable step forward, wood always being in short supply. But it was an early model of kerosene stoves, and not only acted up regularly but imparted a smoked kerosene flavor to the biscuits Mama still baked three times a day.

There had been houses burned down by kerosene stove explosions, and Mama took no chances. When the stove sputtered or flickered, when it did not burn steadily or true, she called Bert and me. We lifted the stove gingerly, and carried it far out into the rock yard. If it did not explode there within the next half hour, we carried it back into the house.

Then Mama resumed cooking supper. Her war with the stove was an endless and unsatisfying thing. It should have blown up, just once, out in the yard. But it never did.

I came home from school on a misty November afternoon, with the coolness on my face, and stepped around the brimming potholes in Mama's cherished rock yard. I saw a bedding roll lying on the front gallery, and that could mean that Dee had come in from the ranch. I ran into the house yelling, "Hooray—Dee's home!" and went through the living room without looking.

Mama was in the kitchen, very flustered about something. I thought at first that it was the stove again, because she stood there fiddling with one of the burners.

But she looked at me in a strange way, and when she took me by the hand I was scared out of seven years' growth. She hadn't done that for years: it was kid stuff, sissy stuff.

"Come in here with me, Allie boy," she said in a strained voice.

I thought something had happened to Dee. Like the time his horse took him under a tree when he wasn't looking, and a limb scratched him out of the saddle, gashing his head and knocking him unconscious. I thought maybe Dee had fallen from a windmill tower. It couldn't be anybody else, with that bedding roll on the gallery.

We went back into the living room, into what Mama called "the house." In the far corner, knees hugging the hot-smelling little wood stove, a man sat in Mama's rocking chair. The sallow light of the wet November afternoon filtered uncertainly through the windows of the west bedroom and was reflected on Mama's yellow straw-matting carpet; it gave the whole place a sober, autumnal hue, and touched the visitor's face with jaundice. He was a stranger, a small man, bald with a fringe of gray hair; a man in his fifties. His eyes looked small behind steel-rimmed glasses, and he had on a wrinkled brown suit that had been worn successively in rain and in blowing alkali dust, until the stains became a part of the fabric. On the floor beside the chair was a case of some sort, so that my mind leaped to the explanation that he was an agent, come to sell us lightning rods, or to take orders for enlarged crayon portraits, or to repair Mama's old Singer sewing machine.

"Howdy, Adam," the man said.

I didn't answer, since it was obvious that the stranger did not know my name. But Mama was still holding my hand, and that made me ill at ease. The stranger got up, and I stood taller than he did, and we faced each other through an awkward silence.

"Don't you know who this is?" Mama asked.

I shook my head. The stranger smiled.

"This," Mama said very softly, "is your Papa."

Twenty-six

The first shock of disillusionment was almost physical. It was like a wave, rolling me under, and when the stranger sat down again, small and drab, a hundred dreams had drowned, and all of the Old West had shrunk to his size. A hundred striking, life-sized pictures had faded, too. *Papa Ropes a House, Papa Rides as Ringleader of the Hide Stealers, Papa Sets the Quail Free, Papa Smuggles Gold Through the Enemy Lines. Papa Tall in the Saddle, Papa High on the Wagon Seat, Papa in Quest of New Country* . . .

They were all gone, and forever. Before me was a new one, *Papa in the Rocking Chair*. I was embarrassed with shame for him.

"Did you hear me?" Mama pleaded. "This is your Papa."

"I've got to get down to the pool hall and fire up my popcorn wagon," I said. The mail stage would be coming in, and there would be a crowd at the post office.

"You'll do nothing of the kind. You'll stay right here and talk to your Papa."

I was halfway to the door, and I came back reluctantly. Papa, looking around the room, had just discovered the enlarged crayon portrait with the .22 bullet hole squarely between his eyes.

[312]

Mama told him the shooting had been an accident. He said nothing, but I could see that the indefensible attack had shattered whatever dignity Papa may have had. Mama went back to the kitchen. I sat down, dreading the interview.

"Let's see, Adam," Papa said jovially. "You're about thirteen."

"My name is Allie," I said. "I was fourteen on the twenty-ninth of October."

Papa studied me for a moment. "I always wanted to name you Adam. *She*"—he nodded toward the kitchen—"named you Allie, after an old beau."

"After an old beau, my foot!" Mama called through the open door. "You know very well why I named him Allie. I told you before he was born. I dreamed that I had a son named Allie, and he became famous."

Papa smiled a dry, deprecating smile, a plea for man-to-man understanding. "I always wanted to name you Adam," he said again, and leaned over to pick up the case. He laid it across his baggy knees, opened it, and took out a violin, which he held up with an air of reverence. "Do you know what this is?" he asked.

My resentment rose at such a question. "Of course I know what it is! It's a fiddle—a violin."

"It's more than just a fiddle. This is a Stradivarius. I found it in Mexico, during the panic of 1909. I bought it cheap enough, considering, but it's worth a sight of money! With this, you might sure enough become famous!"

I grunted. Papa turned the violin to catch the light. It was beautiful, all right. He stroked it lovingly, and then he held it out to me so I could read the signature.

"I will give you this violin, this genuine Stradivarius," he said slowly and impressively, "on one condition."

I was wary. In the first place, I had never heard of Stradivarius, and was not really impressed. In the second place, I was not sure that I wanted a violin of any make; one of my friends was taking violin lessons, and he and all *his* friends regarded it as sissy stuff. Then Papa's benevolent air, with its implied assumption of power to bestow or withhold, irritated me. Papa apparently didn't know that I was no longer a child. He was unaware of the fact that I was the popcorn-and-peanut king of Ozona, Texas—the article in the weekly paper had called me that—and could damn well buy my own violin, if I wanted one.

"On one condition," Papa repeated. "That you be known as Adam."

I remembered miserable days at Sunday school, and the series of infantile colored alphabet cards, illustrating Biblical scenes, that were passed out as rewards for attendance. The first one said, "A is for Adam." It showed Adam lurking in brush up to his navel, with nothing on. It met the decency standard of the Southern Baptist Church, but left a bad impression on my young mind. All the brush in West Texas was thorny, and at the time I received the card I studied it and concluded that Adam must have been a very uncomfortable person, suffering from sunburn and thorn scratches and chigger bites. At the same time, I was trying to figure out the vulgar meaning of the stuff we were being told about the tree of knowledge and the apple and the serpent. It remained a mystery, and the name Adam was still synonymous with the raw, painful, and unexplored.

"No," I told Papa. "Nothing doing!"

Papa looked hurt. "Listen to the beautiful tone," he said. He tucked the Stradivarius under his chin. He put rosin to the bow, and sawed over the strings a few times. My interest rose to excitement—Papa was actually going to play! Mama came out of the kitchen, nervously smoothing a freshly starched apron.

It is very probable that I knew more about violin music than Papa did. Among the fine Red Seal records Albert-the-Dutchman-the-Bootmaker had thrown into the canyon after having a few fine drinks were some Fritz Kreisler—"Souvenir," "Humoresque," and "Schön Rosmarin."

I was waiting to hear Papa play like Fritz Kreisler on his Stradivarius.

Papa began by patting his foot. One—two—three—four, he patted, and then he launched into a violent rendition of "Turkey in the

Straw." The Stradivarius groaned, but Papa ran through a whole flock of turkeys. Then he played "Pop Goes the Weasel," his foot coming down hard on each pop. Mama sighed, and went back to the kitchen.

"Would you change your mind, Adam?" Papa asked.

"My name ain't Adam!" I said.

It began to rain, slowly, monotonously, and above the drone on the roof were mandolin and harp overtones of water dripping in Mama's tin wash boilers at the corners of the house, and the bright chuckle of tiny waterfalls on the shelving rock. The light faded and Mama brought in a kerosene lamp, and I was losing money by the minute because people would be waiting for the mail. Papa ran through "Turkey in the Straw" again. Then he sighed, and put the Stradivarius away, and I left, heading for the pool hall and my pop-corn-and-peanut machine.

On the way, I saw Papa had a Studebaker wagon standing under the big liveoak tree under our hill, the horses waiting with their heads resigned to the rain. I was old enough to wonder about that bedding roll on the gallery, and to know that if he stayed at the house it would create gossip in Ozona. But I need not have worried. Before I left the rock yard, Papa said good night. He wrapped the Stradivarius case in the bedding roll—I remembered then that I had forgotten to ask if he had a rattlesnake's rattles in the violin to pro-tect it from dampness—and he put the bedding in the Studebaker.

Then he drove down to the wagon yard, where he could build a fire and camp out.

II

The return of a prodigal parent might have been expected to call for a gathering of the clan, but it didn't. Dee and Jay rode in briefly from the ranches and visited with Papa at the wagon yard. Floyd said he was too busy at the store, and Papa could come see *him*. Bert saw him after he got off the night shift at the telephone office, but only once or twice.

"I'll just swanee!" Mama said, using her strongest expletive.

"I think you boys ought to show your Papa a little more respect. After all, he's getting old."

"He hasn't changed much," Jay said. "You remember him, Allie?"

I said I didn't know. If I remembered him at all, he sure had shrunk.

"Well," Dee said thoughtfully, "I reckon he *has* shrunk a little. He's kind of falling in on himself, the way a man does when he gets old."

"Your Papa's not old," Mama said, reversing herself. "He's just in his fifties, and that's the prime of life. But he's been having some eye trouble. The doctor told him to go back to the piney woods country, where there isn't so much glare."

Floyd came up to Mama's house with his wife and baby daughter. "I don't feel too sorry for him," he said. "What did he ever do for us?"

Papa ate a few meals with us, and brought his violin along to play for Dee. Dee listened respectfully to "Turkey in the Straw," and withheld comment. Then he shook hands with Papa and saddled his horse and went back to his ranch job, and whatever there had been of family unity fell apart; Dee had been the real head of the family for twelve years.

Papa did not go east to the piney woods country. It rained, and he remained in Ozona about ten days, visiting part of the time with Aunt Docia, but still camping out at the wagon yard. Then, one Sunday afternoon, he came to the house with a spring in his step and an air of excitement about him. He was there to tell us good-bye. He had heard about some new country. It was a couple of hundred miles away, west of the Pecos and deep down in the Big Bend of the Rio Grande. Papa had passed by on the north of it once, long ago. It was the kind of country you can see from a long way off. "It's wild, and there's a lot of it!" he said. "Mountains! Not little rocky anthills like you've got around here, but sure-enough mountains!" He looked at me. "Better pack your duds and come with me, Adam."

"My name's Allie," I said.

For a moment, Papa stood beside the wagon looking out over the western hills, where the level rimrock ran toward the Rio Grande, as if he could see far beyond the hills, into tomorrow and the next day. "Like I told you, *she* named you Allie, after an old beau," he said.

Mama didn't say anything. I thought she was going to cry.

Papa said, "Well, I reckon I'd better roll." He stepped on the hub of the front wheel, and I saw that he had on a new pair of boots. He climbed up briskly, and unwrapped the reins from the brake handle. At that moment, mounting the Studebaker wagon, he took on stature, and importance, and dignity. He settled himself on the wagon seat, and waved his hand to us. "Good-bye!" he called. *"Adiós!"*

We said good-bye. Mama turned away and looked up at the house on the rocks. The trace chains jingled and the wheels turned. Papa did not look back. He drove across a vacant lot to reach the main road, and the earth there was still soft from the rain. The tracks he left were deep. They ran straight west.

III

Nineteen hundred sixteen, just a few weeks away, was the most notorious of all the years along the troubled Mexican border. On the ninth of March, Pancho Villa raided Columbus, New Mexico, killing nine residents of the town and eight cavalrymen, and setting off the Pershing Punitive Expedition. Late in April and during the first week of May, while high officials from Washington and Mexico City were meeting in El Paso in an attempt to avert war, Villistas staged a swift succession of smaller raids—one near Eagle Pass, and three west of the Pecos, near Dryden and at Glenn Springs and Boquillas.

That week Mama received a telegram from Marathon. It was sent by the sheriff of Brewster County. It said that Papa was among several people killed in the Boquillas raid, but added, mysteriously, that his body had not been recovered.

Mama received the news dry-eyed, only half believing it. Why should the Mexicans, or anyone else, carry Papa's body away? She telephoned the ranch where Dee was working, and Dee came to town at once.

A family consultation was held. Dee said he had better go down into the Big Bend and investigate.

Jay and Floyd advised against the trip. "If he's dead, he's dead," Floyd said. "If he's alive, he can take care of himself, and we'll hear from him someday. Besides, what did he ever do for you?"

Dee went, nevertheless, and Mama worried that there might be other Mexican raids while he was there. Boquillas, Texas, was nothing but a ranch store, across the wide Rio Grande canyon from a Mexican town—a cluster af adobe houses—also named Boquillas, which means "Little Mouths." It was and is a wild place, with the walls of Boquillas Canyon rising more than sixteen hundred feet above the river; Dee had to leave the train at Marathon and hire a horse to ride nearly a hundred miles, and he was gone for two weeks.

He found men around Boquillas who were hiding out from the law on both sides of the Rio Grande, and a few small, scattered, trigger-jumpy cavalry patrols who couldn't afford to take chances. Survivors of the raid told him that the *bandidos* had come at night, shouting both *"Viva Villa!"* and *"Viva Carranza!"* so that no one could be sure who they were. They rode around a house where eight cavalrymen were billeted—it had galvanized iron walls and a *sacaguista*—thatched roof. They had fired shots into the house and then set fire to the dry *sacaguista*. Papa was among the people inside, and he had been shot down as they ran out to escape being roasted alive.

But one man swore he had seen Papa on the day after the raid— on foot, leading a pack mule along a rugged canyon, heading westward. The man added that Papa was dressed about like Mexicans dressed around there, and that he was dark as a Mexican. The Studebaker wagon was gone, perhaps burned in the raid, and nothing belonging to Papa was ever found. Not even the Stradivarius that could have made me famous.

Many years afterward, Dee and I went to Boquillas—so long afterward that we rode in a jeep instead of a Studebaker wagon. The Big Bend was still remote, still wide and wild and mysterious, and some of its rocky, winding canyons had never been explored. We found some old-timers who remembered Papa in 1916. Sure, they said, Papa been killed in the raid. Sure, he had been seen headed west the following day.

Papa had become a legend again.

Twenty-seven

"These autobiographies of our generation are going to be important because they record the most spectacular upheaval in human affairs in all history. There has been more change in the way of living—you'll note I did not say 'the way of life'—since 1880 or 1890 than in any 5000 years of human history. These autobiographies are the primary sources." —WALTER PRESCOTT WEBB,
in a letter to the author

Mama survived Papa by more than thirty-three years. She lived to see the West Texas skies lighted by the strange and portentous flash over White Sands, and to read and hear about Hiroshima. She did not pretend to understand the dawn of the Atomic Age, but characteristically translated its first dire accomplishments into peril for her children. Long before fallout shelters were devised, Mama said, "I swanee, the way things are, I just wish we could dig us a hole in the ground and pull it in after us!"

She lived to see all her children with families of their own, and never failed to glow with pride at their endeavors. When war ruined my popcorn-and-peanut business, and I clerked successively in Bunger's store and Watters' store, and drove the delivery flivver for Chris Meinecke & Son, Mama said, "Allie boy, I was in the store today, and it just looked to me like you were busier than anybody else in the whole place!" When Dee first began windmill work, it was, "I declare, honey boy, you can just do anything! But I just worry half to death about your falling off one of those high towers. You be careful, hear me?" When Jay's scale-model locomotive ran under its own steam, and he came up with a set of cleverly designed trench-digging tools he was offering to the War Department, Mama hailed him as "just as smart as Thomas Edison." Bert painted a series of canvases showing Alpine lakes and mountains that never were, and then made a tour of San Angelo and Ballinger and Coleman doing signs. For a number of years his signature was legible upon restaurants, where he had been so bent on artistic lettering that he spelled it "Sandwitches." Mama said she knew all along that there was artistic talent in the family. Floyd continued to shock and astonish and please her in various ways: he never stopped having fights, but he always won, and even when Mama reproved him her eyes were shining. For a short time, and on a short track, Floyd was probably the youngest passenger train engineer in the nation. He manned the throttle on the Roscoe, Snyder & Post, a railroad of some thirty miles built in the Sweetwater country by Mr. Post of Post Toasties. Mama was very proud of this. (She never heard the nickname that vulgar wits gave to the R. S. & P.)

I drew cartoons and wrote what was alleged to be poetry for the first high school annual ever produced in Ozona, and Mama was ecstatic. And when the long-time janitor of the school—a man of family—was lured to the new oil fields of Burkburnett and Ranger (Bert went there too), I applied for the janitorial job, which paid seventy-five dollars a month, and got it. I planned to be the janitor and still go to school. I carried an alarm clock to classes, so that I would be reminded to ring the bell.

Mama was fifty-six years old. She came down every afternoon after school was out, and helped me sweep out the two-and-a-half-story building. On weekends we washed windows.

I was in the tenth grade, and Mama was determined that I would be graduated.

Mama was of an earlier generation than that of which Dr. Webb speaks. She lived to see almost everything but space shots, but she viewed the changes in a more impersonal way: Mama rode in an automobile with me at sixty miles an hour, but she never drove a car. She lived, fortunately, in her own unhurried way, at the pace of the Studebaker wagon, with the dusty road slowly unrolling toward tomorrow.

Her pictures were clear and sharp. She never had the transition from wagon speed to the sudden blur of thirty miles an hour behind the wheel of a Model T Ford. She hadn't watched Karl Kuhl's tan-colored biplane, lazily circling over the San Angelo fairgrounds, preparing to beget shrieking monsters that traveled faster than sound.

For Mama, the years marched at their accustomed leisurely pace, and she really never understood why her boys had to be off and doing—she never saw that Time was cutting the road out from under our feet.

But she came to accept the fact that we were Papa's children, and wore his restlessness, and not once did she say, "Stay!"

Floyd had a wife and two children—both babies—in 1917. When war was declared on April 6, he went to San Angelo and enlisted in the Navy. I was fifteen, and tried to enlist, but Mama would not sign the consent papers. "You're still my baby, bless Patty!" she said. "I won't have you going off to fight a war."

Bert tried, but he had had surgery for an osteomyelitis infection in his left leg, and he was rejected. My unofficial duties as bugler for a unit of the Texas Cavalry (later ignominiously known as the Stick Horse Cavalry, because it did not get off the ground) didn't count: Mama had only one star on her service flag. Floyd was on the U.S.S. *Stringham,* a coal-burning destroyer, fighting U-boats. He was in a Navy radio school at Harvard. One day on the interurban train for Boston, he got up to give his seat to a woman, and a man pre-empted it. Floyd hit the man's jaw so hard he broke a bone in his hand, and spent several weeks in Chelsea Naval Hospital.

I imagine, as the man lay on the deck of the swaying trolley, Floyd said, "Now, let that be a lesson to you."

Mama never had all five of her boys at home, at one time, after World War I. The former janitor became disenchanted with the oil fields, and wanted his old job back; my tenure became a cause célèbre defended by Miss Coral Clark, who was the high school principal; we lost, and I left the halls of learning forever, sans diploma. Mama was heartbroken.

But I told her I would make it up to her. I would finish my education in the Navy.

I went to Houston, where Maude lived, and called at the recruiting office. The Navy was overmanned. A salty and tattooed chief petty officer sat with his feet on the desk, and said, "Son, I don't even know what they're going to do with me!"

I worked at the magazine stand in Union Station, and then joined a hardy crew selling magazine subscriptions from door to door; I went to Amarillo, and shoveled coal as a fireman on the Fort Worth & Denver, with Floyd, and news-butched on the Santa Fe. I went back to Ozona and dug postholes in solid rock with a crew building barbed-wire fence. It was nearly two years before my sporadic calls on recruiting stations coincided with the Navy's desire for my services. When I finally enlisted, as apprentice seaman, in the summer of 1922, I was twenty years old.

II

This is not intended to be my autobiography. I should like to take the story back to the house on the rocks, where Mama and Dee were still living, but I do not know what occurred there during the next year and more. When I went to Ozona on leave, Dee was considering moving across the Pecos to Sanderson, where he would eventually set up a windmill business of his own. I made the trip there with

Dee and Mama—wearing Navy whites—and it was a little like old times. We traveled in Dee's Model T, but not very fast; it was more than 125 miles over dirt roads, through the ranch country, and we took all day. At noon we made camps beside a windmill. I shot a duck on the tank, and four quail in the chaparral; Dee made a fire, boiled coffee, fried potatoes, and cooked the game. It meant a lot to me to find that the family was still self-sustaining on the road.

We saw Norah in Sanderson, and after I had gone back to the West Coast and the battleship *Maryland,* Dee and Mama sold the house on the rocks, where Mama had lived for more than seventeen years, and moved west of the Pecos.

I went directly from the Navy into a newspaper job in San Diego, and began to write magazine material. I was married, and had a son. Mama and Dee came out to spend a month in California—they traveled in the old way, camping out at night, except they rode in a truck instead of a Studebaker wagon. I had Mama come to the West Coast for another visit, a few years later, when I was the news editor of the San Francisco *Chronicle*. I had been back to Texas every year at vacation time, to see Mama. She was now seventy, and Dee was fifty-three, and still a bachelor.

Mama stayed in San Francisco for three months. She saw the red-woods, and Golden Gate Park and Seal Rocks; she was extremely proud of my newspaper work and my magazine stories. Her dream, she said, had come true. In her eyes, at least, I was famous.

But she wasn't happy. The San Francisco fog depressed her, after so many years in the high, dry West Texas air. She still suffered from stomach ailments, real or imaginary, and wanted me to get her a bottle of Peruna. I knew that Peruna had a rather high alcoholic content, and—San Francisco being what it was in the days of Prohibition—I got her a gallon of port wine, instead.

"Why, Allie boy, you know I'd just never drink wine!" she said, aghast.

"But it's good for you. And the Bible says to drink a little wine for your stomach's sake."

"Well," Mama said, "you were in the medical department in the Navy" (I had been a hospital corpsman) "and I guess you're almost a doctor. And if you say so . . ."

She tippled the port, and thrived. But she worried about "Dee boy." Who was taking care of Dee boy? She would just have to get back to Texas and cook for him, and see that his clothes were washed.

I reminded her that Dee was fifty-three years old. It didn't make any difference. Dee was still just a child as far as Mama was concerned, and I had to get her rail tickets to take her back to Sanderson.

Before she left, we had a telegram from Dee. He had married a widow with a little girl and two other children.

"Well, I'll just declare!" Mama said, and then she cried, and both joy and sadness were in her tears. She went home to face something new and strange. Dee had always been her favorite son, and now she would have to share him with another woman.

I had long held a Naval Reserve commission. In 1938, I left news-paper work to do free-lance writing, and Mama was terribly proud when I had short stories and a serial in the *Saturday Evening Post,* and stories in *Collier's* and *Liberty,* and other magazines. The Navy interrupted this literary splurge by calling me to active duty, as a lieutenant, a year before Pearl Harbor. I wrote Mama from the North Atlantic and from Iceland; the war broke, and I went back to San Francisco, and was promoted to lieutenant commander.

The duty officer in my office telephoned me at home one evening. "A man came in here," he said hesitantly, "claiming he is your brother. He—er—had on a leather jacket. Said he had just come down from White Horse, in the Yukon. Said—"

"I'll be damned!" I said. "Floyd! Where is he?"

The duty officer gave me the name of a third-rate hotel. I called there, and found Floyd in a temper rivaling any Papa ever had.

"I came down here under contract to the Navy," he said. "They put me in this flophouse until I go to Pearl Harbor—I'd be doing plumbing work out there. Went up to my room, and found another man in the bed. Supposed to share it with him. I'm breaking the contract!"

I laughed, knowing the hotel situation at the time, and told Floyd we had room at our apartment, and that I would drive down and get him. He met me with a strange attitude.

"I want to go out and visit with you," he said. "But staying there —that's different."

"Why?" I asked.

"Well, you're a naval officer now. I'd be doing plumbing work, and wearing clothes like this." He was neatly dressed in khaki trousers and an Eisenhower jacket. "It wouldn't look good for people to see me leaving your place."

"Oh, for Christ's sake!" I said impatiently. "Get your gear, and get in the car!"

Floyd was just turning fifty years old. He was rather bald, and had dentures, but he was still very wiry and muscular, and as quick as a cat. I said, "What happened up in the Yukon?"

"I was working for the Government," he said, and laughed. "Had a fight, and got fired."

"You still fighting?"

"Well," he explained, "we all ate in a big mess hall, and paid a dollar a meal—family-style meals, and it didn't matter what you ate, you still paid a dollar. Now, you know, for a long time I haven't gone much for lunch. Just a piece of apricot pie and a cup of coffee, and I do better work. This day they had beef stew on the table, in big tureens. The guy across the table spooned a big pile of stew on his plate and tore into it, and then saw I was eating apricot pie. He said, with his mouth full, 'Ain't you going to have some beef stew?' I said, no, I wasn't going to have any beef stew. He said, 'But you're paying for it, ain't you?' and I said, yes, I was paying for it. He said, 'Well, it don't make sense, not having beef stew if you're paying for it!' and by that time I was pretty sore. I waited till he had cleaned his plate, then said, 'Have some more beef stew.' He said, 'No, I guess I've had all I want.' I said, 'Oh, come on—have some more

[326]

beef stew—you're paying for it!' and then I picked up the tureen and dumped it into the glutton's plate, and some of it spilled into his lap, and the fight was on."

Floyd chuckled happily. "He outweighed me by forty pounds, but he wasn't as fast. We went outside—the other boys formed a ring—and I cut him down to my size, and whipped hell out of him. They said I started the fight, so I had to call for my time."

He looked at my crew cut, and said, "I know it's regulation, but it's a mistake. You ought to wear your hair longer. Never can tell when somebody might lay a piece of pipe across your head in some dark alley, and a head of hair might save your life."

I remembered when he had told me the same thing, more than twenty years before, when we were in Amarillo and I was a student fireman on the railroad. We made a trip in which Floyd was the regularly assigned fireman, and I did the work. At the day's end we found ourselves switching freight cars around Clarendon, which was not far from Vernon, where Papa did not cross the Red River. We went to the railroad Y.M.C.A., but only had showers there to remove the soot and coal dust.

"No use spending money for a room, Bit-fit," Floyd told me. "I'll show you something. It'll make a man of you."

We went back down to the railroad yards, pulled some hay out of a boxcar, and slept alongside the tracks. And Floyd said then that I ought to wear my hair longer, in case somebody hit me with a piece of pipe. . . .

"When was the last time you saw Jay?" I asked him at our San Francisco reunion.

He laughed. "Last summer. We were camping in our trailer, on the San Saba River. I went into town to get some ice, and saw a man stooping over to put a block of ice in his car. I knew from the rear view that it was Jay, and it was. He said he was camping out down on the river with a little bunch of goats, and I thought he was goat ranching. But when I went down there with him, he had a trailer, and hitched behind it he had a sub-trailer that he had built. It was a very fancy rig, with air brakes and electric lights and everything. In it were about a dozen goats, of all ages. I told Jay I thought he meant he was ranching. He said no, they were milk goats. He said, 'Couple of years ago I had some bad stomach trouble, and like to have died. The doctor told me to try goat's milk. So I got her'— and he pointed out a goat in the trailer—'and she saved my life. These two are her kids, and these others are their kids. What can I do? She saved my life, and I've got to take care of them.'"

Floyd remained in San Francisco for about six weeks, working for a government contractor. I was about to make my first trip to Australia in a troop transport, as troop commander, but at the last minute I was ordered to Admiral Halsey's staff in the South Pacific instead. I swore my eighteen-year-old son into the Navy one day, and saw him off for boot camp at Farragut, Idaho. The next day I flew to the South Pacific.

Floyd left for Texas by bus. The bus was crowded, and all the way across Southern California and Arizona a man who sat at the window seat, across the aisle, kept sipping from a bottle and then climbing over the lap of a pretty girl to go to the rest room. The bus made a twenty-minute lunch stop somewhere in Arizona, but Floyd did not eat his apricot pie that day. Instead, he took the man around the corner of the bus station and chided him for his lack of manners. There was a fight. Floyd boarded the bus and left his opponent sitting propped up against the building, and the pretty girl rode the rest of the way unmolested.

I saw him again, in Alpine, Texas, after the war. I was a captain in the Navy, on my way to Japan.

"I can remember when I was in the Navy," Floyd said, "and you hardly ever saw a captain. A captain was like God."

"Dime a dozen now," I said, but I could see that he had finally given up his campaign of making a man of me. "What do you hear from Jay?"

Floyd laughed again. "He's camped out on the river near Brady. I was over there this summer. I went to the biggest store in town, and asked the proprietor if he could tell me where to find Jay. He looked at me suspiciously, and said, 'What do you want with Mr. Bosworth?' I told him I was Jay's brother, and then he unbent. He said, 'Well, that's different. If you're his brother, I reckon you know Mr. Bosworth is a kind of a—well, kind of a character. I figure he's a sort of poet. One day he may come to town looking like a tramp. The other day he came driving up in front of this store on a brand-new tractor. Had on new boots and a Stetson, and his mustache was waxed. You know, he's down on the river, with a tent, and he's got a big Majestic cooking range out under the trees, and he cans stuff for some of the big outfits around here—canned something like fifteen thousand quarts for them this spring. And when the town bought a new Diesel rig for the power plant, they sent for Mr. Bosworth to come in and install it. Think a lot of him around here."

III

Ivanhoe died in New Mexico, when I was first in newspaper business. The rest of my brothers and sisters are living. Each time I see them, I know that they have changed much less than I, for they have remained in Texas; and the Lone Star State, for all of its amazing growth and proud progress, is essentially changeless. Even though they are bound with pavement, the prairies still run wide from Sweet Home to the postoak country; the Panhandle plains are limitless, and the rimrocked hills of Crockett County dream under the sun, as they always did, of half-naked Comanche warriors with feathers in their hair.

It remained for Papa's youngest child to go farther and stay away longer than any of the family, and perhaps to lose more than he gained by doing that. But my generation came of age with the automobile, and moved, already dizzied by speed, into the age of aviation. The earth and everything in it shrank; time was accelerated, and Aesop to the contrary, the race was to the swift. In the present state of affairs, national and world-wide, I cannot escape the conclusion that men's souls and moral values also have been diminished, and that the world would be better off traveling in an old Studebaker wagon, looking for a place to spend a peaceful night.

[329]

I shall always be grateful, however, for the highways and the speed of a British sports car which enabled my son and me to make time from Washington, D.C., to Sanderson, Texas, in the summer of 1949. We reached Dee's house the day after Mama had suffered a stroke. She was eighty-five.

I sat by her bedside. She rallied a little, and Dee asked her if she knew me.

"It looks like Allie boy," Mama said, and smiled happily. She slept awhile, and then opened her eyes.

"Where's Dee, honey boy?" she asked me.

"He's eating supper," I told her.

"Well, why aren't you eating supper too, honey boy?"

I told her I thought I would sit with her while Dee and the others had their meal.

Mama studied me for a moment. I was forty-seven years old, a commander in the Navy, a war veteran, a former newspaper editor, and the author of several books.

"You poor little feller!" she murmured softly. "If they'd just let me get up out of this bed, *I'd* fix you something to eat!"

Those were her last words.

Bibliography

PRIMARY SOURCES:

Family Letters.

Family Bible.

Written "Memories" of my sister Norah, and tape-recorded reminiscences of both Norah and my brother Dee.

Courthouse records in Lavaca and other Texas counties.

Contemporary Texas newspapers.

Federal Census.

Civil War Records.

SECONDARY SOURCES:

BOETHEL, PAUL C., *A History of Lavaca County*. Austin, Von Boeckmann-Jones, 1959.

———, *Sand in Your Craw*. Austin, Von-Boeckmann-Jones, 1959.

BREIHAN, CARL W., *The Day Jesse James Was Killed*. New York, F. Fell, Inc., 1961.

BURKE, JAMES, JR., *Texas Almanac and Immigrant's Handbook*, 1881.

CLARKE, MARY EMELINE BOSWORTH, *Bosworth Genealogy*. Oakland, Calif., the author, 1930.

———, *Bosworth Bulletin*. Oakland, Calif., the author, 1930–1940.

COCKRELL, MONROE F., *After Sundown*. Evanston, Ill., the author, 1952–1960.

Compendium of American Genealogy, *First Families of America, Vol. IV*. Chicago, The Virkus Company, 1930.

DALE, EDWARD EVERETT, *Cow Country*. Norman, University of Oklahoma Press, 1945.

DOBIE, J. FRANK, *A Vaquero of the Brush Country*. Boston, Little, Brown and Company, 1929.

———, *Coronado's Children*. New York, Grosset and Dunlap, 1930.

———, *The Longhorns*. Boston, Little, Brown and Company, 1941.

[333]

EMMETT, CHRIS, *Shanghai Pierce; A Fair Likeness.* Norman, University of Oklahoma Press, 1953.

FEDER, SID, *Longhorns and Short Tales of Old Victoria.* Victoria, Texas, Victoria Advocate Publishing Company, 1958.

GARD, WAYNE, *The Chisholm Trail.* Norman, University of Oklahoma Press, 1954.

GIPSON, FRED, *Cowhand: The Story of a Working Cowboy.* New York, Harper & Brothers, 1953.

HOLLON, W. EUGENE, *The Southwest: Old and New.* New York, Alfred A. Knopf, 1961.

HORGAN, PAUL, *Great River: The Rio Grande in North American History.* New York, Rinehart and Company, Inc., 1954.

HUNTER, J. MARVIN, *100 Years in Bandera.* Bandera, Texas, The Bandera Bulletin, 1953.

Louisiana Federal Writers' Project, *Louisiana, a Guide to the State.* New York, Hastings House, 1941.

McGREGOR, STUART, editor, *The Texas Almanac.* Dallas, Dallas Morning News, 1961.

McKENNA, JAMES A., *Black Range Tales.* New York, Wilson, Erickson, Inc., 1936.

Mississippi Federal Writers' Project, *Mississippi, Description and Travel.* New York, Viking, c. 1938.

PHARES, ROSS, *Texas Tradition.* New York, Henry Holt and Company, 1954.

RIDER, FREMONT, editor, *The American Genealogical-Biographical Index to American Genealogical, Biographical and Local History Materials.* Middletown, Conn., Godfrey Memorial Library, 1956.

ROSE, VICTOR, *The Texas Vendetta.* New York, J. J. Little and Company, 1880. Reprinted by Frontier Press, Houston, 1956.

TOLBERT, FRANK X., *An Informal History of Texas.* New York, Harper & Brothers, 1961.

WEBB, WALTER PRESCOTT, *The Great Plains.* New York, Ginn and Company, 1931.

————, *The Texas Rangers: a Century of Frontier Defense.* New York, Houghton Mifflin, 1935.

WHITELY, EDYTHE JOHNS RUCKER, *History of the Rucker Family and Their Descendants.* Tennessee, Hermitage Printing Company, 1947.

WOODSON, HENRY MORTON, *Historical Genealogy of the Woodsons and Their Connections.* Memphis, the author, 1915.

About the Author

Captain Allan R. Bosworth was born in Texas and attended high school in Ozona, Texas. In 1926, after four years in the Navy, he joined the staff of the San Diego *Union* as a reporter. From there he went to the Los Angeles *Examiner*, the San Francisco *Chronicle,* the San Francisco *Examiner* and, after his wartime service, to the San Francisco *Call-Bulletin.* Later he was recalled to active duty with the Navy.

During the past thirty years he has had at least five hundred stories published in the *Saturday Evening Post, Liberty, Collier's, The Ladies' Home Journal, Esquire* and many other magazines. His most recent books are *The Lovely World of Richi-san, The Crows of Edwina Hill,* a novel, and *New Country.*

Captain Bosworth retired from the Navy on June 1, 1960, and is now living just outside Roanoke, Virginia, in a two-story British colonial house.